BUILDING
THE LOCAL ECONOMY

cases in economic development

Edited by

Douglas J. Watson and John C. Morris

Carl Vinson Institute of Government
The University of Georgia
© 2008 Carl Vinson Institute of Government
All rights reserved
Printed in the United States of America
13 12 11 10 09 08   1 2 3 4 5

ISBN 978-0-89854-229-5

Library of Congress Cataloging-in-Publication Data

Building the local economy : cases in economic development / edited by Douglas J. Watson and John C. Morris.
     p. cm
   ISBN 978-0-89854-229-5
  1. Economic development projects—United States—Case studies. 2. Community development—United States—Case studies. 3. Local government—United States—Case studies. 4. Economic development—United States—Case studies. I. Watson, Douglas J. II. Morris, John C. (John Charles), 1959– III. Title.

   HC110.E44B85 2008
   338.973—dc22

                    2008018711

Contents

Preface

State and local governments have increasingly engaged in competition and, on occasion, cooperation for economic development. Elected officials often are judged by voters by the success or failure of their efforts in economic development. Most city managers and mayors report that they spend a large percentage of their time on economic development projects and efforts. In most states and localities, elected officials are held accountable for how well they fare in the competitive wars of economic development. In some cases, these officials have faced allegations of giving away too much in incentives to win a project for political reasons.

Economic development is a relatively new priority among local officials. Over the past quarter century, they have played an active role in developing local economies. State governments have competed for industrial projects since the 1930s, when Mississippi authorized the first issuance of industrial development bonds. The intense competition among states, regions, and localities is the result of a "winner-take-all" tax system in which taxes from an economic development project located in one jurisdiction are captured by that jurisdiction and thus are not available to others. Occasionally, states or regions of states will cooperate to compete against other states or regions with the goal of attracting jobs and taxes. In other cases, these cooperating entities may be in the running for the same project and will be competitors. While this notion of "coopertition" may seem counterintuitive, many jurisdictions believe their ability to compete is enhanced by cooperation with others: even if they lose a specific project, they probably were more competitive than they would have been otherwise, and they may be successful in subsequent efforts.

The chapters in this book describe how governments are competing, why they are competing, what tools or weapons they are using, and the consequences of competition. Local governments in most states have incentive programs such as tax abatement loan programs that they can implement if authorized to do so by their state legislatures. Since state elected officials are anxious to attract new jobs and create new taxes, incentive packages are competitive with surrounding states. If one state offers an incentive for development and gains a temporary advantage, other states follow suit.

After describing the broad context of economic development in the introduction, we present 15 case studies of state and local governments that have engaged in economic development competition and/or coopertition. The cases are from states as geographically spread as Oregon, Texas, Michigan, and Alabama. The reader will discover that, interestingly, the tools of economic development are strikingly similar from one state to the next. This homogeneity reflects both the diffusion of innovation and the determination of governments to stay competitive with their rivals for jobs and tax growth.

Economic development is no longer merely synonymous with industrial development, where governments compete to attract manufacturing facilities from other states to their own. While industrial development is still important because of the significance of manufacturing to the economy, local governments that are heavily dependent on sales taxes recognize the potential of other enterprises, such as a major shopping center, to generate tax revenue. Economic developers also are heavily involved in redevelopment, community development, and infrastructure projects.

Economic development practice is a fairly new academic discipline but is becoming increasingly popular in public affairs graduate programs. Students aspiring to be local government managers realize that they must be knowledgeable in this important new field as much as they are in human resource management or public financial administration. Our own experience in developing courses in economic development reveals a shortage of in-depth case studies that illustrate the complex environment in which local economic development takes place. We believe that the topics illustrated in the studies presented here will be helpful in the education of aspiring local government managers and economic development specialists.

Local officials involved in economic development will also find these case studies helpful. The pressure to engage in economic development can be fierce, and local government managers are constantly searching for information and ideas that will increase economic activity in their jurisdictions. The cases here illustrate strategies and techniques that have proved successful in different locations around the nation as well as several cases in which techniques were not so successful. Knowledge of "worst practices" can be just as important as knowledge of "best practices" in sorting out the complexities of economic development, and practitioners already in the field can learn important lessons from these case studies.

We wish to express our gratitude to our contributors in this venture as well as to the men and women in state and local governments who are committed to creating better opportunities through economic development for their fellow citizens. Although not compensated at the same level as private developers, they are motivated by a strong sense of public service and community betterment, and we are all better off for their efforts.

Douglas J. Watson
John C. Morris

INTRODUCTION

Competition, Coordination, or "Coopertition?"

Douglas J. Watson and John C. Morris

Over the past 25 years, local governments in the United States have become major players in economic development. Almost all of the nation's cities and counties have accepted as their responsibility the building of their local economies through a wide variety of economic development efforts. Like their counterparts at the state level, candidates for mayor often run for election based on promises to create jobs for local residents and tax revenue for the local government's coffers. The condition of the local economy and the impact elected officials have had on it often determine the fate of those elected and appointed officials and possibly even the underlying form of government based on promises of prosperity (Hassett and Watson 2007). Indeed, economic development often is the defining issue (Hassett and Watson 2007).

Other researchers have noted the role of local government in economic development. In her study of economic development agencies in 31 southeastern cities, Bowman (1988, 511; see also Watson 1995, 6) concluded that they were highly competitive and that the competitive ethos among the agencies was "pervasive." Local governments, particularly their economic development agencies, cooperate with each other when it is to their benefit, but "when the benefits cannot be shared by all, the incentive to cooperate is removed and cities become competitive with each other" (Bowman 1988, 512; see also Watson 1995, 6). Moreover, "[by] virtue of their existence, jurisdictions are self-interested entities. Competition is said to occur when benefits are returned to a subset of the jurisdictions seeking them. Cooperation is precluded by the simple fact that it leads to no joint gains. Self-interest dictates competitive behavior" (Bowman 1988, 512; see also Watson 1995, 6).

Key leaders in a community make the decisions that commit the resources of the community to economic development "deals" (Sharp 1990, 18). Because of their fiduciary responsibility over the funds, infrastructure, and property of a local government, they are required to make the nonroutine decisions of committing substantial community resources to a project. Sharp (1990, 18) argues that political leaders feel a need to be involved because the "questions of who gets what and assessments of the winners and losers in economic development tend to focus on city-to-city comparisons." Economic development is competitive—not cooperative—because it "pits communities (and regions) one against the other and forces local officials into an entrepreneurial, risk taking role that contrasts with the more traditional roles of the urban service policymaking and administrative oversight" (Sharp 1990, 19; see also Watson 1995, 6).

While competition is the ethos that dominates local economic development, communities may combine their forces to compete with other communities or regions. On occasion, states demand cooperation of local agencies when a large project, such as the Mercedes Benz factory in Alabama or the Toyota plant in Kentucky (Milward and Newman 1989), is at stake. For example, the cities of Tuscaloosa and Birmingham both contributed sizably to the package of incentives granted to Mercedes by the state of Alabama. In Kentucky, the Pulaski County government and the City of Somerset created a third entity to recruit industrial and other projects to the area. Oftentimes, smaller governmental units find that they must partner with others in order to be competitive with other regions.

Others have argued that there are pressures on local governments to partner with business for the purpose of economic development. Because members of the "growth machine" in a community benefit economically, local governments often are key players (Logan and Molotch 1987). Realtors, developers, bankers, news media, construction companies, attorneys, and numerous others play an important role in encouraging local governments to invest in growth. Because the organizations and individuals in the growth machine often are more well organized and influential than those who oppose growth, they tend to have a greater effect on local policies.

Although the current competition for economic development among state and local governments is more heated than at any time in the nation's history, its roots go back to the founding of the country. New Jersey "granted tax exemptions, the power to condemn property, and control over water resources to a private business founded by future president, James Madison" (Sugg 2007, 41). The federal government granted lands and bonds to the builders of the transcontinental railroads in the 1860s even while the Civil War raged (Ambrose 2002, 43–57). With the urging of Abraham Lincoln and the support of Congress, the railroads were built in six years thanks to the public subsidies of the Union Pacific and Central Pacific. The owners of the railroads gained tremendous wealth under sometimes scandalous circumstances, allegedly misusing government funds and lands (Ambrose 2002, 52–53).

The excesses of the 19th century, especially in states such as Pennsylvania, led by the end of the century to federal and state controls over the actions of governments in the use of public funds to intervene in the market (Babcock 1990, 9–43; see also Watson 1995, 10–12). The cities of Philadelphia and Pittsburgh made large investments in banks, railroads, and public infrastructure to serve private interests. When corruption was uncovered in many of these ventures, a state constitutional amendment was passed making it illegal to use public money to invest in private companies (Babcock 1990, 11; Watson 1995, 11). Similar actions by other states to rein in local governments' investment in private enterprise took place simultaneously.

The modern era of competition among governments, especially for industrial projects, started in 1936 when the state of Mississippi authorized the use of tax-free industrial development bonds to attract Realsilk Hosiery Mills (Rollinson 1976, 16; Watson 1995, 17; Sugg 2007, 41–42). A decade later, the state of Kentucky passed similar legislation after the Supreme Court ruled that there was no "substantial federal question" involved in the Mississippi law (Rollinson 1976, 16). Other southern states offered the same incentives by the early 1950s. By the early 1980s, all states were granting tax-free financing for manufacturing and many other businesses. Congress finally stepped in with the Tax Reform Act of 1986, eliminating tax-free bonds that took money from the federal treasury (Watson and Vocino 1990, 427–34).

During the 1980s, the relationship between the public and private sectors at the local level in the United States changed because state and local governments became much more involved in trying to influence market decisions. During that decade, local officials became markedly more proactive in their quest to create economic development in their communities than at any other time in the 20th century (Watson 1995, 1–3). Various explanations have been offered for the rise of the "entrepreneurial city," including the pressure for tax revenues resulting from the recession of the early 1980s and the establishment of the Urban Development Action Grant program by the U.S. Department of Housing and Urban Development. The program encouraged local governments to intervene in the marketplace by creating jobs and generating taxes. The amount of the grant to a local government depended on the size of the private investment and the number of new jobs created.

Many local governments are now viewed as entrepreneurs in activities that traditionally are considered to be reserved for the private market. One publication proclaimed, "The history of cities in the United States is entering a new era of public entrepreneurship. . . . This profound change in the way cities operate may best be termed 'urban entrepreneurship.' Cities are acting as risk-takers and active competitors in the urban economic game, and the key to each city's success is its ability to invest and to market shrewdly" (Duckworth, Simmons, and McNulty 1986, 4–5; Watson 1995, 1).

The political pressure to show results in economic development has led to this highly competitive situation among local governments. Although much has been written about privatization, public-private partnerships, outsourcing, and "government by proxy," local governments have become increasingly entrepreneurial, often intervening in the marketplace to affect decisions that private company executives make. In some cases, this intervention in the market has created opportunities for businesses that otherwise would not have been available. For example, many cities fund and operate business "incubators" for start-up companies that often emerge from partnerships between state and local governments and research universities. Others offer grants, loans, or free utility connections; construct speculative buildings; and provide infrastructure and free land for larger projects.

In other cases, however, local governments are fighting over the same projects. In these situations, companies realize that the jobs they offer and the taxes they pay are leverage they can use to gain incentives from local governments. Since the local governments are judged on how many new jobs they generate, it matters greatly whether the project is in their corporate limits or across the line in another jurisdiction. For example, in the suburbs of Dallas, the City of Plano believed that it had a commitment for a major retail mall. On the day the final paperwork was signed, Plano officials were told by the developer that the neighboring city of Frisco had offered a much more lucrative incentives package. As a result, the developers chose a site across the city limits in Frisco, which benefited from the residual development despite rebating most of the sales taxes to the developers.

In 1993, Alabama offered approximately $350 million in incentives to attract a Mercedes-Benz manufacturing facility. At the time, then-governor Jim Folsom and the state legislature were roundly criticized for using excessive incentives to buy the project (Watson 1995, 67–82). Since then, Honda, Hyundai, and dozens of suppliers have moved to Alabama based on the success that Mercedes has enjoyed there. Each successively larger automobile project has received even greater incentives. As Sugg (2007, 38) recounts, "In 2006 the Korean car maker Kia decided to build a $1.2 billion plant in West Point, Georgia. To land the project, the state offered a $420 million incentive package that included free land (bought from the previous owners at about 2.5 times the market value), tax-funded employee training, and a new $30 million Interstate interchange. Altogether, the subsidies amounted to $168,000 for each of the 2,500 jobs at the plant."

One economist argued that West Point was chosen because it is on the Alabama-Georgia line and Alabama has a trained force of autoworkers (Sugg 2007, 40). If that is the case, the benefit to Georgia would be minimal. There have been numerous calls from scholars to scale down the incentives war (see Chapter 1 of this book). However, there have been few serious efforts among practitioners to roll back incentives in our winner-take-all tax system. For example, as a result of uncontrolled raiding of businesses from one jurisdiction to another, the governors of New York, New Jersey, and Connecticut signed a pact that banned advertisements aimed at luring businesses from one state to another. Before the ink was dry on the agreement, New Jersey had recruited a company from New York (Dvorchak 1992, 15A). As Bowman (1988) pointed out, states and localities are competitors and will remain that way as long as the political stakes are based on economic success or failure.

Although all states participate in the incentives war, southern states have been especially notorious in the granting of incentives. According to Sugg (2007, 41), "It's hard to get a precise total of the dollars involved, but almost every major business relocation in the South is accompanied by a cornucopia of publicly funded grants, despite ample evidence that the subsidies have little impact on corporate site selection. Other regions of the nation, especially ones experiencing protracted economic downtowns, are increasingly emulating the South."

Bills that limit the moving of industries from one state to the next are introduced regularly in Congress. The argument of those proposing such legislation is that there is no net gain to the nation by an industry relocating from Wisconsin to Alabama, for example. However, in our system, it is unlikely that the federal government will attempt to stop competition among states in a meaningful way. Congress can limit federal tax abatements, as it did with the Tax Reform Act of 1986, and it can require industries to give workers adequate notice before they close their factories and move them to other locations (Watson 1995, 114; see also Watson and Vocino 1990).

There is no regulation of the awarding of incentives except when it is self-imposed by local or state governments. As long as elected officials are judged based on their ability to create and maintain a prosperous local economy, they are unlikely to try to alleviate the competitive situation. Once it becomes no longer politically acceptable to constituents to give major tax breaks to private companies, the "new civil war" over economic development will end (Watson 1995, 6–7). The few elected officials who decry the granting of incentives, such as former Dallas mayor Laura Miller (see Chapter 11), are usually marginalized by fellow elected officials and members of the growth machine.

Local economic development comes in many forms, as the contributions to this book will demonstrate. Oftentimes when one mentions economic development, industrial development comes to mind. The battles over major industrial projects over the past two decades have been featured prominently in the professional and academic literature. Projects such as Mercedes-Benz's selection of Alabama for its new site, Boeing's choice of Chicago over Dallas for its headquarters (Rast and Carlson 2006), United Parcel Service's decision to remain in Louisville (Koven and Lyons 2003), and Texas Instruments' selection of Richardson, Texas, for its $3 billion computer wafer plant (see Chapter 3) are well known.

Local leaders are innovative in not only fostering new businesses and creating jobs in their local areas but also addressing social and community problems. Local governments may encourage businesses to locate in low-income areas through the use of incentives, as was done in Detroit and Grand Rapids (Chapter 1). Alternatively, they may build public facilities or infrastructure to address the needs of the poor or homeless through cooperative efforts with the nonprofit and private sectors, as the case studies of Cleveland's transit construction (Chapter 9) and Dallas's homeless facility (Chapter 14) illustrate.

Local government involvement may be especially pronounced following natural disasters such as hurricanes and floods. At times, state governments may join local governments in assisting in the recovery of local economies (see, for example, Hassett and Handley 2006; Waugh and Smith 2006; Reese 2006). For example, following the devastation of Hurricane Katrina, a number of Mississippi's Gulf Coast cities were faced with the daunting task of rebuilding. State leaders in Mississippi took a lead role in helping cities devise a plan for reestablishing the gaming and tourism industry that has been so critical to the economy of South Mississippi. The state also facilitated public involvement at the local level to rebuild infrastructure, stimulate the economic recovery of the respective cities, and formulate an intergovernmental regional recovery plan (Hassett and Handley 2006).

Even in the era of "fend-for-yourself" federalism, the federal government plays an important role in local economic development, especially after disasters occur. Sometimes in these circumstances, governments are allowed to make investments they would not otherwise consider. For example, Sugg (2007, 40) questioned the decision of Mississippi senators Trent Lott and Thad Cochran in the immediate aftermath of Hurricane Katrina to allocate nearly $1 billion from the federal treasury to CSX railroad to move its rebuilt train tracks 10 miles to the north. The senators' justification for the subsidy to CSX was economic development. One critic charged the senators with "carrying the water for the developers and casino operators who now can build along the coastal land where the tracks originally ran" (Sugg 2007, 40).

Many local economic development programs are targeted to the specific needs of a community and are important elements of a community's strategic plan. Some local governments' approach to development is to accept any and all projects that are chosen for their communities (Rubin 1999). Most governments realize that they have limited resources and direct their funds toward reaching certain community objectives, as demonstrated by the efforts of large cities like Dallas and Detroit to create projects in their downtowns.

Major Themes

In the chapters that follow, case studies are presented that illustrate the wide variety of activities that local governments engage in to attract new development projects. Cities across the country that are investing heavily in economic development are represented. Some are using the typical tools offered by state governments such as tax incentives to create investment in deteriorating areas or to entice a major industry. Others are addressing social issues in partnerships with nonprofits, building new town centers where none existed before, luring (or hoping to lure) major projects through heavy public investment in infrastructure, or facilitating efforts to recover from natural or man-made disasters.

Perhaps the most pervasive theme in the case studies is the importance of cooperation and collaboration as competitive tools—a notion that may seem counterintuitive. Cities or states in competition with one another would seem to have little to gain by working closely with their competitors; such actions can obviate comparative advantage. As many of the cases highlight, however, cooperation often enhances a government's ability to be competitive by bringing to bear additional resources or options that are beyond the scope of individual actors. This cooperation can cut across local units of government (Chapters 3 and

10) or state boundaries (Chapters 6 and 7). Even in cases that mostly are limited to local jurisdictions, state governments and even the federal government can play important roles in ensuring that legal authority or fiscal resources are available (Chapter 13). This phenomenon of "coopertition" may significantly enhance a community's chances of success. Moreover, the ability of governments and businesses to leverage existing collaborative networks can prove to be an effective strategy. All of the cases in this book highlight the relative importance of cooperation and collaboration and illustrate the significant advantages of a competitive strategy founded on coopertition.

The second theme of the book is the tremendous variation in the organizational structures that exist to support economic development goals. Although it is often assumed that local governments are typically the driving force behind economic development efforts, a broad range of actors across all sectors of society are active in this arena, including planning agencies and districts, universities, nonprofit organizations, state governments, federal agencies, utility companies, and transportation agencies, among others. Through cooperative and collaborative actions, these actors enhance the ability of communities to compete for favorable development outcomes. However, many of these entities have their own organizational agendas that must continually be balanced against the policy goals of economic growth and sustainability.

The paramount importance of available space and physical infrastructure is a third theme. Chapters 8, 9, and 15 highlight the need for land on which to build new infrastructure. The benefits of having basic infrastructure already in place are emphasized in Chapters 4, 12, and 13. As evidenced in these cases, localities are able to be much more competitive—and much more successful—when fundamental needs are easily met. Communities that must invest heavily in basic infrastructure (whether in transportation, education, or utilities) will have a harder time attracting new development to their area.

A fourth theme is the importance of vision and leadership. Vision is necessary to be able to articulate a future plan, and leadership is essential to pull disparate actors together and focus their efforts toward a clearly defined goal. Leaders may be of two varieties: A political leader is one who is able to muster the political will and resources of governments across both space and time and to convince people that a particular project is worthwhile (Chapters 6 and 7). An entrepreneurial leader is able to leverage available resources to sustain a workable, feasible, and palatable plan (Chapters 3 and 11). The importance and abilities of both types of leader come through in many of these case studies.

Finally, it would be remiss to overlook the most intangible factor of all—luck—which although clearly beyond human control is nonetheless crucial to the success or failure of economic development efforts (Chapters 1 and 13). The vagaries of natural disasters (Chapter 10), changes in national demographics (Chapter 7), or the particular interests in a community (Chapter 14) may be deciding factors. Some of these factors may be mitigated or overcome by other conditions: communities can, in some circumstances, make their own luck. Still, as Kingdon (1984) notes in his discussion of the convergence of policy streams, there is no certainty that all the factors will align at the right moment in time.

The Case Studies

The following chapters feature a variety of scenarios to illustrate these themes. In Chapter 1, Gary Sands and Laura Reese present scholarly evidence against the effectiveness of incentives in swaying corporate location decisions and point to the importance of using incentives as part of a broader approach to economic development. By examining a range of incentives provided by cities in Michigan, the authors find that even though all cities use some combination of economic incentives, there is little to suggest that any particular incentive or package of incentives is any more effective than another and that other factors may be equally important in determining the ultimate success of any city pursuing economic development.

Julia Melkers and Laura Czohara ask in Chapter 2 whether state and local governments are providing the kind of information prospective firms need and whether that information makes locations competitive in the selection process. Examining the results of surveys of site location officials, economic development professionals, and state economic development directors, they explore what type of information is important to businesses and what information governments and economic development agencies produce. They find that states and communities that communicate effectively with prospective firms are generally more competitive than governments that do not.

In Chapter 3, Kimberly Aaron and Douglas Watson analyze the use of economic development networks as an effective competitive strategy. Drawing on the case of the siting of a semiconductor plant in Richardson, Texas, the authors discuss the development and operation of a collaborative network that included state, county, and municipal governments; business and industry leaders; a state university; and other local groups and citizens. This network provided a conduit for information and ideas and was instrumental in both the removal of barriers and the creation of incentives to entice an international firm to locate in Richardson.

The ability of second-tier regions to compete for high-technology jobs is the subject of Chapter 4. Heike Mayer presents the case of Portland, Oregon, a city trying to compete with California's Silicon Valley for high-tech jobs. Mayer reports that the critical factors were the ability of local governments to work collaboratively with the high-tech firms and to meet their demands for both traditional economic incentives and critical public goods such as higher education. Realizing that a steady supply of trained and educated workers was critical to the long-term viability of the area, these firms pressured local and state officials to invest in engineering and computer science programs. They also sought and obtained venture capital to create technology incubators that would enable them to work directly with universities to produce both graduates and high-tech research.

The use of regional cooperative structures is the focus of Chapter 5. John Lombard presents two examples of regional partnership: Team New England, fostered by a regional utility company, and the Hartford-Springfield Economic Partnership, a cross-state initiative to encourage economic investment in the Hartford-Springfield corridor. Each works to promote New England as a viable alternative for new business investment. Lombard concludes that the success of the partnerships is due in part to the fact that they built on existing structures and did not require additional resources from participating governments. He also finds that cooperation did not obviate competition: the partnerships aim to attract business to the region, and state and local governments still compete to be the chosen site.

Chapter 6, by Joe Sumners, details a series of economic development projects in Alabama and Mississippi. This region has struggled economically for many years, yet there are several stories that illustrate success. These cases highlight the importance of leadership, community involvement, determination, and goal definition. Sumners also examines a regional economic development agency in Alabama that was formed to market resources and publicize locations in the region, much like the partnerships discussed in Chapter 5 were intended to do.

The dilemma of economic loss in the Rust Belt states of the Northeast is the subject of Chapter 7. The author, Wendy Hassett, turns the traditional model of economic development on its head. Drawing on the case of Youngstown, Ohio, Hassett outlines the choices available to civic leaders when faced with declining traditional "smokestack" industries. Rather than recruit new heavy industry, civic leaders sought to attract high-technology firms and identified a vision for improved quality of life: more green space, better schools, revitalized neighborhoods. The case highlights the importance of not only leadership and vision but also collaboration with civic groups, business leaders, and education officials and the creation of incentives and projects that can leverage these resources.

In Chapter 8, Bob Sharp describes the competition among cities in the Hampton Roads area of Virginia to turn town centers into economic development engines. Spurred largely by tremendous growth in suburban sprawl in the area, these communities are adopting this approach to both create a sense of identity and attract high-end restaurant, retail, and entertainment establishments. The two cases presented here illustrate the efforts of two adjoining cities (Newport News and Hampton) to create such a district: one by using largely undeveloped land and the other by redeveloping an existing retail center. Sharp concludes that while the initial impetus for the projects was a desire to keep pace with their neighbors, both communities also sought developments that would be unique, economically viable, and lasting.

Chapter 9 by Floun'say Caver and Grace Gallucci presents a case in which a transportation project was used as a catalyst for economic development. The Euclid Avenue corridor in Cleveland, Ohio, had lost much of its past luster but remained an important conduit to downtown Cleveland. City leaders secured funding from the U.S. Department of Transportation to build a bus rapid transit demonstration project along Euclid Avenue, which in turn generated mixed-use development in the form of revitalized residences, new retail shops, and increased office space. It also provided a convenient connection between downtown Cleveland and its northeastern suburbs, thus enhancing the economic success of businesses in the city center. Caver and Gallucci conclude that while transit-oriented development is not a "utopian" solution, it does provide potential that goes well beyond the movement of people through the corridor.

The destruction wrought by Hurricanes Katrina and Rita in 2005 along the Gulf Coast exacted a stiff price in terms of not only human lives but also the ability of the region to remain economically viable in the future. The loss of population along with the near-total destruction of critical infrastructure, housing stock, and business and retail space left the region with significant challenges. In Chapter 10, Paul Battaglio details some of the economic recovery efforts in Louisiana, including collaboration and partnership among federal, state, and local governments and the enactment of a range of economic incentives and programs to help existing businesses rebuild and attract new business investment. Although recovery efforts are still in the formative stage, early indicators suggest promising outcomes.

The competition to host professional sports teams is often intense. In Chapter 11, Kimberly Aaron discusses the efforts of cities in the Dallas–Fort Worth Metroplex to become the new home of the Dallas Cowboys, a competition ultimately won by the City of Arlington, Texas. The story is one of competition among cities, negotiations with the franchise owner, and the importance of political unity within jurisdictions. Aaron ultimately concludes that the outcome was due to the combination of incentives offered, unity of purpose among the city's leaders, and the ability of the city to build an effective political coalition to attract the new stadium.

In Chapter 12, Donna Handley recounts the efforts of the City of Birmingham, Alabama, to build a domed stadium. Unlike the case presented in the previous chapter, Birmingham did not have a professional sports team ready to move into the new facility; rather, the idea was to build the new facility as a means to attract a franchise or other large sporting events to the area. The new stadium was to be the crown jewel in an ongoing effort to expand and improve the facilities in the Birmingham-Jefferson Convention Complex. Underlying the story are the myriad struggles over political control, public credit for success (or failure), squabbling between the county commission and the state legislature over funding mechanisms, and a lack of effective leadership in the community. In spite of these shortcomings, Handley reports that many actors are still optimistic that the project eventually will materialize.

Perhaps one of the more economically devastating things that can happen in a community is the closing of a military installation. These bases often are tremendous economic engines, and their loss can be catastrophic. With the ongoing efforts to downsize the military installations through the Base Realignment and Closure process, many communities have felt this pain directly. In Chapter 13, Paula Loomis and John Morris analyze the redevelopment of the former Williams Air Force Base near Phoenix, Arizona, which ceased military operations in 1993. They highlight the importance of the articulation of a vision; careful planning; collaboration among governments, public authorities, and private industry; and prevailing conditions and needs. Their conclusion is that the long-term economic effect of the facility is likely to exceed its impact as a military installation.

In Chapter 14, Alicia Schortgen examines the role of nonprofit organizations in economic development efforts. Although nonprofits often are critical partners in the provision, production, and delivery of services, these agencies can be caught in the middle when economic development interests collide with community needs. The clash of values inherent in the relationship between the public and private sectors forms the basis for analysis in the case of a project in Dallas to transform an abandoned building into an affordable housing development project. Schortgen concludes that the nonprofit sector is uniquely positioned to facilitate collaboration between business and government.

The NIMBY ("not-in-my-back-yard") syndrome is a common factor in decisions to locate industries, waste dumps, and other less-than-desirable forms of economic activity. Often included in this list are prisons; most citizens would prefer to live as far away from a prison as possible. In Chapter 15, Michelle Hoyman, Jenn Weaver, and Micah Weinberg describe a program in North Carolina to treat prisons as economic development projects. Rather than building a few large facilities, state leaders reasoned that smaller facilities spread across the state could be conducive to local economic development. In interviews with community leaders in counties with prisons, Hoyman, Weaver, and Weinberg find that job creation tends to be the most important factor but that local leaders are also concerned about the costs of land, sewage, and water. The authors conclude that North Carolina's use of "managed competition" in siting decisions helps prevent a "race to the bottom."

Collectively, these chapters develop the themes broached in this introduction through the telling of stories drawn from cases around the nation, cutting across project types and development goals and illustrating the notion of coopertition. Although similar issues are involved, no two cases are truly alike—yet they are bound together by commonalities that can help form the basis for a greater understanding of the necessary factors for successful economic growth.

References

Ambrose, S. E. 2002. *To America: Personal reflections of an historian*. New York: Simon and Schuster.

Babcock, R. F. 1990. The city as entrepreneur: Fiscal wisdom or regulatory folly? In *City deal making*, ed. T. J. Lassar, 9–43. Washington, DC: Urban Land Institute.

Bowman, Ann O'M. 1988. Competition for economic development among southeastern cities. *Urban Affairs Quarterly* 23:511–27.

Duckworth, R. P., M. Simmons, and R. H. McNulty. 1986. *The entrepreneurial American city*. Washington, DC: Partners for Livable Places and the U.S. Department of Housing and Urban Development.

Dvorchak, R. 1992. Business incentives incite new civil war. *Montgomery Advertiser*, October 4, 1A, 15A.

Hassett, W. L., and D. M. Handley. 2006. Hurricane Katrina: Mississippi's response. *Public Works Management and Policy* 10:295–305.

Hassett, W. L., and D. J. Watson. 2007. *Civic battles: When cities change their form of government*. Boca Raton: PrAcademics Press.

Kingdon, J. W. 1984. *Agendas, alternatives, and public policies*. Boston: Little, Brown.

Koven, S. G., and T. S. Lyons. 2003. *Economic development: Strategies for state and local practice*. Washington, DC: ICMA Publications.

Logan, J. R., and H. L. Molotch. 1987. The city as a growth machine. In *Urban fortunes: The political economy of place*, 50–98. Berkeley: University of California Press.

Milward, H. B., and H. H. Newman. 1989. State incentive packages with the industrial location decision. *Economic Development Quarterly* 3:203–22.

Rast, J., and V. Carlson. 2006. When Boeing landed in Chicago: Lessons for regional economic development. *State and Local Government Review* 38:1–11.

Reese, L. A. 2006. Economic versus natural disasters: If Detroit had a hurricane.... *Economic Development Quarterly* 20:219–31.

Rollinson, M. 1976. *Small issue industrial development bonds*. Chicago: Capital Publishing Company.

Rubin, H. J. 1999. Shoot anything that flies; claim anything that falls. In *Approaches to economic development*, ed. J. P. Blair and L. A. Reese, 263–77. Thousand Oaks, CA: Sage.

Sharp, E. B. 1990. The meaning of economic development. In *Urban politics and administration*, 215–35. New York: Longman.

Sugg, J. F. 2007. The folly of southern hospitality. *Reason* (May): 38–44.

Watson, D. J. 1995. *The new civil war: Government competition for economic development*. Westport, CT: Praeger.

Watson, D. J., and T. Vocino. 1990. The changing nature of intergovernmental fiscal relationships: The impact of the 1986 Tax Reform Act on state and local governments. *Public Administration Review* 50:427–34.

Waugh, W. L., and B. R. Smith. 2006. Economic development and reconstruction on the Gulf Coast after Katrina. *Economic Development Quarterly* 20:211–18.

CHAPTER 1

Implementing Economic Development Incentives: The Case of Grand Rapids, Michigan

Gary Sands and Laura Reese

Older cities throughout North America are increasingly faced with the challenge of attracting investment and people to ensure continued vitality. As businesses and households of means opt for suburban locations, central cities and older suburbs are left with needy populations and aging infrastructure to be served by a diminishing tax base. In many instances, the quality of urban life declines, further encouraging those businesses and residents who can to move to newer environments with fewer immediate problems.

Efforts to address these issues have often relied on limited interventions to offset the disadvantages of a central city or older suburban location through combinations of subsidies and abatements. Already stressed urban governments are often required to "buy" residents and business by offering financial incentives designed to mitigate the perceived disadvantages of urban locations or lower the costs of living for the former and production costs for the latter. Because cities generally, and those in the state of Michigan in particular, lack sufficient local resources to offer subsidies, economic development techniques have often focused on incentives. They are most typically based on an array of tax abatement schemes, providing a temporary, partial reduction in local property taxes.

The literature on the effectiveness of tax abatements and other forms of economic development incentives generally has been rather skeptical of their effectiveness. Over the past two decades, scholars and critics have made a number of recommendations for reshaping local economic development policies. No analyst has recommended increasing the use of property tax abatements. Yet their continued use belies the many concerns about their effectiveness raised in evaluations spanning decades (see, for example, Due 1961; Ahlbrandt and DeAngelis 1987; Schwarz and Volgy 1992; Fisher and Peters 1998; Peters and Fisher 2004).

Although some research has found positive outcomes related to tax incentives under particular conditions—such as when they are targeted or focused on a limited geographic area (Bartik 1991; Gramlich 1997; Dardia 1998; Oakland and Testa 2000)—a recent meta-analysis by Peters and Fisher (2004) concludes that their overall effectiveness remains in doubt. Among the 10 studies examined, 3 showed at least minor benefits, another 3 showed no discernable impacts of incentives, and 4 had completely ambiguous effects. Overall, the authors concluded that even after four decades of research, there is no consensus on whether tax incentives have any effect at all: "[T]he best case is that incentives work about 10% of the time, and are simply a waste of money the other 90%" (2004, 32).

Why, then, do states continue to create such incentive programs, and why do local governments continue to use them? In part, the answer may lie in the perceived competitiveness of economic development: incentives must be offered because other localities are offering them. It also may reflect political realities. Local officials who refuse to offer incentives and thereby lose a large investment opportunity are likely to be seen as derelict in their duties and may face a difficult reelection (Wolman 1996).

This chapter does not attempt to resolve these larger questions inherent in the use of incentives. Rather, it is presumed that local governments make use of the incentive programs available to them. The concern here is whether such programs can be more effective when they are not used indiscriminately. That is, can incentives be used strategically to achieve maximum benefits, at least for the locality that employs them? Examining how localities can make the best of this situation may be a more useful approach than arguing for the abolition of all incentives.

Nature of Economic Development Tools

The State of Michigan's strategy for local economic development is particular rather than general. That is, rather than granting municipalities a broad mandate within which economic development strategies can be designed, state enabling legislation provides municipalities with a number of narrowly defined tools that can be used in specific circumstances.[1] Most Michigan economic development incentives are targeted to "distressed" communities, although several (most notably, industrial tax abatements) are widely available.

This examination focuses on three representative economic tools available to municipalities in Michigan: industrial facilities tax abatements, neighborhood enterprise zones, and renaissance zones. The first of these is effectively available to all local governments in the state while the latter can only be used by a limited number of distressed communities. Each program has been available to local governments for at least a decade.

Industrial Facilities Tax Abatements

The Industrial Facilities Tax (IFT) Abatement program (created by Public Act [PA] 198 of 1974) allows local governments to establish plant rehabilitation or industrial development districts if the property tax levy equals or exceeds 30 mills. Eligible industrial property may consist of both real and personal property related to a manufacturing operation under the same ownership, including office, engineering, research and development, warehousing or parts distribution facilities, and research and development laboratories of suppliers to manufacturers.

A tax abatement may be granted for a maximum of 12 years from the completion of the facility, although the local legislative body may grant the abatement for a shorter time period. The abatement can be revoked if industrial facility improvements or construction are not completed within two years or if the company leaves the area.

PA 198 permits municipalities in Michigan wide discretion to abate industrial property taxes, which they do at one of the highest levels in the nation (Reese and Fasenfest 1997; Reese and Sands 2007). More than 14,000 IFT abatements were granted in Michigan between 1980 and 2001. Because of its widespread availability and use, PA 198 might best be considered an effort to increase the state's competitiveness rather than a program designed primarily to assist specific distressed communities. Most of Michigan's local governments are eligible to participate, and about one-third have granted at least one IFT abatement (Sands and Zalmezak 2001).

Neighborhood Enterprise Zones

PA 147 of 1992 established the Neighborhood Enterprise Zone (NEZ) program. The program offers tax incentives for development or rehabilitation of owner-occupied housing. Any one of the state-designated Core Communities is eligible to designate areas as an NEZ. The goals of the program are to "spur the development and rehabilitation of residential housing in communities where it may not otherwise occur." An NEZ also "promotes neighborhood revitalization [and] encourages owner occupied housing and new investment by lowering property taxes" (Citizens Research Council of Michigan 2007, 58–59).

Property taxes within an NEZ are reduced for eligible projects: rehabilitated facilities (i.e., a rehabilitated existing structure with a cash value of $80,000 or less per unit) or a new facility with one or two units, one of which must be owner occupied as a principal residence. This latter definition excludes rental apartments but does permit new condominium units. NEZs are not widely used in the state, even among communities eligible to designate them. Of the 33 eligible municipalities, only 12 have implemented NEZs. Several municipalities have established multiple NEZs.

Renaissance Zones

In 1996, the State of Michigan created the Renaissance Zone (RZ) initiative (PA 376 of 1996), an economic development program that offers greater tax concessions than any previous development incentive program (Michigan Jobs Commission 1997; Tyszkiewicz 1997; Rothwell 1997). PA 376 allows all occupants of RZs exemptions from a dozen different state and local taxes, including state and local income taxes and most property taxes: state sales tax and any ad valorem taxes pledged to the repayment of bonded indebtedness are the only nonfederal taxes that continue to be collected.

State-designated distressed communities may apply to the State Administrative Board for RZ designation. Within the broad parameters of enabling legislation, localities have considerable latitude in the design of zones. The initial zones were created in aging industrial centers, declining rural communities, and relatively prosperous small towns and suburbs. In 1999, the Michigan legislature amended the RZ Act through PA 98 of 1999, allowing for the creation of additional RZs. This same legislation allowed existing zone communities to make changes to zones, including creating additional subzones, enlarging existing subzones, and extending the life of zones. Currently, there are 156 RZs in Michigan.

Overall Program Comparison

Table 1 summarizes the characteristics of these programs. There are substantial differences among them in terms of not only the benefits provided but also the costs to municipalities and the likelihood that public benefits will actually accrue. In most cases, there are obvious trade-offs among the three techniques in terms of forgone revenue and community paybacks. For example, RZs and NEZs imply greater levels of tax revenue loss for cities (and income tax loss as well for the former), but their duration is limited, at least affording the possibility that at some point the community will recoup some of the tax revenue. Because firms may be granted multiple IFT abatements for a single location (so long as they make multiple qualifying investments), it is likely the communities will never recoup the 50 percent of foregone property taxes.

Table 1: Characteristics of Incentive Tools

Characteristic	Renaissance zones	Neighborhood enterprise zones	Industrial facilities tax zones
Duration	12(+3) years	12 years	12 years (renewable)
Investment potential	possible	likely	certain
Tax loss (property)	100%	60%–70%	50%
Tax loss (income)	100%[a]	0	0
Deferred revenue	yes	yes	yes
Increased cost of services	yes	yes	yes
Increased cost of schools	uncertain	yes	no

Source: Citizens Research Council of Michigan (2007).
[a] Zone workers who reside outside the renaissance zone pay income tax at regular rates.

Homeowners in NEZs receive the benefit of reduced taxes only if they make qualifying investments in property located in the zone. On the other hand, some level of investment is guaranteed with PA 198 abatements while, particularly for RZs, the creation of the zone is largely speculative. Investment will only occur if businesses and residents find the zone an attractive place in which to relocate or reinvest.

Finally, the three incentive programs differ significantly in terms of "who benefits" from the tax breaks. In the case of IFT abatements, the beneficiaries are exclusively industrial facilities whereas NEZs benefit only residents. RZs have the broadest potential beneficiaries since any investment in the zone is covered: commercial, industrial, or residential. In RZs, it would be up to an individual municipality to designate the desired emphasis for zone development. Of the three incentives, the most speculative involving the greatest cost in forgone revenue are RZs. Thus, it might be expected that cities would be more judicious in their use of incentives and would attempt to employ them more strategically in cases in which investment is likely to occur but only with particular incentives. Clearly, the designation of RZs covering a large portion of the municipal land area would mean extensive forgone revenue. RZs, followed by NEZs, entail the greatest levels of foregone revenue if investment in the zones actually occurs. IFT abatements, for which the highest level of taxes are paid upfront, are only given when actual investment occurs, making them perhaps the safest bet, particularly when they are granted for new jobs and investment.

Case Methodology

The Data

The data for this analysis come from several sources. First, data on tax abatements come from the files of the Michigan Economic Development Corporation and its predecessor agencies. These data cover all abatements awarded from 1980 to 2001 and include the number of abatements, projected real and personnel property investment, and projected retained and created jobs. Census and property assessment information for the years 1980, 1990, and 2000 were added to the abatement data set.[2]

Currently, no state or local source collects comparative data on the RZ or NEZ programs. Information about these incentives comes from the files of the Michigan Economic Growth Corporation and the cities being compared. Face-to-face interviews were conducted with local officials to assess the nature and extent of strategic behavior on the part of local decision makers.

The primary focus of this chapter is the City of Grand Rapids; however, to put that city's use of incentives into perspective, specific comparisons are made with Detroit. Both Grand Rapids and Detroit have made extensive use of IFT abatements over the life of the program, although the former has done so at a higher rate and, indeed, is the most active user of tax abatements in the state. Overall the propensity for communities on the west side of the state to issue tax abatements has been far greater than those in the Detroit metropolitan area even though the latter is more populous. Wayne, Oakland, and Macomb Counties, in which most of Metropolitan Detroit's population resides, reported fewer IFT abatement certificates between 1991 and 2001 than did Kent and Ottawa Counties, two counties in the Grand Rapids metropolitan area with less than one-fifth of the total population in Wayne, Oakland, and Macomb Counties.

Detroit has made much more extensive use of NEZs; currently, there are roughly 100 NEZs within the city. Grand Rapids, on the other hand, has only three NEZs. The two cities are relatively similar in their use of RZs: 16 of the state's 156 RZs are within Detroit, and 10 are in Grand Rapids.

Community Profiles

It is a common perception in Michigan that Grand Rapids (along with other areas in West Michigan) has become a dynamic and prosperous urban center while in Detroit, a period of decline that began a half century ago continues. Indeed, many empirical measures support this contention (Table 2).

Table 2: Community Profile Data

Variable	Detroit		Grand Rapids	
	2000	2005	2000	2005
Population (N)	951,270	836,056	197,800	193,568
Foreign born	4.8%	6.3%	10.5%	3.4%
Bachelor's degree or higher	11.0%	12.1%	23.8%	26.1%
Labor force participation	56.3%	57.6%	65.8%	70.9%
Unemployment	7.3%	14.0%	4.4%	8.0%
Median household income	$29,526	$28,069	$37,224	$38,229
Per capita income	$14,717	$15,042	$17,661	$18,608
Individuals in poverty	26.1%	31.4%	15.7%	20.8%

Source: U.S. Census Bureau (2000).

In Detroit, post-2000 population decline has resulted in a 7 percent increase in the residential vacancy rate, leaving one of every six homes in the city empty. The property tax base in Detroit was just over $10,000 per capita in 2000. About 6 percent of the total represented industrial real property. By 2005, the total property tax base had increased to $16,000 per capita, with industrial property maintaining its 6 percent share. After homestead exemptions and tax abatements, the city's taxable value per capita was about $11,100 in 2005.

In Grand Rapids, the property tax base in 2000 averaged almost $19,000 per person, with about 8 percent of the total consisting of industrial real property. By 2005, the tax base in Grand Rapids increased by almost half, to $27,800 per capita. Industrial property values rose by only 14 percent, however. Nevertheless, the total taxable value in 2006 was $23,300 per person—more than double the comparable figure for Detroit.

Use of Tools

Industrial Facilities Tax Abatements

Both cities were active in granting PA 198 abatements during the 1990s; Grand Rapids provided more than twice as many of these tax breaks than did Detroit (Table 3). The total investment generated in

Detroit as a result of IFT abatements was more than $4.5 billion. Abatements involving real property (i.e., industrial buildings) represented less than 3 percent of this total. Grand Rapids granted only $438 million in abatements, with almost 30 percent of the investment going toward new manufacturing plants.

Table 3: Industrial Facilities Tax Abatement Activity, 1991–2001

	Total		Per 1,000	
Activity	Grand Rapids	Detroit	Grand Rapids	Detroit
Certificates (N)	221	107	1.12	0.11
Investment real property	$129,418,000	$130,254,000	$654	$137
Investment personal property	$308,512,000	$4,406,243,000	$1,558	$4,770
Total investment	$437,930,000	$4,536,497,000	$2,212	$4,770
New jobs (N)	3,286	2,510	16.6	2.6
Retained jobs (N)	12,184	24,742	61.5	26.0
Total jobs (N)	15,470	27,252	78.1	28.7

Source: Authors' analysis of 1980–2006 state tax abatement application data (Michigan Department of Treasury 2000; 2005).

As noted earlier, Detroit—although more distressed than Grand Rapids in terms of any measure—issued far fewer certificates in total and even fewer per capita than did Grand Rapids. Total projected investment associated with abatement certificates over the 20-year period was higher in Detroit, however. Despite having issued a larger number of abatements, Grand Rapids had less total projected investment, about half a billion dollars.

Detroit—and to a somewhat lesser extent, Grand Rapids—has relatively little real property investment per capita associated with abatements. Overall, projected investment in personal property (i.e., new equipment) is more common than investment in real property (i.e., new facilities). Industrial facilities tax abatements in Michigan most typically are used for the retooling of existing factories.

Detroit does better than Grand Rapids in terms of projected investment per certificate; average investment per certificate was about $20 million in Detroit but less than $1 million in Grand Rapids. Again, investment figures are projections drawn from applications. Absent outcome data (which are neither collected nor required by the state), it is not certain how reliable these figures are. It seems reasonable to assume, however, that Detroit has substantially higher investment than Grand

Rapids as a result of the abatements granted, regardless of the accuracy of the estimates.

Detroit issued just over 100 abatements designed to attract more than $4.5 billion in investment. Grand Rapids granted twice as many abatements but received only $438 million in investment. Detroit secured more than 14 times the amount of investment in personal property through abatements (i.e., machinery and equipment) than did Grand Rapids. On the surface, then, it appears that Grand Rapids has a higher transaction cost for each dollar invested. Indeed, the city has granted on average one abatement every two weeks for the last 20 years but is well down on the list of overall total investment purportedly attached to abatements.

Abatements in Detroit also involved many more projected jobs than in Grand Rapids. Indeed, Detroit's abatements involved almost twice as many jobs as did those in Grand Rapids. In Detroit, each certificate involved an average of 200 jobs while Grand Rapids averaged fewer then 60. However, in Grand Rapids, abatements promised a greater number of new jobs, although only half as many jobs were retained there as a result of abatements compared with Detroit. Abated jobs in Grand Rapids accounted for about 16 percent of the city's labor force—double the proportion in Detroit.

These differences are even sharper when the respective populations are considered. Relative to population, Grand Rapids was 12 times more likely to grant a request for a tax abatement than was Detroit. Investment per capita in Detroit was about $4,600 compared with about $1,550 in Grand Rapids. However, the number of employment opportunities in Grand Rapids relative to its population was more than two and a half times higher than in Detroit.

There are two ways to view these projected investment figures. On the one hand, the amount of investment projected to be generated by each abatement generally is higher in central cities (and Detroit in particular). However, most of the investment is in personal property, meaning abatements are being used in central cities and older suburbs primarily for retooling existing facilities. If these businesses would have remained or retooled regardless, then the value of the investment would be, in effect, a measure of forgone tax revenue. Based on this reasoning, Detroit clearly is paying a very high price in terms of foregone taxes for each job while Grand Rapids pays a much lower price. Detroit gave up over $33,000 in property tax revenue for each promised job; the cost to Grand Rapids was about $1,500. In part, Detroit's costs are the result of the city's high tax rates; if Detroit's property tax rate was 50 mills (roughly the average of other metropolitan Detroit communities), the cost per job would be about $23,000—still much higher than in Grand Rapids.

Overall then, although it issues far more abatements than Detroit, Grand Rapids appears to be paying lower costs in forgone revenue per job and has greater investment in personal property and new jobs than Detroit. Detroit, however, appears to garner greater investment and more jobs per abatement.

Neighborhood Enterprise Zones

Detroit's use of the NEZ program can only be described as indiscriminate. Since NEZs were first made available, Detroit has created more than 100 districts; from 2003 through 2005, 50 new NEZs were established, with the potential of providing more than 6,000 homeownership opportunities. While initially NEZs were established to facilitate sales of new single-family homes and condominiums, some of the more recent designations have included substantial amounts of existing housing, allowing for both rehabilitation and new infill development. Currently, more than 5,400 Detroit homeowners are benefiting from NEZ property tax abatements.

In July 2006, the City of Detroit began using the new Homestead NEZ program. Detroit is one of only two cities in the state that has elected to participate in the program, which provides a relatively modest reduction in total property taxes to owner-occupants who invest at least $500 in their homes.[3] The intent of this program is to encourage middle- and upper-income homeowners to move into or remain in the designated areas. It has been estimated that this initiative could cost the city as much as $9.3 million in foregone property taxes annually. Under this program, Detroit has designated 26 areas; net acreage is just over five square miles, or almost 4 percent of the entire area of the city. Despite its recent introduction, more than 1,870 Detroit homeowners have received this property tax reduction.

The NEZ program has been highly successful in attracting new housing construction to designated areas. Unfortunately, this success has resulted in a culture of dependency in which no new owner-occupied housing is being built in the city without the award of tax abatements. Because property tax concessions have also been granted for virtually all new rental housing developed in the city in the past decade, the short-term effect has been a disproportionate increase in demand for services relative to revenue gains.

An implicit assumption of the NEZ program is that during the period of reduced taxes, sufficient improvements will be made in the quality of services (including public safety, education, and environmental services) such that zone residents will willingly accept the steep rise in property taxes at the expiration of the abatement. Neither of these assumptions is proving to be correct. Because overall quality of public services in NEZ neighborhoods has not improved substantially, home-owners have petitioned for abatement extensions. Although short-term fixes have been implemented, the potential effects of the expiring abate-ments on the city's housing market are not clear.

The City of Grand Rapids has been much more parsimonious in establishing NEZs. No NEZs were created until 2003; currently, there are only three such zones in the entire city, and these zones cover only about 35 blocks. They consist primarily of built-up areas as op-posed to vacant sites. Nevertheless, 62 of the 64 NEZ certificates in Grand Rapids are for new construction units.

What is most notable about the Grand Rapids NEZs is that the city continues to enjoy new residential development outside the zones. Downtown Grand Rapids alone has added more than 1,000 units in the past decade. The city has consciously followed a policy of using other forms of incentives (such as Historic Tax Credits and Brownfield and Obsolete Property Redevelopment Incentives) to support new housing in most locations.

Renaissance Zones

The City of Detroit Renaissance Zone consists of 16 subzones, which total 1,434 acres, or 1.6 percent of the total area of the city. To date, the city has reported $737,250,000 in total private investment in the zone and the creation of 1,872 jobs. About 11 percent of the invest-ment occurred before 2000. This earlier period accounted for over 53 percent of the reported job growth, however.

The initial RZ designations were largely speculative; that is, relatively large areas were designated in hopes that tax benefits would attract investors. The later expansions and new subzones were more specific, targeting the requirements of identified development projects. While the city has extended the life of several of the initial RZs, a few will no longer offer tax breaks as of 2008.

Grand Rapids pursued a clear strategy in its RZ proposal. The City of Grand Rapids Renaissance Zone is made up of 10 subzones, totaling approximately 648 acres, or about 2.2 percent of the city's area. Three of the subzones include most (i.e., three-quarters) of the total RZ acreage in Grand Rapids. The zones were selected based on a review of commercial and industrial areas, the property records of which indicate that there has been little or no investment in recent years. A conscious effort was made to exclude residential areas from the designated sub-zones, with the result that most of the subzones are linear. Although residences were excluded, in several instances subzones were selected to improve available services in targeted neighborhoods.

To date, the city has reported $247,078,167 in total private investment in the zone and the creation of 1,747 jobs. About 30 percent of the investment and half of the jobs were in place by 1999. Survey data from the late 1990s indicate that the average wage rate was just over $10 an hour and that 40 percent of the job growth benefited Grand Rapids residents.

During the first few years the RZ program was in existence, both Detroit and Grand Rapids continued to grant abatements under the PA 198 program to industrial firms outside the RZs. In both cities, total investment under the IFT abatement program was higher than in the zones (Table 4).[4] Detroit, however, granted property tax relief amounting to more than one-sixth of its total increase in property values. In Detroit, about 17 percent of the growth in property values is attributable to investments that benefited from property tax abatements. The comparable figure for Grand Rapids is less than 7 percent.

Table 4: Investment and Growth in Tax Base, 1997–99

City	Growth in property values	Reported investment		Total growth	
		RZ	IFT	RZ	IFT
Detroit	$1,876.0	$79.8	$236.8	4.3%	12.6%
Grand Rapids	$255.3	$77.5	$83.4	3.0%	3.3%

Source: Authors' analysis of 1980–2006 state tax abatement application data (Michigan Department of Treasury 2000; 2005).

Note: RZ = renaissance zone; IFT = industrial facilities tax zone.

Discussion

Detroit and Grand Rapids have made extensive use of economic development incentives over the past decade. The two cities differ considerably in their approaches, however. In terms of industrial tax abatements, Detroit has been able to attract more private investment than Grand Rapids. Investment per capita is higher in Grand Rapids, however. Grand Rapids has also been much more successful in using IFT abatements to attract promises of new jobs and new real property investment. To the extent that these economic tools are indicators of growth, it would appear that Grand Rapids has been more successful.

There are a number of important caveats to the foregoing conclusion. For one, the data reflect presumed results of abatements that have been granted. Since neither city was selective in granting industrial tax abatements, the apparent advantage for Grand Rapids might be the result more of "who asked" than strategic choices.[5] Even though a requirement of the IFT abatement program is that the applicant certify that the investment would not occur "but for" granting of the abatement, it is not clear that there would have been no investment or job activity absent abatements. Thus, a more realistic conclusion would seem to be that Grand Rapids has had better outcomes from the firms that have decided to remain in or relocate to the city. That the economic base in Grand Rapids tends to comprise smaller, locally owned firms than is the case in Detroit likely accounts for the more numerous smaller investments. That firms also find Grand Rapids a more desirable location accounts for the large number of requests to that city and—since all requests are granted—the larger number of abatements.

Other variables are at work, however. City officials in Grand Rapids have been specifically counseled by economic development specialists to underestimate the numbers used in applications for prospective jobs and investment. Presumably, local expectations are easier to meet if initial estimates are lower and the city is able to show a pattern of investment and job creation success. Thus, the prospective jobs and investment information in applications might look similar for the two cities if Detroit also consistently underestimates.

Abatements seem to have done more for Grand Rapids than for Detroit. Yet even with a policy of granting abatements to all comers, it is possible that some steering is going on, particularly in Grand Rapids. Because it has relatively greater local resources to support economic development staff, this city has the capacity to do more proactive work with firms potentially interested in relocating or expanding. Officials indicate that the city works actively with firms to identify investment plans, advertise abatement opportunities, and assist firms in abatement applications. All aspects of abatement paperwork then move through a streamlined local review process. In this way, the city can target upfront—the sorts of employers it wants to assist with abatement applications. Thus, although the city's formal policy is to grant all requests for abatements, it is possible for officials to encourage more abatement applications from firms or industries that are considered desirable.

Somewhat different circumstances exist with regard to the other two incentive programs. For both NEZs and RZs, local governments generally have more discretion in establishing zones (determining both the size and number), and in the case of RZs, directing the type of investment desired. Moreover, there is no requirement for necessity as a condition for creating a zone, so they can be located in areas that are already developing and that could use a boost (that is, in areas where development success is more likely).

Whereas NEZ designation has become an entitlement for any new owner-occupied housing development in Detroit, this tool has been used in a highly targeted way in Grand Rapids. The few NEZs that exist in Grand Rapids are intended to support other economic development initiatives, particularly RZs geared toward neighborhood commercial or industrial development. Although new for-sale housing has been developed in the downtown area of Grand Rapids, it has been done without NEZ designation, in part because new tax revenue from residential development is needed to support the activities of the Downtown Development Authority. Indeed, the city has specifically denied applications for expansion of downtown RZs or creation of NEZs within its boundaries, arguing that the market will clear new housing without incentives. Other incentive requests have been denied because of the poor rates of success of specific developers or because the projects were insufficiently tied to other types of commercial or industrial development. City officials have expected projects to provide an anchor for future development, diversify housing options in the downtown, stimulate a diverse downtown population, and bolster future market housing.

The designation of RZs in Detroit was broadly inclusive. Large areas of the city were designated as zones without clear plans for marketing properties. Although much zone property was in public ownership (often due to tax foreclosure, resulting in clouded titles), designation nevertheless reduced tax revenues substantially, most likely well beyond any reasonable expectation of what the market could absorb within the tax holiday period. The city's ability to provide infrastructure improvements to facilitate new development also was quite limited. Put another way, Detroit could have designated a much smaller geographic area for tax-free RZs and still have accommodated the same amount of new development. This potential seems to be implicit in the city's subsequent strategy with respect to RZ extensions or the creation of new RZs.

Grand Rapids based its RZ designations on two principles: foregone tax revenues were viewed as an investment in economic development, and the city was willing to forgo a limited amount of tax revenue if tangible results could be attained, such as new jobs (which even if held by nonresidents of the zones, would generate income tax revenue) or enhanced quality of life in abutting residential areas. Overall, the city concluded that new jobs in the RZs provided sufficient increases in revenue to justify expansion of the zones as well as creation of new zones.

Local officials were counseled to emphasize industrial and commercial activity in zones, along with residential uses. Linear commercial strips were included in at least two of the zones to anchor neighborhood shopping and employment opportunities. Careful assessment of past land use and value data was conducted before zones were designated, and outcome data needed for continued monitoring of zone success were collected over time. Indeed, this monitoring allowed the city to include some areas in the zones that were on the cusp of development anyway. As with the NEZs, this strategy increased market confidence for future development.

It is difficult to conclude whether either municipality's use of these economic development incentives is responsible for improving the economic well-being of the communities and residents, however. Indeed, incentives may not have contributed substantially to making either city better off. It is certainly the case that Detroit must give up more in terms of tax revenues than Grand Rapids for each promised job or dollar of investment. However, it seems clear that Grand Rapids has made more limited and likely strategic use of both the RZ and NEZ incentives. If costs and benefits are any indication, the city makes more indiscriminate use of tax abatements that almost certainly produce at least some benefits with only a 50 percent tax reduction. The other tools that entail more risk, uncertainty, and greater forgone revenues are used with more caution. In Detroit, by contrast, almost the reverse is true.

It is possible that some cities are so distressed that neither strategic nor wanton use of development incentives is likely to achieve significant long-term success. For other cities that have relatively strong economies, such as Grand Rapids, strategic use of incentives does appear to enhance larger economic development efforts. A final caveat, though: officials in Grand Rapids were quick to point out that in no cases were incentives used in a vacuum. The successful downtown redevelopment was part of a larger effort that included NEZs and abatements in combination with investment in public parks, the arts, public safety, transportation, and flexible zoning that allowed mixed uses. The incentives alone likely would not have been successful absent the larger local investment. In cities like Detroit that have very limited resources for ancillary public investment, incentives alone—no matter how they are strategically employed—are unlikely to do the job.

Notes

1. This approach is opposite to that of the federal government, which has replaced categorical assistance with bloc grants.

2. Property values are drawn from 1982, 1991, and 2001 because each of these years captures the previous year's valuation, thereby allowing property value data to be more closely correlated with decennial census data. Data from 1982 are used instead of 1981 data because electronic files were not available until then.

3. The homestead NEZ provides a 50 percent reduction in city and county property taxes for up to 12 years, which in most jurisdictions amounts to a property tax savings of about 15 percent to 20 percent.

4. In part, this difference may be the result of the more stringent reporting requirements for the PA 198 program compared with those for the renaissance zones.

5. Some observers suggest that the Grand Rapids open-door policy on abatements encourages a wide range of applicants, including small firms that are likely to be put off by lengthy or costly application processes.

References

Ahlbrandt, R. S., and J. P. DeAngelis. 1987. Local options for economic development in a maturing industrial region. *Economic Development Quarterly* 1:41–51.

Bartik, T. J. 1991. *Who benefits from state and local economic development policies?* Kalamazoo, MI: W. E. Upjohn Institute.

Citizens Research Council of Michigan. 2007. *Survey of economic development programs in Michigan.* 2nd ed. Livonia, MI: Citizens Research Council of Michigan.

Dardia, M. 1998. *Subsidizing development in California.* San Francisco: Public Policy Institute of California.

Due, J. 1961. Studies of state-local tax influences on location of industry. *National Tax Journal* 14:163–73.

Fisher, P. S., and A. H. Peters. 1998. *Industrial incentives: Competition among American state and cities.* Kalamazoo, MI: W. E. Upjohn Institute for Employment Research.

Gramlich, E. M. 1997. Subnational fiscal policy. In *Perspectives on local public finance and fiscal policy*, ed. J. M. Quigley, 3–27. Greenwich, CT: JAI Press.

Michigan Department of Treasury. 2000. 2005. *Taxable valuations.* Lansing: State Tax Commission, Michigan Department of Treasury.

Michigan Jobs Commission. 1997. *Michigan's Tax-Free Renaissance Zones.* Lansing, MI: Michigan Jobs Commission.

Oakland, W. H., and W. A. Testa. 2000. The benefit principle as a preferred approach to taxing business in the Midwest. *Economic Development Quarterly* 14:154–64.

Peters, A., and P. Fisher. 2004. The failures of economic development incentives. *Journal of the American Planning Association* 70:27–37.

Reese, L. A., and D. Fasenfest. 1997. What works best? Values and the evaluation of local economic development policy. *Economic Development Quarterly* 11:195–221.

Reese, L. A., and G. Sands. 2007. Making the least of our differences? Trends in local economic development in Ontario and Michigan, 1990–2005. *Canadian Public Administration* 50:79–99.

Rothwell, D. 1997. Tax-free renaissance zones. *Planning Michigan* (Fall): 3–4.

Sands, G., and P. Zalmezak. 2001. *Michigan industrial property tax abatements: A summary of activity under Public Act 198 of 1974, 1985–98.* Paper presented at the Urban Research Seminar, Detroit.

Schwarz, J. E., and T. J. Volgy. 1992. The impacts of economic development strategies on wages: Exploring the effect on public policy at the local level. Paper presented at the annual meeting of the American Political Science Association, Chicago.

Tyszkiewicz, M. 1997. Michigan's renaissance zones. *Notes on the Budget and Economy* (November–December). Lansing, MI: Senate Fiscal Agency.

U.S. Census Bureau. 2000. *2000 census of population and housing.* www.census.gov/prod/cen2000/index.html. Accessed March 10, 2008.

Wolman, H. 1996. The politics of local economic development. *Economic Development Quarterly* 10:115–50.

CHAPTER 2

Peering into the Economic Development Black Box: Insight into Firm Location Decisions and Information Needs

Julia Melkers and Laura Czohara

Who wins in the economic development game? For some time, states have engaged in a virtual Olympics in which state and local governments jump through hoops, offer incentives, and reach deep into the state and local coffers for ways to entice businesses to locate within their jurisdictions. While the incentive game has evolved into a "third wave" that involves a broader approach to offering incentives and engaging partners (Bradshaw and Blakely 1999), many state and local economic development policies remain focused on attracting businesses (Reese and Rosenfeld 2004). In practice, tax-related incentives in particular are viewed as critical to state competitiveness. For example, the 2005 meeting of the National Governor's Association highlighted the importance of offering such incentives. Despite evidence that incentives may not be as important in firm location decisions as practitioners might think (Dewar 1998), governments continue to offer them in order to remain competitive. Further, governments expend considerable resources to provide incentives that have questionable and modest payoffs (Bartik 2005).

Over time, economic development incentives have changed somewhat: they are not limited to direct financial incentives but also include other benefits that make locales attractive to potential firms, such as employee training and infrastructure development. Among practitioners, there is some expectation that the value of incentives

The authors thank the Georgia Department of Industry, Trade and Tourism and the Georgia State University Fiscal Research Center for their generous support and input into this research.

matters most, yet recent research has suggested that incentives may have only marginal value and that qualitative factors beyond economic incentives matter most in the final decision process (Dewar 1998; Rondinelli and Burpitt 2000; Bartik 2005). Thus, economic development practitioners are continually faced with the challenge of crafting strategies to meet the existing and potential needs of firms.

In examining these strategies, economic development research has for some time focused on the prevalence, weight, and value of incentives in the site location decision process (see Buss 2001 for a recent review of the literature). What have not been explored to the same extent are the information needs of prospective firms as they go through these processes. Firms assess locations and make choices based on available information, reevaluating their options as new information is received. State and local economic development agencies, together with other partners such as public utilities, are important sources of information. Thus, it follows that if state and local economic development practitioners are not providing useful information to prospects (including professional site location consultants), they are less competitive overall. As Graber (1992) has noted, the effectiveness of public organizations is in part based on their ability to communicate well. Firms relocate or select new locations based on a complex set of factors; in turn, economic development practitioners struggle to present information that will put their communities in the best competitive light. This study uses recent survey data to determine what information is most useful to business prospects in the process of location decisions.

Understanding the Site Location Process

The economic development literature has given most attention to the general factors that inspire firms to relocate and aspects of a community that ultimately determine their decisions. Firms seek new locations for a variety of reasons including cost savings, consolidation of operations, accommodation of business growth or decline, proximity to relevant networks, property costs, and quality of available workforce, among others (Buss 2001; Ghosh, Maurico, and Sirmans 1995; Luce 1994; Leitham, McQuaid, and Nelson 2000). The most frequently cited reason is profit maximization (Buss 2001; Ghosh, Maurico, and Sirmans 1995; Hack 1999; Hayter 1997; Luce 1994). Understanding the site location selection process is complicated by intangible factors that may not have a direct effect on cost calculations but nevertheless are important such as educational resources; housing and quality of life; public services such as fire, police, and emergency services; recreational activities; and community values. Communities must recognize that it is necessary to provide useful and relevant data that address these factors, which—although difficult to measure—are consequential.

In their study of how and why relocation decisions are made, Gilliland, Wood, and Schmitt (1994) found that firms chose states whose values aligned with firms' preferences and desires. A firm's stated preferences may not always correspond with its final choice, however. Barkley and McNamara (1994) found that firms compromised their values and made trade-offs in their decisions. Other research suggests that it may be difficult to change a firm's impressions about a particular location once they are formed. Preconceived notions about a state may enter into relocation decisions. Thus, if communities are to be competitive, then the content and mode of information exchange with prospective firms and/or site location consultants who are engaged in this process must be relevant, appealing, timely, and appropriate.

The issue of how, why, and to what net effect incentives are used in the firm location process continues to dominate local economic development discussions. To provide and maintain a sought-after business climate (Buss 2001), state and local governments increasingly are offering land or tax exemptions or other capital for infrastructure, training programs, and even cash gifts to cover moving expenses (McPherson 1995). As the use of economic incentives has become more prevalent, attention has been paid to their relative importance in the site location process. The assumption is that economic development incentives must be available in order for a community to be competitive.

Recent research, however, challenges the importance of incentives in site location decisions. In a study of the location decisions of multinational firms, Rondinelli and Burpitt (2000) found incentives to be less important than other qualitative factors and questioned whether states should be directing their monies toward economic incentive programs (Rondinelli and Burpitt 2000). Other research has reached similar conclusions. O'Mara (1999) analyzed the motives, behaviors, and trends that informed the relocation decision-making processes of 40 corporations and firms. Findings showed that "information-age" telecommunication firms value the presence of a qualified local workforce foremost; quality-of-life factors were rated the next highest. According to O'Mara (1999, 365), "overall, economic development incentives are less important than the 'ease of living' and labor market support found in the community."

Research in this area has focused primarily on site location factors but has not given direct attention to how firms perceive information about those factors and the process by which information is exchanged with prospective firms. The literature is limited to guides that provide suggestions for where firms can find useful community information. For example, Whitehouse (1990) outlines the basic steps that small businesses can take to gather information. Similarly, Hack (1999) suggests that firms use the services of outside site consultants as well as economic development organizations that are located within a community. McPherson (1995) advocates using economic data sheets that provide brief, factual answers to the questions most often asked about communities. As McGuire (2000) notes, information and knowledge are dispersed among many sources such as city government, utility companies, chambers of commerce, and development corporations, and firms must seek out information from multiple sources. There is no evidence regarding the weight firms assign to this practical information when making their site location decisions, however.

Methodology

The data for this study were drawn from two national surveys conducted in 2002 of state location consultants and economic development personnel as well as a survey of local economic development professionals in one state.[1] To ascertain local government information dissemination processes and products and gather impressions of the information needs of consultants, directors of chambers of commerce and economic development authorities throughout Georgia were surveyed. The mailing list was compiled with the assistance of the Georgia Department of Industry, Trade and Tourism (now the Department of Economic Development) and the Georgia Economic Development Association. Overall, 99 usable surveys were returned, for a response rate of 23 percent. Survey respondents represented 73 of 159 counties across Georgia. Although the results may be useful in recommending policy in this particular state, they are not generalizable to other states. Nevertheless, an understanding of local government perspectives, particularly those of smaller cities and communities, may be gleaned from the descriptive findings.

Professional site location consultants across the United States also were surveyed to explore their information needs. The mailing list for this survey was drawn from that compiled by the International Development Research Council. Although surveying individual firms that had recently relocated may have been an option, the availability of a small pool of professionals who could comment on a range of experiences yielded unique and rich data. (Informal polling of economic development practitioners suggests that the core site location community is limited to approximately 200 individuals.) The activities within this profession are confidential and secretive, however, and turnover is high, making survey responses difficult to obtain. Identification of site location contacts within individual firms is therefore problematic.

Overall, 58 surveys were returned for a response rate of 17 percent. The relatively low response rate may be accounted for by the fact that survey recipients operate on billable hours and may have been reluctant to take the time to respond. Moreover, the list included individuals within real estate divisions of larger firms for whom site location is only a small part of their overall responsibilities. Respondents did include individuals from major consulting firms and corporations.

Finally, questions regarding site location issues were included in a survey sent to state economic development division directors (Melkers and Czohara 2004). Respondents from international trade and business recruitment divisions were asked about their information needs and whether they were involved in forming location decisions. The final data set included 24 respondents from these two divisions in 21 states.

Findings

Survey Respondents

The extent to which professionals provide site location assistance varies. For some, it constitutes the bulk of their activities while for others, it is a relatively small part of their overall jobs. Most of the 58 respondents (47 percent) were real estate professionals employed within larger corporations; only 14 percent were employed by firms solely dedicated to site selection. Other respondents hailed from corporate real estate firms, architecture/engineering firms, and financial/business consulting firms. Respondents reported having 2 to 40 years' experience in the field; 65 percent had 10 years or more. Most respondents stated that they spend 5 percent to 25 percent of their time on site selection; others indicated that half or more of their time is spent on this activity. Most respondents (83 percent) had graduate degrees, mostly in general business or business and finance.

Local entities are important partners in the site location process, and professionals' responses to questions about site location decisions and information needs are instructive. Of the 99 respondents from local entities within Georgia, 75 percent were from development authorities, and the remaining 25 percent were from chambers of commerce. Typically, the president or executive director of the chamber of commerce or the development authority responded to the survey. Respondents ranged from seasoned practitioners in economic development to new professionals. Twenty percent indicated that they had worked in the field of economic development for four years or less; another 20 percent had 20 to 40 years' experience. Further, respondents were well educated: about 40 percent had college degrees, and another 40 percent reported having graduate degrees.

In terms of involvement by consultants in the site location decision process, only about half the local chambers of commerce and development authorities in this study reported that consultants were engaged in development deals in their community. Of these, 17 percent indicated that consultants were involved in 10 percent or fewer deals in their community; in another 17 percent, consultants were used in 15 percent to 50 percent of deals. It should be noted that this relatively low level of interaction may not hold true for other states.

Information Needs and Sources in the Site Selection Process

Site location consultants tap a variety of sources in the site selection process. Most first look to internal databases (large compilations of their ongoing work) when seeking information about possible sites. State and local Internet sources also are important: for 42 respondents (80 percent), these sources are among the first three they consult. The findings of this study underscore the importance of quality Internet-based resources at both the state and local levels.

Site location consultants and local economic development practitioners were asked about the kind of information they seek when selecting sites. Local economic developers in Georgia were asked how frequently they received requests for certain types of information (see Table 1). There were some distinct differences. Site location consultants more often desired information about transportation and related costs, business taxes, utility costs, and tax incentives. Local economic development practitioners placed more importance on tax incentive information than did site location consultants; information to do with transportation, utility, and other costs was less important. Site location consultants expressed less need for education-related data, including technical school information, than did local economic development practitioners. There were striking differences of opinion between local economic development practitioners and site location consultants regarding information concerning loan packages and loan opportunities: the former more often requested this kind of information than did the latter.

Regarding modes of communication, site location consultants considered Internet-based information as being more important than did state and local economic development practitioners. Local economic development practitioners accessed Web-based and electronic information about as much as did site location consultants, but the former cited mailed information as being more important. Site location consultants indicated that they prefer Web-based and e-mailed information for themselves and their clients; mailings were rated much lower. In an age of e-government, the issue of appropriate Web-based information is foremost in the minds of those involved with economic development.

Table 1: Frequency of Information Requested by Prospective Firms or Site Consultants Considering a Community for Relocation

Information Type	Site location consultants[a]		Georgia local economic developers[b]	
	Mean	N	Mean	N
Transportation	2.70	56	2.44	85
Business tax	2.65	57	2.41	85
Utility costs	2.54	57	2.41	88
Opportunities for tax incentives	2.52	56	2.78	86
Transportation costs and alternatives	2.41	56	2.02	87
State income tax	2.29	55	1.92	83
Quality of life	2.16	57	2.40	88
University facilities	2.11	55	1.90	84
Housing cost	2.04	57	2.00	87
Technical school	1.96	55	2.24	86
School district	1.96	55	2.17	86
Residential property tax	1.70	56	1.99	83
Recreational opportunities	1.69	55	1.87	87
Arts and cultural attractions	1.63	57	1.76	84
Loan opportunities and local bank services	1.49	55	2.08	84

[a]Responses ranged from 1 = "never/infrequently need" to 3 = "always need."
[b]Responses ranged from 1 = "never/infrequently requested" to 3 = "always requested."

The findings underscore the importance of electronic modes of information transmittal while pointing to differences in perception among economic development practitioners regarding the value of this technology.

Responses to the question about what information should be provided on a state or local Web site were diverse. Information about the labor force, such as a firm's number of employees and history, was regarded as especially important. One respondent noted that it is beneficial to include "[anything] that can't be obtained from a subscriber database [such as] headcount, downsizing, expansions, [and] recent magazine write-ups." Another pointed to "comparative and detailed labor rates by skill level." With regard to prospective sites, detailed cost and site-specific information was sought. Respondents also desired information about the financial aspects of a community, including property, utility, cost-of-living, sales, school, and tax information. There also were a number of comments regarding tax incentives. Other comments addressed the need for communities to keep Web site information current and provide contact names, addresses, and phone numbers.

The Quality of State and Local Information

In terms of the usefulness of information in the site selection process, respondents indicated that state and local economic development practitioners are important sources for information and that the information they provide is generally reliable. Site location consultants were asked to describe the community and other information typically provided to them by practitioners. Forty-four percent considered the information to be very reliable, and 55 percent deemed it somewhat reliable. Fifty-three percent of the respondents indicated that they usually have the information verified through independent sources.

Respondents also were asked about the quality of their interactions with economic development practitioners. These professionals were ranked highly in terms of responsiveness and professionalism (although local-level practitioners were rated lower than their state-level counterparts) but lower in terms of the confidentiality they provide. Thus, if local economic developers wish to be viewed as partners in the firm recruitment process, attention should be given to improving the quality of information and interrelationships at the local level.

Site location consultants were asked a series of open-ended questions regarding the strengths and weaknesses of information and assistance they receive from state and local economic development practitioners. Consultants considered easily accessible, timely, current, reliable, accurate, easily understood, and readily available information as most useful and "canned" data, "cookie-cutter responses," and lack of urgency as problematic. Well-organized, easily understood data with a comparative component also were cited as being very useful. Overall, site location consultants valued tailored and targeted information, emphasizing public relations and political issues less than costs of doing business. Information overload and outdated data were seen as troublesome. In terms of mode of information transmittal, consultants tended to favor electronic sources over paper or verbal sources.

Responses to the question about what state and local economic development practitioners could do better to help site location consultants were grouped into two general categories: type of information provided and overall behavior of economic development practitioners. Comments tended to focus on information or the relaying of information more so than on the provision of resources or incentives (only one person pointed to the need for building permits and fee waivers). Site location consultants expressed the need for good data regarding labor, costs, business, and other information. In terms of the behavior and activities of economic development staff, consultants stressed the need for better liaison activities and improvement in the areas of accuracy and timeliness in addressing information requests and other questions.

How economic developers perceive the information needs of their clients determines to some extent the information they provide to a community. Similarly, economic developers' assumptions about the information needs and decision criteria of prospective firms and site consultants play a role in the information exchange among economic developers and business prospects. The extent to which state and local economic developers understand and can predict the information needs of prospective firms, the better and more appropriately they can direct useful information, thereby giving them a competitive edge.

To this end, local economic developers, site location consultants, and division directors in state economic development agencies were asked, "In your opinion and based on what you have observed, how important are each of the following to businesses as they consider communities for expansion or location?" Overall, state and local economic development practitioners placed more importance on almost all of the factors listed in Table 2 than did the site location consultants. Among consultants, the availability of skilled and trainable labor along with telecommunications capacity were the most significant factors, whereas state and local practitioners perceived transportation and labor to be most important. In the area of finance, local and state tax incentives were accorded approximately the same degree of importance by all groups, but state and local practitioners placed a great deal more emphasis on the availability of loan packages than did site location consultants. This disparity in perspectives indicates that local economic developers may not always understand the decision and information priorities of the business prospect community.

Conclusion

Understanding the decisions that firms make in the site selection process is at the core of economic development business recruitment strategies. Scholars and practitioners alike question the effectiveness and the value of offering incentives to firms that may or may not stay in a location or bring benefits that outweigh the costs of incentives (Peters and Fisher 2004). This study has taken a slightly different approach to the issue of why firms decide to locate in certain areas by examining how and what kind of information governments communicate rather than attributing their reasons to the use of incentives.

Although it is not always possible to predict the factors that ultimately affect the decision of an individual firm to locate in a certain area, the findings here suggest that it behooves state economic developers to better target their strategies to the information needs of prospective firms and site location consultants. State governments' ability to respond—and therefore their competitiveness—depends in part on the quality of their communication (Graber 1992).

According to respondents in this survey, many states provide useful information, but others do not. In all cases, however, Web-based information and electronic communication play a critical role. Technology is not the only factor, however: the fact that state and local economic development staff are perceived very positively and are looked to as purveyors of reliable information points to the importance of human interaction in responding to the needs of the client community. As one

Table 2: Factors Important to Prospective Businesses When Considering a Community for Expansion or Location

Factor	Site location consultants[a]	Local economic developers[b]	State economic developer practitioners[c]
Community Issues			
Availability of skilled labor	2.84	2.85	2.95
Easy access to transportation	2.74	2.80	2.95
Telecommunications capacity	2.72	2.51	2.67
Availability of trainable labor	2.70	2.83	2.86
Proximity to customers	2.41	2.60	2.52
Quality of the elementary and high school system	2.35	2.68	2.33
Proximity to suppliers	2.24	2.53	2.57
Proximity to technical school	2.07	2.47	2.19
Assistance from local community	n/a	2.65	2.52
Government Assistance			
Assistance from state economic development agency or other state agency	2.51	2.51	2.62
Local government assistance in establishing operation	2.40	2.57	2.48
State-funded training for new employees	2.34	2.63	2.62
Assistance from U.S. Department of Commerce	1.68	1.78	1.52
Finance and Incentives			
Availability and attractiveness of local and state tax incentives	2.61	2.79	2.62
Availability and attractiveness of loan packages	1.89	2.52	2.38

Note: Numbers are mean responses. Responses ranged from 1 = "not very important" to 3 = "very important."
[a] n = 58.
[b] n = 99.
[c] n = 24.

site location consultant noted, these practitioners "provide insight and knowledge of a community that only an insider could have."

As firms expand and relocate, the relationship between site location consultants and business prospects and state and local economic developers becomes ever more important. Future research should pay attention to the mode and nature of information exchange between economic developers and business prospects and the ultimate implications for the site selection process. Such studies will lend greater insight into how communities can meet the needs of firms and thereby improve their chances of success in economic development.

Note

1. The data were gathered as part of a project for the State of Georgia and are therefore limited in scope (Melkers, Rushing, and Thomas 2001).

References

Barkley, David L., and Kevin T. McNamara. 1994. Manufacturers' location decisions—Do surveys provide helpful insights? *International Regional Science Review* 17:23–47.

Bartik, Timothy. 2005. Solving the problem of economic development incentives. *Growth and Change* 36:139–66.

Bradshaw, Ted K., and Edward J. Blakely. 1999. What are "third-wave" state economic development efforts? From incentives to industrial policy. *Economic Development Quarterly* 13:229–44.

Buss, Terry F. 2001. The effect of state tax incentives on economic growth and firm location decisions: An overview of the literature. *Economic Development Quarterly* 15:90–105.

Dewar, Margaret. 1998. Why state and local economic development programs cause so little economic development. *Economic Development Quarterly* 12: 68–87.

Ghosh, Chinmoy, Rodriguez Maurico, and C. F. Sirmans. 1995. Gains from corporate headquarters relocations: Evidence from the stock market. *Journal of Urban Economics* 38:291–311.

Gilliland, Stephen W., Lisa Wood, and Neal Schmitt. 1994. The effects of alternative labels on decision behavior—The case of corporate site selection decisions. *Organizational Behavior and Human Decision Processes* 58:406–27.

Graber, Doris A. 1992. *Public sector communication: How organizations manage information*. Washington, DC: Congressional Quarterly.

Hack, George D. 1999. *Site selection for growing companies*. Westport: CT: Quorum Books.

Hayter, Roger. 1997. *The dynamics of industrial location: The factory, the firm and the production system.* New York: John Wiley & Sons.

Leitham, Scott, Ronald McQuaid, and John Nelson. 2000. The influence of transport on industrial location choice: A stated preference experiment. *Transportation Research Part A: Policy and Practice* 34:515–35.

Luce, Thomas F. 1994. Local taxes, public services, and the intrametropolitan location of firms and households. *Public Finance Quarterly* 22:139–67.

McGuire, Michael. 2000. Collaborative policy making and administration: The operational demands of local economic development. *Economic Development Quarterly* 14:278–93.

McPherson, Edwin M. 1995. *Plant location selection techniques.* Park Ridge, NJ: Noyes Publications.

Melkers, Julia, and Laura Czohara. 2004. *Performance measurement in state economic development agencies: Lessons and next steps for GDITT.* Report to the Georgia Department of Industry, Trade and Tourism. Fiscal Research Center report no. 92. Atlanta: Georgia State University.

Melkers, Julia, Francis W. Rushing, and Jeanie Thomas. 2001. *The application of local economic development incentives in Georgia.* Report to the State of Georgia Office of Planning and Budget. Fiscal Research Center report no. 63. Atlanta: Georgia State University.

O'Mara, Martha A. 1999. Strategic drivers of location decisions for information-age companies. *Journal of Real Estate Research* 17:365–87.

Peters, Alan, and Peter Fisher. 2004. The failures of economic development incentives. *Journal of the American Planning Association* 70:27–39.

Reese, Laura A., and Raymond A. Rosenfeld. 2004. Local economic development in the United States and Canada: Institutionalizing policy approaches. *American Review of Public Administration* 34:277–92.

Rondinelli, Dennis A., and William J. Burpitt. 2000. Do government incentives attract and retain international investment? A study of foreign-owned firms in North Carolina. *Policy Sciences* 33:181–205.

Whitehouse, Kay. 1990. *Site selection: Finding and developing your best location.* Blue Ridge Summit, PA: TAB Books Inc.

CHAPTER 3

Networking in Economic Development:
The Case of Project Emmitt

Kimberly Aaron and Douglas J. Watson

One of the frequent criticisms of local economic development is that it is not targeted but rather follows the philosophy of "shoot anything that flies, claim anything that falls" (Rubin 1999, 263). Most communities spend considerable time and resources—in terms of both money and staff—responding to inquiries or requests from businesses considering establishing sites in their area. Generally, the mission of an economic development office is to create jobs and taxes for the local government (Koven and Lyons 2003; Wolman and Spitzley 1999; Watson 1995). Local economic developers often react to opportunities to generate jobs and taxes by deploying incentives that can help them win the battle against other communities seeking the same economic prize, whatever that may be.

It is rarer for a community to have a clear strategic plan for economic development and then stick with it, even through difficult times. Richardson, Texas, is one such community. It identified the telecommunications industry as the one on which it wished to bank its economic prosperity and persevered with that strategy even through the devastating "telecom bust" of the late 1990s and early 2000s. As the telecom industry began to recover, Richardson deftly put together a sophisticated plan to lure one of the top economic development prizes of the decade: a $3 billion Texas Instruments manufacturing plant, which was completed in 2006. This case study is the story of Richardson's determination (despite broadening its recruiting efforts to other industries in recent years) to remain true to the strategy, which it accomplished by developing a network of key public and private partners. The result has been a thriving business community.

Some of the most groundbreaking work today is done by "dream teams" composed of experienced individuals who collaborate to achieve a common purpose (Barabasi 2005). Over the past decade, these networks have assumed more importance for public administrators. With the move toward public-private partnerships, outsourcing, downsizing, and productivity improvement, government managers have become more dependent on developing networks with other organizations—both public and private—to attain their goals (O'Toole 1997; Goldsmith and Eggers 2004). O'Toole (1997, 45) defines networks in public administration as "structures of interdependence involving multiple organizations or parts thereof, where one unit is not merely the formal subordinate of the others in some larger hierarchical arrangement. . . . The institutional glue congealing networked ties may include authority bonds, exchange relations, and conditions based on common interests, all within a single subunit structure. In networks, administrators cannot be expected to exercise decisive leverage by virtue of their formal positions."

For public managers to be successful in the modern era, they must be adept at "governing by network," according to Goldsmith and Eggers (2004, 24), who argue that the "era of hierarchical government is coming to an end." It is being replaced by an entirely new model that requires public managers to be coordinators of resources with other public, nonprofit, and private entities that must be brought into the network. The case of Richardson, Texas, attests to the successful networking of numerous independent public, private, and nonprofit organizations to garner one of the largest economic projects of the decade. Parts of the network had been in place for many years; other players were quickly and successfully brought in based upon their common interests.

Background

With an estimated 2003 population of slightly less than 100,000, Richardson is the 10th most populous city in the Dallas–Fort Worth Metroplex. It is noted for the Telecom Corridor®, an area along U.S. Highway 75 that is home to approximately 700 telecommunications and information technology–related businesses and the University of Texas at Dallas (UTD). UTD, a research institution on the cutting edge of science and technology, has a current enrollment of more than 14,000 students and a faculty that includes two Nobel laureates.

Richardson's city limits are located within both Dallas and Collin Counties and their respective school districts. It has a council-manager form of government. Residents elect the seven-member city council, which then chooses a mayor and mayor pro tem from among its members. The council is responsible for passing city ordinances, planning for capital improvements, issuing and selling municipal bonds, purchasing and selling property, establishing city departments, determining city services, approving the annual budget, and setting the city's tax rate. The city manager is responsible for the city's daily operations, hiring department heads, supervising city personnel, directing and coordinating all municipal programs, enforcing all municipal laws and ordinances, and recommending an annual budget.

Richardson and the "Growth Pole" Theory

Historically, Richardson has had a robust business community. It is the second-largest employment center in the Dallas metropolitan area. The commerce of local businesses generates much of the city's revenues, initially through permit and construction fees and on an ongoing basis through property taxes (i.e., real estate, fixed assets, and inventory), sales tax, franchise taxes, permits, fines, and utility fees.

Richardson boomed under the "growth pole" theory, with two closely related industries (high technology and telecommunications) driving the economy. According to Koven and Lyons (2003), growth pole theory hypothesizes that growth depends on one or more "propulsion industries." In growth poles, backward linkages develop when employees set up companies to supply a parent company with material needs, and forward linkages arise when employees set up companies to market products that originally were developed by the parent company. In the case of Richardson, Texas Instruments (TI) served as a major member of a propulsion industry that led to highly successful linkages with other spin-off firms in telecommunications. Hill and Brennan (2000) describe industries like TI and the companies that developed from it as "driver industries" because they have the effect of catalyzing the local or regional economy.

TI established itself in Dallas, near the Richardson border, in 1951 and has played a significant role in Richardson's economic development. As TI grew over the decades, other companies providing ancillary services emerged in nearby Richardson. Collins Radio, established in 1957 and acquired by Rockwell International in 1971, also became an important player in the economic development of Richardson when it located its defense communications operations in the city. Expanding its work to all phases of communications, Rockwell Collins began making the first telecommunications switches.

Although the combined presence of TI and Rockwell Collins prompted the city to focus on technology and telecommunications, the breakup of AT&T in 1982 was the spark that generated the development of the Telecom Corridor®. With AT&T's breakup, the opportunities for telecommunications companies increased dramatically. As a result, Richardson started offering technology companies fast-track zoning and tax abatements of 25 percent to 50 percent. Expanding international firms such as Ericsson, Nortel, Alcatel, and Fujitsu established themselves in Richardson over subsequent decades.

Engineers with an entrepreneurial bent who started their own telecommunications and technology companies further spurred growth, adding new linkages to the major companies that had settled in the area. Further, in 1992 MCI, which had established an office in Richardson in 1972, began relocating its network engineering operations to Richardson along with thousands of its employees. This expansion fueled more white-collar jobs, research and development, and manufacturing growth around telecommunications. Furthering this growth was the passage of the Telecom Act of 1996, which signaled massive deregulation, and the establishment of the Telecommunications Infrastructure Fund, a $1.6 billion grant program designed to facilitate the deployment and use of advanced telecommunications technologies in Texas public schools, hospitals, libraries, and other public institutions. The Telecommunications Infrastructure Fund was created in 1996 and was expected to be administered by the state through 2006. However, in 2003 the Texas legislature determined that the fund had met its purpose and transferred the funds into a technology allotment for public education.

From 1997 to 2001, over 24,000 net jobs were added within the Telecom Corridor®, and the city's tax base increased by $1.5 billion. Twenty-five percent of the firms were information technology and software related; the balance consisted of semiconductor and other high-technology businesses. However, with the subsequent weakening of both the economy and the telecommunications industry, city sales tax revenues began to decline from a high of $24.9 million in 2000–2001 to $19.7 million in 2005. Also as a result of the downturn in the economy and the saturation in wireless services and related products, technology companies significantly reduced staff and cut back operations. Vacant offices and a loss of business personal property undermined the property value assessments critical to the city budget. Richardson's unemployment rate more than doubled between 2000 and 2002 from 2.2 percent to 5.6 percent, slowing economic development.

Economic Development Strategy

Despite the downturn of the last several years, Richardson continues to target telecommunications and related high-technology companies, believing that the global economy will depend even more on the sophisticated products manufactured there. The city's strategy for economic development is summarized by certain points in its mission statement:

- continue to nurture and build upon the existing clusters related to high-tech such as telecom, software, and semiconductors and to develop new clusters in nanotechnology and biotechnology

- strengthen Richardson's role as the leading high-tech city in the Dallas–Fort Worth area

- encourage high-quality retail growth in appropriate locations

- capitalize on opportunities for redevelopment

Richardson emphasizes an agglomeration, or clustering, approach to economic development that builds synergy around "like-minded" firms (Koven and Lyons 2003; Feldman and Francis 2004; Held 2004; Hill and Brennan 2000; Porter 2000). Clustering can be described as "geographic concentrations of interconnected companies, specialized suppliers, firms in related industries, and associated institutions (e.g., universities, standards agencies, trade associations) in a particular field that compete but also cooperate" (Porter 2000, 15). Porter (2000, 16) argues that government's most important role in economic development is found at the microeconomic level, at which it can remove obstacles to growth of clusters and facilitate dialogue that "can and must take place among companies, government agencies, and institutions such as schools, universities, and public utilities."

Hill and Brennan (2000, 66) state that competitive advantage is gained when "the various factors of production are combined, genius is harnessed, and business strategies are executed." In their comprehensive study of the Cleveland-Akron Consolidated Metropolitan Statistical Area, the authors identify 29 separate driver industries that form 10 industry groups. Of the 10 industry groups, 5 were considered industry clusters that gave the area a competitive advantage. Feldman and Francis (2004) and Held (2004), among others, also have studied the concept of clustering.

In accordance with Porter's (2000) argument that government plays an important role in cluster development, the Richardson city government has adopted the clustering approach through not only targeted recruitment but also careful planning and zoning. For example, the city has helped to establish industrial and office parks that appeal to telecommunications companies anxious to project an image of success. Within the Telecom Corridor®, six business clusters have been established: telecommunications, network and information technology, software, electronic equipment, semiconductor, and other high technology. This clustering allows companies to build stronger customer/supplier/partner relationships, share a common pool of skilled workers, and take advantage of the "knowledge spillover" that is critical to the growth of technology-based companies.

Richardson Economic Development Partnership

Richardson accomplishes local economic development primarily through the Richardson Economic Development Partnership, which was established in 1984 as a joint effort of the city and the local chamber of commerce. It provides services to companies that are considering Richardson for expansion or relocation. These services include the analysis of building selections, land sites, incentives, and costs of business; site tours; executive introductions; coordination of development projects; and assessment of special relocation needs.

The City's Role

The city identifies itself as being the "community developer," particularly in terms of infrastructure support and development. It focuses on the development of transportation systems, the delivery of utilities and other public services, planning for appropriate land use, and collaboration with other organizations such as the school systems, the counties, and the Dallas Area Rapid Transit (DART) system in order to meet the needs of both business and the citizenry. Richardson's intention is to cultivate a fertile business environment that reflects the academic and economic vitality of the city.

Within the city government framework, the Planning Division is responsible for formulating the long-range comprehensive plan for the physical development and redevelopment of the city. This plan addresses future land-use designations, zoning, transit-related development, and street and utility mapping. The city maintains future land-use plans, reviews them every two years, and revises them entirely every five years. Major goals of the city are to protect and encourage the development of property in a manner designed to preserve the integrity of the Telecom Corridor® relative to land use and quality of construction and to identify businesses and industries compatible with the Richardson environment. Recognizing the importance of technology-related industries to the local economy, the city regards programs and policies that maintain and improve the business environment for research and development, high-technology manufacturing, and services that support the high-technology industries as important priorities.

Richardson continues to offer as its primary incentive tax abatements in the 25 percent to 50 percent range for a period of 5 to 10 years. Most abatements are single-business deals, and each incentive proposal is reviewed on its own merits. The criteria for determining which projects warrant a tax abatement include number and quality of jobs a project will generate, environmental and community impacts, the longevity and creditworthiness of the company, and whether local facilities will be leased or owned. Local property taxes (excluding land) and business personal property added as a result of either relocation or expansion are abated. Once the city offers abatements, other taxing jurisdictions such as school districts and counties decide whether to participate.

The city offers additional incentives. It does not assess impact fees and may waive zoning and building permits, and it may provide some or all infrastructure construction at no cost to expanding and relocating businesses. Richardson also has an Industrial Development Corporation that makes tax-exempt financing available, providing that a project is primarily manufacturing and the company's total capital expenditures in the county (including the bond debt) do not exceed $10 million for a six-year period. The city recently established its first tax increment financing zone.

The Chamber's Role

The chamber acts as the city's marketer and has primary responsibility for directing development endeavors. Historically, it has focused on technological innovation as a means of economic progress. Accordingly, the chamber established the Metroplex Technology Business Council (MTBC), a regional trade association for Dallas–Fort Worth high-technology companies, as an affiliate in 1994. The MTBC comprises more than 200 companies and has an independent board with 24 chief executive officers as directors. Concentrating on building the "soft infrastructure" for technology-based businesses, the MTBC provides weekly programs, peer-to-peer education, lead generation and introductions, direction on business development opportunities and possible funding sources, and tech-business advocacy. A main source of information regarding the high-technology industry in the Metroplex, the MTBC fields inquiries from the media, international trade groups, venture capitalists, entrepreneurs, and various governments. Founding members include MCI, Nortel, Fujitsu, and Rockwell Collins.

Much of the chamber's efforts are directed toward providing information and assistance to facilities wishing to locate in the area and recommending financial inducements. Fledgling enterprises look to local business incubators such as STARTech, Incucomm, and Genesis Campus for growth opportunities. In addition to its focus on business attraction and new enterprise development, the chamber has recently increased its business retention efforts.

Relationship with Texas Instruments

Although other companies such as Blue Cross Blue Shield, Countrywide Financial, and Sherwin-Williams have located to Richardson, the city has not altered its basic economic development strategy of courting high-tech companies, despite the downturn in the economy generally and in the telecommunications industry in particular. In 2003, TI offered the State of Texas the opportunity to vie for a large new semiconductor plant. The story of how Richardson quickly expanded its network of partners to win this $3 billion plant is instructive for other communities wishing to stimulate their economies by attracting new business.

TI was founded in 1930 in New Jersey as Geophysical Science but established its corporate headquarters in Dallas. Initially, its business was based on seismic exploration services for the petroleum industry, but it later built electronics equipment for the U.S. Army during World War II. The company, which changed its name to Texas Instruments in 1951, patented many of its breakthrough discoveries in the burgeoning computer technology field, including the discovery of the solid circuit in 1958.

As TI grew, its four founders became important civic figures in the Dallas area. Among their many contributions was the founding of the Southwest Center for Academic Studies, which was established as a graduate school in Richardson to produce engineers for TI and other emerging high-tech companies. In 1969, TI donated the land and buildings of the center to the UT system with the understanding that a campus would be located there. As a result, UTD became primarily a graduate school. Numerous buildings on campus are named for the TI founders, and their influence in moving UTD toward prominent standing in engineering and science is well known (Starner 2004; Engibous 2003).

In 2001, TI opened in Dallas "the world's most modern semiconductor plant," the DMOS 6, the first TI facility to produce semiconductors on 300-millimeter silicon wafers. A seemingly risky venture at the time, it turned out to be highly profitable. Despite the financial success of the DMOS 6 plant, observers were surprised to learn that TI was considering building a second semiconductor manufacturing plant somewhere in the world. The intention was to construct the building and infrastructure ahead of market demand, with subsequent equipment installation to be staged based upon demand. *Site Selection* magazine noted that speculation centered on non–U.S. locations such as China, Mexico, or Korea as the site of the second plant (Starner 2004).

TI had begun the process of locating its second semiconductor plant in 2000 but decided not to proceed when the market weakened. By the end of 2002, the company revived its plans and developed an in-house team to begin the worldwide search for the best location. TI investigated sites in 25 states and several foreign countries but finally narrowed its choices to four sites in Texas, New York, Virginia, and Singapore (Harrison 2003; Bruns 2003). The Richardson site was a 90-acre tract located a few miles from the UTD campus (also in Richardson) and within short commuting distance to other TI facilities in North Texas. While Richardson may have had a "home court" advantage, Singapore offered an essentially tax-free environment, and both New York and Virginia had specific policies in place to attract semiconductor businesses. New York's granting of tax concessions to acquire an IBM facility likely influenced TI's financial criteria for proposals (City Manager Bill Keffler and Bill Sproull of the Richardson Chamber of Commerce, joint interview with the authors, April 2006).

However, as the company's history suggests, TI's ties to the Dallas area are very strong. Of its 34,100 employees in 25 countries, nearly one-third work in Texas and most in the Dallas metropolitan area. Out of a sense of loyalty to Texas, TI told state officials in late 2002 about the project and offered them the opportunity to meet the financial targets for its new location. Richardson was a natural choice. TI already owned land in the city, and in 1995, TI and the city had worked together on TI's Twin Star economic development project. This effort served to "prep" the economic development team on what was needed to satisfy TI (Bill Keffler, interview, June 2005). Consequently, the essential hub of the network was in place and positioned to expand its associations to bring the plant to Richardson.

Project Emmitt

No one investment in the history of Texas was as large as the $3 billion plant planned by TI, and Richardson officials were anxious to have it be located within their city limits. It was consistent with their long-standing goal of recruiting high-technology firms and would at nearly a single stroke rekindle the momentum the community had lost after the telecom bust several years earlier. As a result, Richardson's city manager and mayor decided that a project team had to be assembled to develop a proposal that included an incentive plan that would meet TI's financial expectations. State and local governments, school districts, and institutions of higher learning, in addition to the standing network of economic development professionals within the partnership, would be key players. The task force was named for Emmitt Smith, the star running back of the Dallas Cowboys who had recently left the Dallas team to move to Arizona. The task force did not want another "star" in the form of the TI plant to slip out of the state (Bill Keffler and Bill Sproull, interview, April 2006).

Starting in December 2002, the Project Emmitt team began meeting on a formal basis. It was led by the executive director of the Texas Economic Development Council, the Richardson city manager, the vice president of economic development for the Greater Dallas Chamber of Commerce, and the dean of the School of Engineering and Computer Science at UTD. The senior vice president of public affairs for TI also participated. At the onset, state officials ran the meetings, with leadership shifting to local officials as the specifics of the deal began to materialize. All team members had their own assignments and reported to each other at regular meetings (Bill Keffler and Bill Sproull, interview, April 2006). Communication via telephone, e-mail, and fax was ongoing.

The city manager focused on networking with trustees from the Plano Independent School District (PISD) and officials from Collin County and the Collin County Community College system. The chamber vice president concentrated on working with officials in the state capital of Austin, including members of the governor's economic development department and the Texas legislature. Members of the governor's economic development team with ties to North Texas provided valuable insight into how the state and the local community could work together (Bill Sproull, interview, September 2005).

TI had a compelling reason to consider the Richardson location. The company wanted to use the new facility to introduce the next generation of semiconductors and needed the intellectual capital of engineers at its Dallas location. However, the company also needed financial incentives that would satisfy its board of directors. To establish a location in Texas, TI had two requirements: (1) the guarantee of new investment that would fund programs, research, and facilities at UTD to make it a top-tier engineering school and (2) what it considered "normal" tax benefits from local governing bodies including the city, county, and school district.

The city manager knew that the most difficult challenge in assembling the financial package was to obtain the support of the PISD in granting property tax abatements (Bill Keffler, interview, June 2005). Although located in Richardson, the project would be situated within the boundaries of the PISD. Thus, the PISD was being asked to abate a significant amount of tax revenue even though the project would be sited in the neighboring city. The school district had never before approved a tax abatement. TI, the city manager, and the other members of the Project Emmitt task force, working with local legislators, approached the PISD and were persuasive in demonstrating the impact of the TI project on the entire North Texas area. Even though the PISD and other local government entities were abating some property taxes, task force members contended that the estimated 1,350 jobs and other benefits from the project would more than offset any loss in tax revenue.

The Texas Enterprise Fund and UTD

A significant factor contributing to the success of Project Emmitt was the creation of the Texas Enterprise Fund (TEF), a $279 million fund controlled by the governor that was established in 2003 to encourage economic and community infrastructure development and create job training programs and business incentives. The lieutenant governor and the speaker of the state House of Representatives must approve the governor's expenditures from the fund. The TEF is known as the "deal-making fund" because it provides a pool of funds for use by the governor "to respond quickly and aggressively to opportunities to bring jobs to Texas" (Richardson 2003, 1). The Texas legislature created the TEF to provide the state with more flexibility to compete against other states on economic development projects after losing the Boeing headquarters to Chicago. The Project Emmitt team worked with the governor's office and the state legislature to ensure that the TEF was created in time to respond to TI's proposal request.

One of the requirements of TI to locate in Richardson was a commitment from the governor of $50 million from the TEF to UTD's Erik Jonsson School of Engineering and Computer Sciences, named for the former mayor of Dallas who was also chief architect of DFW Airport and cofounder of TI (along with Eugene McDermott and Cecil Green). The Jonsson School has one of the fastest-growing engineering programs in the country (Texas Instruments 2003). In addition, the state and the university had to agree to raise another $250 million from public and private sources to be dedicated to technology education at the university. The money was to be paid over a five-year period, during which time the university would build a new research facility that would expand its education facilities in engineering and computer science. Believing that engineers and computer scientists would be in short supply in the future, TI wanted to locate its plant in "a climate that encouraged advanced research and extreme innovation," according to the chairman of the board and chief executive officer of TI (Engibous 2003).

At the time it was set up, the TEF was the largest cash fund of its kind in the country (Ward 2005), and its $50 million commitment to UTD as part of the TI project was essential to sealing Richardson's deal. It also represented the first time the State of Texas had committed funds to such a project (Bill Keffler and Bill Sproull, interview, April 2006). The investment in UTD would facilitate the institution's move into the ranks of the premier engineering schools in the country, resulting in a highly educated local workforce and top research and development programs (Engibous 2003).

Incentives and Advantages

By June 2003, just six months after the formation of Project Emmitt, TI was satisfied that all commitments had been made by the governing bodies of Richardson, PISD, Collin County, and the Collin County Community College system, and it accepted the incentive package (Post 2003). TI's chairman/chief executive officer, the governor, lieutenant governor, mayor of Richardson, UTD president, and other federal, state, and local officials gathered to make the formal announcement that TI would remain in North Texas.

In addition to the sizable incentives offered by the State of Texas, the city of Richardson provided a 10-year 75 percent tax abatement on the facility. Further, taxes on any investments made within the first 14 years of operation also would receive tax abatements. These abatements would correspond to the phases of investment, which meant that some form of tax abatement would be in place for up to 24 years. An economic analysis of the tax abatements estimated that TI would save $173 million over the first 24 years. In turn, during the same period, Richardson would earn $116 million in taxes, utility fees, and other direct and indirect revenue (Post 2003). The success of this and other economic development projects that were under way at the time of the TI deal demonstrate the resiliency of the city in weathering an economic downtown.

Estimates regarding the net economic impact of the TI plant in return for the public and private investment vary, but it is expected to be substantial. The Perryman Group (2003) determined that the facility would bring a temporary stimulus to the Collin County economy of $2.99 billion in total expenditures, $1.54 billion in gross product, and 21,944 person-years in employment. For the Dallas Metroplex, the Perryman Group estimated total expenditures at $4.9 billion, gross product at $2.5 billion, and person-years in employment at 34,290. For Texas as a whole, the manufacturing facility is expected to generate approximately $157 million in revenue.

Once the TI plant is fully online, it likely will generate $518 million in yearly total expenditures and $281 million in yearly gross product and will create 3,532 permanent jobs for the local area (Perryman Group 2003). For the state, these values increase to $626 million in yearly expenditures, $323 million in yearly gross product, and 4,035 in new jobs. Even more importantly, "the project positions Texas to become a world leader in such fields as nanotechnology and advanced materials. In short, the TI 300-mm wafer plant represents an outstanding mechanism to locate an important manufacturing enterprise in a dynamic region of Texas while supporting academic excellence in a synergistic manner. . . . It is a catalyst to future business expansion and job creation that is critical to the long-term outlook for the state" (Starner 2004, 337).

Ground breaking and construction of the new semiconductor plant took place earlier than expected in November 2004, and the building was completed in 2006. With its multiple buildings on 92 acres, the facility is the size of 12 football fields (Hundley 2004). It includes over a million square feet of office, manufacturing, and office support space and will employ 1,000 people when fully operational (Texas Instruments 2004a). Once the plant starts production, it will be one of the most advanced semiconductor manufacturing facilities in the world and will produce digital signal processing and analog-based systems-on-chip devices for wireless, broadband, and digital consumer applications. Employees will include engineers, operators, and technicians. A few miles west of the UTD campus, construction on the $85 million, 192,000-square-foot natural science and engineering research facility has been completed. The building, now known as the Natural Science and Engineering Research Laboratory, houses 350 faculty, graduate students, and postdoctoral scholars in the fields of electrical engineering, materials science, chemistry, biology, and behavioral and brain sciences. In addition to laboratories, a clean room, and other areas dedicated to research, the facility will include space for a business incubator, which will be used to move scientific innovations into commercial production (Texas Instruments 2004b).

Conclusion

This example of successful partnering to achieve an economic development goal offers lessons for other communities. Richardson's cultivation of high-tech telecommunications industries—which began two decades earlier and continued despite economic downturns—points to the need to stay focused instead of "shooting anything that flies, claiming anything that falls."

Also, timing is a crucial element. When the opportunity with TI emerged, the key players in the city's economic development network reacted quickly in order to win this very large prize. Richardson was fortunate to have the opportunity to develop a proposal for the TI project, which could have been built anywhere in the world. Although TI's affinity for its home region and for UTD may have influenced the company's decision to locate a plant in Richardson, its own financial interests as a major international company were foremost. If the city had not moved decisively to form Project Emmitt, the plant likely would not be located in Richardson.

Finally, this scenario highlights the importance of fostering relationships among all sectors of the community. It was imperative that the basic elements of the network of economic development leaders that had been in place for nearly 20 years be expanded to bring other critical players to the table. In the case of Richardson, the city manager acted as the "strong integrator" (Goldsmith and Eggers 2004, 75). In addition to working with all the members of the network, the city manager kept governing officials well informed about the progress of the negotiations and involved them when necessary (for example, when approval was needed for the infrastructure projects and the tax abatement agreement). Thus, even with the challenges of coordinating multilinked networks composed of several entities, Richardson demonstrated that such complex structures could operate both efficiently and effectively.

References

Barabasi, A. 2005. Network theory—The emergence of the creative enterprise. *Science* 308:639–41.

Bruns, A. 2008. Microprocessor makers seek solid state. *Site Selection Online* (September). www.siteselection.com. Accessed March 24, 2006.

Engibous, Tom. 2003. Speech delivered to Texas Instruments, Richardson, Texas, June 30.

Feldman, Maryann P., and Johanna L. Francis. 2004. Homegrown solutions: Fostering cluster formation. *Economic Development Quarterly* 18:127–37.

Goldsmith, S., and W. D. Eggers. 2004. *Governing by network: The new shape of the public sector*. Washington, DC: Brookings Institution Press.

Harrison, C. 2003. The making of a UTD windfall; secret meetings with Texas Instruments, state yield $300 million. *Dallas Morning News*, July 1, 1A.

Held, J. R. 2004. Regional variation and economic drivers: An application of the Hill and Brennan methodology. *Economic Development Quarterly* 18:384–405.

Hill, E. W., and J. Brennan. 2000. Methodology for identifying the drivers of industrial clusters: The foundation of regional competitive advantage. *Economic Development Quarterly* 14:65–96.

Hundley, W. 2004. Richardson is optimistic over TI groundbreaking; computer chip plant, research facility at UTD hold promise of jobs. *Dallas Morning News*, November 21, 6B.

Koven, S. G., and T. S. Lyons. 2003. *Economic development strategies for state and local practice*. Washington, DC: International City/County Management Association.

O'Toole, L. J., Jr. 1997. Treating networks seriously: Practical and research-based agendas in public administration. *Public Administration Review* 57:45–52.

The Perryman Group. *2003. The economic and fiscal impact of the Texas Instruments 300mm semiconductor manufacturing facility and a collateral educational initiative at the University of Texas at Dallas on Texas and the Dallas–Fort Worth area: A prospective analysis of a key investment in future prosperity*. www.perrymangroup.com. Accessed February 2004.

Porter, M. 2000. Location, competition, and economic development: Local clusters in a global economy. *Economic Development Quarterly* 14:15–34.

Post, S. 2003. City looks for ripple effect from TI deal. *Dallas Morning News*, July 6, 1S.

Richardson, G. D. 2003. "Slush" fund may lure much-needed businesses. *Fort Worth Star Telegram*, July 6, 1.

Rubin, H. J. 1999. Shoot anything that flies; claim anything that falls: Conversations with economic development practitioners. In *Approaches to economic development*, ed. J. P. Blair and L. A. Reese, 263–77. Thousand Oaks, CA: Sage.

Starner, R. 2004. TI's Texas two-step. *Site Selection* (May): 336–39.

Texas Instruments. 2003. TI taps Texas as site for next semiconductor manufacturing facility. June 30. www.ti.com/corp/docs/press/news.htm. Accessed March 2006.

————. 2004a. Texas Instruments prepares for the future. October 25. www.ti.com/corp/docs/press/news.htm. Accessed March 2006.

————. 2004b. Texas Instruments and UTD hold joint groundbreaking for facilities critical to region's future. November 18. www.ti.com/corp/docs/press/news.htm. Accessed March 2006.

Ward, M. 2005. How Texas plays "Let's Make a Deal" for jobs. *Austin American-Statesman*, February 21, A1.

Watson, D. J. 1995. *The new civil war: Government competition for economic development*. Westport, CT: Praeger.

Wolman, H., and D. Spitzley. 1999. The politics of local economic development. In *Approaches to economic development*, ed. J. P. Blair and L. A. Reese, 225–62. Thousand Oaks, CA: Sage.

CHAPTER 4

Competition for High-Tech Jobs in Second-Tier Regions: The Case of Portland, Oregon

Heike Mayer

Collaboration between the public sector and private industry—a phenomenon that is becoming more prevalent—often is at the heart of a region's economic success. The case of Portland, Oregon, illustrates how governments can stimulate competitiveness and economic growth by attracting and retaining businesses through tax incentive programs and provision of higher education opportunities for the workforce. This chapter provides a critical analysis of the role of high-tech firms such as Intel in influencing policy and pushing for an economic development agenda that advances their own interests while stimulating a region's prospects.

Portland is known as a second-tier high-tech region and is commonly referred to as the Silicon Forest. Compared with Silicon Valley, Portland's high-tech economy is smaller and younger. Unlike more prominent high-tech regions, the Silicon Forest evolved in the absence of a major world-class research university. Instead, two high-tech firms—Tektronix and Intel—functioned as "surrogate universities," attracting talent to the region, fostering research, and serving as incubators for a plethora of start-up firms (Mayer 2005b). The firms also helped create an innovative milieu by attracting customers, suppliers, and competitors. In addition, their presence catalyzed the development of local business support services like specialized law firms, patent attorneys, venture capitalists, temporary staffing agencies, and specialized public relations firms. More importantly, Tektronix and Intel were significant actors in Oregon and Portland's quest to establish the Silicon Forest as a competitive region. Specifically, the two firms worked in concert with state, regional, and local governments to shape economic development policies.

The Silicon Forest

Unlike Silicon Valley's or Boston's Route 128 high-tech economies (Saxenian 1994), Portland's Silicon Forest evolved as a high-tech region despite the lack of a major research university (Mayer 2003; 2005b) and no military investments (Markusen 1987). The Portland region substituted the presence of an MIT or Stanford University with a combination of home-grown electronics firms, high-tech manufacturing branch plants, and a range of spin-off companies. In 1946, Howard Vollum and Jack Murdock—two Oregon natives—started the electronics firm Tektronix. The two founders returned to Portland from military duty during World War II and began thinking about products for their entrepreneurial venture, eventually deciding on the manufacture of oscilloscopes (i.e., electronic test and measurement equipment). Over the years, Tektronix gained a worldwide reputation for making innovative, high-quality electronic equipment.

At its peak in 1980, Tektronix employed more than 16,000 people at its Portland headquarters. Tektronix's corporate success declined starting in the early 1980s, however, when Japanese and U.S.-based firms began to compete in the same market. Layoffs, divestitures, and organizational restructuring resulted (Mayer 2005a). As part of the changes, Tektronix dissolved its in-house corporate research and development laboratory (Tek Labs) and began to focus on its core competencies.

Surprisingly, Tektronix's corporate crisis influenced the region in positive ways. Former employees who were affected by layoffs and restructuring started innovative high-tech firms. Tektronix began to invest in these firms and provided them with the necessary start-up capital. Business units were sold but retained their presence in the Portland region. Altogether, former Tektronix employees founded more than 48 companies. An additional 23 firms were started by employees of those initial Tektronix spin-offs. In short, these developments seeded a nascent high-tech economy that was later bolstered by the presence of Intel.

Intel moved its first branch plant facility outside Silicon Valley to Portland in 1976. Initial considerations for moving the plant to Oregon included the short commute time to Silicon Valley (under two hours by plane) and the availability of cheap electricity and clean water for the production of semiconductor chips (Mayer 2003). Neither tax incentives nor the availability of higher education opportunities were considered, even though these issues would later emerge as Intel's presence in Oregon grew and became more complex. Consistent with the general trends in the industry, Intel's Oregon operations evolved from mere manufacturing facilities into a complex set of R&D operations. At times, Oregon-based Intel inventors outdid their counterparts at the firm's headquarters in California in terms of number of patents registered. In addition to contributing to an innovation-oriented environment, Intel helped spawn interrelated supplier and customer firms. Over time, competitors—especially from Japan—began to move to Portland's Silicon Forest because of the region's growing high-tech reputation, the availability of skilled talent, and the proximity to leading firms like Intel.

The combination of home-grown electronics firms such as Tektronix, its spin-offs, branch plants like Intel, and other companies have stimulated the region's economy. Firms in the Silicon Forest employed more than 54,960 people (primarily recruited from California, the Midwest, and the East Coast) with average annual wages of $72,601 in 2004 (ECONorthwest 2005). The region's quality of life (including its affordability compared with other West Coast cities, its recreational assets, and its proximity to the ocean) significantly contributed to the retention of employees and entrepreneurs.

Today, Portland boasts not only a vibrant high-tech economy but also a significant cluster of firms operating in the sports apparel market. Many companies call the region home (including Nike, Adidas, Columbia Sportswear, Keen Footwear, and Lucy), as do specialized industries such as coffee roasting, transportation equipment manufacturing, and metals and machinery production. Just outside the urban growth boundary is located a thriving nursery industry that exports shrubs and trees.

Getting Education Right

The absence of a world-class research university in the Portland region did not go unnoticed by business leaders and policy makers. The "Portland problem" affected primarily the high-tech industry in the metropolitan area. In the beginning, the industry was mostly interested in an improved higher education system to supply its workforce needs. Only in recent years has public discourse shifted toward concerns over competitiveness. Support for R&D has become another pressing issue.

Portland's academic infrastructure has not influenced the high-tech industry to a great extent, nor have Oregon's two major land grant universities (located within 100 miles south of the city) played a significant role in the development of the Silicon Forest. Between 1976 and 2002, the two Portland-based higher education institutions (the Oregon Graduate Institute and Portland State University) supplied only 8,161 graduate students who had degrees in engineering and computer sciences (National Science Foundation 2002). Over the same period, the high-tech industry in the Portland-Vancouver metropolitan area added 47,513 jobs. Between 1997 and 2001, a majority of high-tech industry representatives consistently ranked Oregon worse than other states on the availability of an engineering workforce (American Electronic Association 1997; 1998; 1999; 2000; 2001).

In a 2002 survey of high-tech firms in the Portland region, the lack of sufficient higher education infrastructure was the most frequently cited competitive disadvantage. The respondents felt that better infrastructure would not only improve the availability of qualified talent but also support continuing education and research (Mayer 2003). Industry executives such as Jim Johnson, the former Intel Oregon manager, called the lack of qualified high-tech employees a "quiet crisis" (*The Oregonian* 2000). High-tech firms had to compensate for this inadequacy by beefing up their corporate education programs and importing qualified people from outside the region for engineering and computer science jobs. As a result of Oregon's dismal track record, industry (represented by large high-tech employers such as Tektronix and Intel) actively lobbied for increased investments in higher education.

Institutional Involvement

The first efforts to improve higher education in the Portland metropolitan area date to 1959, when Gov. Mark Hatfield called for a report on science and engineering education. He subsequently appointed an eight-person advisory committee to work on suggestions for how to improve higher education infrastructure in the Portland region (Dodds and Wollner 1990). Howard Vollum, one of the founders of Tektronix, was a member of this committee. At the time, Tektronix already was a significant employer, with about 2,950 people working at its Washington County campus. Noting the lack of graduate education and research, the committee recommended establishing a cooperative center for graduate education and advanced research to be situated on the west side of Portland where Tektronix had moved in 1951. The committee proposed a collaborative effort among existing public and private institutions such as Portland State College (now Portland State University), Oregon State University, and the University of Oregon and explicitly rejected the idea of creating a new institution. The center never materialized, however, because opposition from the larger land grant universities and their alumni was too strong. Instead, a 15-member board appointed by Governor Hatfield in 1963 developed a plan to establish an independent graduate-only institution: the Oregon Graduate Center. Tektronix played a pivotal role in getting the center off the ground. Cofounder Vollum and other industry representatives financed its start-up, and the Tektronix Foundation donated the land. This industry support was critical in light of the legislature's subsequent rejection of Governor Hatfield's request to appropriate $1.5 million for the 1965–67 biennium (Dodds and Wollner 1990).

The center started operations in 1966. A year later, the first faculty members were hired, and in the fall of 1969, the first students enrolled. Financed mainly by private funds, the center was an ambitious attempt to fill the void in graduate science education and research and to serve the emerging high-tech industry in the Portland metropolitan area. It was modeled after Stanford University, its goal being to provide applied research and graduate education in engineering-related disciplines. During the 1970s, the center attracted research grants and corporate donations, and in the early 1980s, it established the Oregon Graduate Center Science Park. Modeled after Stanford University's science park, it was intended to attract high-tech companies that would then enter into research partnerships. Policymakers and industry leaders viewed the center as critical in Portland's quest to become a high-tech region. The goal was to "make the Oregon Graduate Center a Pacific Northwest version of the Massachusetts Institute of Technology, and the Sunset Corridor would become the western equivalent of Boston's Route 128" (Dodds and Wollner 1990, 110).

Due to limited endowment funding, lack of state support, and sporadic corporate donations, the Oregon Graduate Center never achieved the status of an MIT-like institution. In 2000, the institution (which by then had changed its name to the Oregon Graduate Institute) merged with the Oregon Health Science University to form Oregon Health and Science University with the hope of leveraging the medical institution's resources and research in biotechnology and other life sciences (Rojas Burke and Carter 2000). With the establishment of the center in the late 1960s, regional leaders hoped to create a stable supply of graduate students and applied research to make the Portland region competitive in high technology. The Oregon Graduate Center never took on a catalytic role, however, and the discussions about "getting education right" in the Portland region continued.

It was not until Oregon's severe economic recession began in the 1980s that policymakers and business leaders became more vocal in decrying the continued lack of appropriate higher education infrastructure in the Portland metropolitan area. This time, state representative Vera Katz (a Portland Democrat who later became the city's mayor) and the Oregon Council of the American Electronics Association led an effort aimed at improving higher education offerings. The coalition secured $500,000 in state funds for the creation of the

Oregon Consortium for High Technology Education (Dodds and Wollner 1990). The consortium was dominated by industry interests and geographically focused on the Portland metropolitan area. Higher education institutions played only a small role in the planning and administration of the consortium. The Oregon State System of Higher Education therefore issued a counterproposal and suggested setting up the Council for Advanced Science and Engineering Education/Research for Industry, a collaborative effort between Portland State University, Oregon State University, and the University of Oregon.

Neither endeavor fulfilled the industry's expectations of elevating higher education institutions in Portland to first-tier status. The Oregon Council of the American Electronics Association and Washington County business leaders felt impelled to approach the issue again in 1985. This time, they were able to obtain funding from the legislature (about $500,000) for the creation of the Oregon Center for Advanced Technology Education.

Although the efforts of the early 1980s did not significantly contribute to the strengthening of higher education in the Portland metropolitan area, the initiatives (most of which were geared toward continuing education and workforce-related training) may have seeded the success of Portland's community colleges. During the boom of the semiconductor industry in the 1990s, community colleges were pushed to improve and adjust their workforce training curricula. The colleges continuously expanded their offerings and partnered with local industry leaders like Intel. Microtechnology programs and semiconductor processor training programs were established at the Washington County Capital Center in Hillsboro and at Mt. Hood Community College in Gresham. Although community colleges do not provide higher-level engineering degrees, they do turn out skilled manufacturing workers who are critical to large-scale high-tech industries.

University-Industry Partnerships

During the late 1980s and early 1990s, the quest to get higher education right continued. At the same time, Oregon's higher education institutions became more entrenched in fierce battles over limited resources and competing suggestions for restructuring. In 1989, Gov. Neil Goldschmidt appointed the Commission on Higher Education in the Portland Metropolitan Area to study the problem (Colby 1989). A year later, the committee released a report titled *Working Together* in which it recommended adding graduate programs at Portland State University and shaping the school into an "urban-grant university" focusing on urban issues (Hill 1990). Another suggestion was the creation of a formal coalition under a council of university presidents to coordinate the efforts of the 31 postsecondary schools in the Portland area. The third suggestion was to create the Oregon Joint Graduate School of Engineering, with oversight to be conducted by an engineering council. To implement and finance these suggestions, a Greater Portland Trust in Higher Education was proposed.

The suggestions reflected a compromise after a contentious public debate during the commission's deliberations. Immediately after Goldschmidt appointed the commission, the Oregon Council of the American Electronics Association submitted a proposal to dismantle Portland State University and fold it into Oregon State University and the University of Oregon (Hill 1989b). The group also proposed to spend $100 million in state funds to upgrade higher education. Frustrated about the lack of state engagement and progress, industry leaders were among the most avid supporters of these suggestions. *The Oregonian* quoted a Tektronix vice president: "[T]he proposal stemmed from 27 years of frustration. Despite the high-tech community's efforts and financial investments, the state has failed to fund high-quality engineering programs, especially in the Portland area" (Hill 1989a). In its rebuttal to the industry-backed proposal, Portland State University suggested setting up a branch campus near the core of the high-tech industry in Washington County and merging with Oregon Health Science University, the local teaching and research hospital. Neither the merger nor the branch campus became a reality.

The most promising outcome of the *Working Together* report was the establishment of the Engineering Council, which was intended to foster collaboration and coordinate engineering and computer science programs at Oregon universities. In 1991, the Oregon State System of Higher Education appointed the first five industry executives to the newly formed council to oversee the Oregon Graduate Schools of Engineering. Among these industry executives were representatives from companies like Tektronix, Intel, and Mentor Graphics (a Tektronix spin-off).

Despite the formation of the council and improvements in technical education at the region's community colleges, higher education continued to suffer during the 1990s. In addition, the system faced deep budget cuts due to the 1990 passage of Measure 5, a property tax limitation bill. The measure reduced the amount of property tax money available to public elementary and high schools and required the state to replace funding using its general funds, which in turn affected the higher education budget. The cuts hit universities hard: during the 1993–95 biennium, the state system had to reduce the universities' budgets by 10 percent (Rubenstein 1995). In addition, the Greater

Portland Trust in Higher Education that was set up following the *Working Together* report failed to raise enough money and consequently was disbanded after only 18 months in operation.

Public debates in the first half of the 1990s revolved around the dire budget situation, and it was not until 1995 that another round of discussions about how to restructure higher education resurfaced. This time it was a bold restructuring proposal from Joe Cox, the chancellor of the Oregon State System of Higher Education. He proposed a seven-school system that would be divided between the University of Oregon and Oregon State University. The proposal was similar to the 1990 Oregon Council of the American Electronics Association proposal to fold Portland State University into the other bigger universities. Cox's proposal spurred four separate suggestions submitted by each higher education institution, including the Oregon Graduate Institute.

In November 1996, the State Board of Higher Education under the leadership of Tom Imeson, then vice president of a local utility company, brokered a compromise. The compromise left the schools separate but centralized financial and policy planning and oversight of Oregon State University's and Portland State University's engineering and computer science programs. The position of Vice Chancellor of Engineering was created with the goal of fostering coordination and integration. The schools promised to double within five years the number of high-tech degrees offered and expand their research and professional training opportunities. Additionally, they promised to respond better to industry needs.

Since the 1950s, Portland's high-tech industry leaders had voiced their concerns about shortcomings in higher education. They continued to argue "that the local higher education institutions weren't big enough [or] good enough to produce the graduates and research that high-tech companies need to compete in a global economy" (Barnett and Hernandez 1995, E06). Yet they persisted in their efforts to forge connections with establishments of higher learning. In particular, industry leaders outlined three benefits of an improved higher education system: increasing continuing education, producing more undergraduates to fill entry-level jobs, and fostering basic research to generate new ideas for commercialization. Even though the universities began to collaborate and coordinate their science and engineering education programs, industry leaders were not satisfied with the progress.

Representatives from the industry continued to lobby the legislature, stressing the need to reform Oregon's higher education system. In 2000, Johnson, the former manager of Intel Oregon, drafted a plan to create a world-class engineering school at Oregon State University. The rationale for picking OSU was that the university already had a good reputation upon which improvement efforts could be built. Out of these industry-based discussions, a new interest group, the New Economy Coalition (NEC), composed of high-tech industry representatives, higher education administrators, and public officials was formed.

Research and Development Efforts

The industry's lobbying efforts to improve higher education infrastructure have yielded some results at the beginning of the new century. In contrast to earlier efforts, recent changes have primarily focused on applied research and university-industry relationships. On the one hand, this shift may reflect the maturing of the Silicon Forest economy from one that was dominated by manufacturing branch plants to one that thrives on innovation and the tight links between R&D and manufacturing. On the other hand, the shift may be attributable to improvements in workforce development and education at Oregon's higher education institutions.

The most notable R&D effort has been the creation of the Oregon Nanoscience and Microtechnology Institute. The initial push for its formation came from a state-level advisory body, the Oregon Council for Knowledge and Economic Development, established in 2001. The council represented the public sector and private industry and recommended the establishment of "signature research centers" (Oregon Council for Knowledge and Economic Development 2002). The most avid supporters of the signature research center were industry representatives, particularly prominent local venture capitalists and large high-tech firms, who argued that applied research rather than basic research would ensure regional economic competitiveness. The objectives of the research center would be compatible with corporate aims and would augment firms' R&D efforts, especially in the areas of nanoscience and microtechnologies.

The Oregon Nanoscience and Microtechnology Institute functions as a network organization for the University of Oregon, Oregon State University, Portland State University, the Pacific Northwest National Laboratory (located in southeastern Washington), and Oregon Health and Science University (Oregon Business 2004). For the first time in the region's history, all major research universities are collaborating on a large research project. They have been successful in receiving support from the state ($21 million) albeit after intense lobbying and pressure from industry. During the deliberations, high-tech representatives made clear that they would follow their plans even if the state did not offer support.

Ultimately, industry was successful in convincing the Oregon legislature to fund higher education. Moreover, the efforts contributed to more collaborative practices among Oregon's universities, which historically have been undermined by fierce rivalries. The network approach to higher education in Oregon is characteristic of larger trends in building university-industry relationships. As industry becomes less reliant on in-house corporate R&D laboratories and more interested in tapping into ideas and innovations from outside the company, universities in high-tech regions like Portland are becoming more important.

The Development of Tax Incentives

Higher education is not the only battleground high-tech firms have chosen in Portland. Firms (especially Intel) have proactively lobbied the state to offer tax incentives in exchange for large-scale capital investments and job creation. Intel has been a pioneer in obtaining tax incentives from states like Arizona, New Mexico, and Oregon. In 2005, Washington County and the City of Hillsboro approved the fourth tax break program for Intel. The achievement was hailed by Tom Hughes, the mayor of Hillsboro: "Intel is at the heart of the economic life of this community. Their continued investment in Oregon takes us a long ways towards building the economy for the 21st century" (Washington County 2005).

Intel has indeed been at the heart of the economies of both Oregon and Washington County since it located a branch plant in the suburb of Aloha in 1976. Until the early 1990s, Intel kept a low profile regarding its public affairs and political influence. That changed around 1993, however, when Intel considered a series of expansions in New Mexico, Arizona, and Oregon, pitting the states against each other in a war over tax incentives. It was at that time that Intel played an important role in shaping Oregon's approach to attracting and retaining capital-intensive high-tech industries.

The granting of Intel's fourth tax break in 2005 represents a continuation in the state and region's quest to create a high-tech economy that began in the early 1980s. Motivated by the decline of the timber industry and a very deep economic recession with double-digit unemployment rates, policymakers changed the state's corporate income tax structure to help recruit foreign-based high-tech firms. Japanese firms had been looking to expand their operations in the United States. Oregon, with its unitary tax on the worldwide revenues of multinational corporations, did not appeal to them, and they threatened to go elsewhere (Dodds and Wollner 1990). In 1984, Oregon became the first state to repeal the unitary tax.

After the unitary tax was repealed, Japanese-owned high-tech corporations such as the NEC Corporation, Epson, and Fujitsu located branch plants in the Silicon Forest. Oregon became more attractive to foreign-owned branch plants, some of which continue to have a significant economic impact. Between 1985 and 1999, Japanese high-tech firms invested about $808 million and created more than 1,950 jobs (Cortright and Mayer 1999). (It should be noted, however, that even though this economic record is impressive, these firms have not contributed to entrepreneurial start-up activity in the region [Mayer 2003].) Some might argue that even without tax incentives, these firms would have been interested in locating in an emerging high-tech region because of the favorable exchange rates at the time and their desire to be near competitors like Intel.

The repeal of the unitary tax paved the way for subsequent tax abatement programs specifically targeted at making the state competitive in attracting and retaining high-tech firms. In 1993, Oregon's legislature approved the Strategic Investment Program (SIP). The program allows counties to issue a property tax break to export-oriented industries that invest heavily in equipment and facilities. Oregon's unique tax situation accommodates the program (the state does not have a sales tax and relies on income and property taxes). Income tax revenues typically fund state programs, while property taxes are used locally by counties to fund programs like education and public safety. Property taxes are assessed on not only the land but also any improvements to it. It has been argued that capital-intensive industries such as high-tech industries (which tend to make larger, more frequent investments than do other sectors) are disproportionately affected by Oregon's property tax.

The SIP is tailored to the particular needs of capital-intensive high-tech manufacturing firms. The program caps the assessed value of a company's investment at $100 million in the first year, with incremental increases of 3 percent in assessed value each year thereafter. The SIP suits manufacturers like Intel (to which the program was primarily targeted when it was first conceived), whose costs for building a semiconductor fabrication facility can run up to $3 billion. In exchange for capping the amount of investment that is taxed, the company pays a community service fee equal to 25 percent of the property taxes saved up to a maximum of $2 million.

The Strategic Investment Program

The evolution of the SIP represents a joint effort. Oregon lawmakers found themselves fighting a war against other states for the expansion of Intel's operations and therefore had good reason to create a tax break program targeted at capital-intensive high-tech industries. Similarly, Intel had a stake in designing and implementing a tax incentive program that would be to its benefit.

In 1993 and 1994, Intel chose to expand in New Mexico and Arizona rather than in Oregon. The company picked Rio Rancho in New Mexico as a site for a $1 billion manufacturing plant (dubbed Fab 11). For this project, Intel invited six Western states (Arizona, California, New Mexico, Oregon, Texas, and Utah) to compete. The company picked New Mexico because it offered the best incentives. "We're going to build where Intel gets the best deal," one company executive commented in a *Time* magazine article (Barlett and Steele 1998). Besides $2 billion in industrial revenue bonds granted by New Mexico's Sandoval County in 1993, Intel received $8 billion in incentives in 1995. The county where the manufacturing plant is located also holds title to the land, building, and equipment, which it leases back to Intel (Barlett and Steele 1998).

Oregon's proposal for the Fab 11 project did not make the cut because the state did not offer tax abatements as an incentive. Subsequently, Gov. Barbara Roberts and officials from the economic development department met with Intel's chief operating officer, Craig Barrett. In the meeting, Intel management made clear that the company's future expansions would happen only if Oregon would be willing to offer similar incentives. After losing the bid for the New Mexico plant, Governor Roberts and economic development officials in conjunction with legislators developed a bill that created a tax abatement program (the SIP) that would be implemented by county governments. Although the bill (HB 3686) passed in August 1993, it was ratified too late to win the bidding war for Intel's Arizona plant (Barnett 1994).

Intel applied for SIP benefits shortly after the law passed and was granted two SIP packages in 1994. A third followed in 1999, and a fourth in 2005 (see Table 1). The 1999 programs had an interesting twist. Because the program is implemented at the county level, local jurisdictions can influence specific requirements. In exchange for receiving a $200 million tax break, Intel agreed to pay a growth impact fee of $1,000 per worker if the company exceeded a ceiling of 1,000 manufacturing jobs on top of the 4,000 that already existed (Verhovek Howe 1999). In 2003, however, after the economy cooled down as a result of a recession, county commissioners voted to repeal this fee and according to the local newspaper, had no interest in restoring it (Rogoway 2005).

Table 1: Strategic Investment Program Agreements in Oregon, 1994–2006

Year	Company	County	Investment ($)	Tax break ($)	Community service fees ($)	Jobs (N)
1994	Intel (D1)	Washington	105	9	2	355
1994	Intel (Ronler Acres)	Washington	2,000	52	19	1,400
1994	Integrated Device Technology	Washington	800	4	1	975
1995	Fujitsu Microelectronics	Multnomah	1,000	23	9	445
1995	LSI Logic	Multnomah	4,000	113	27	2,000
1999	Intel	Washington	13,000	200	27	—
2005	Intel	Washington	25,000	579	—	—
2006	Elk Horn Wind Farm	Union	160	—	—	8–15
2006	Georgia Pacific's Wauna Mill	Clatsop	193	15	—	40
2006	Genentech	Washington	300	26	8	200–300

Source: Gorman (2006), Hill (2006), Mayer (2003), Sickinger (2006a).
Note: Tax break amounts and numbers of jobs (full-time jobs) are based on projections. Fujitsu Microelectronics dropped out of the program in 1997 because it did not meet the stated job-creation goals.

Gaining approval for the SIP at the county level was taken very seriously by Intel. For the 1999 package, the company engaged a Portland-based communications and public relations company and spent a total of about $128,000 on a campaign to convince employees (some of whom were vocal critics during earlier discussions), business partners, citizens, and county commissioners (Intel Corporation and Fiskum & McCormick Conkling 2000). A local consulting firm also was hired to prepare fiscal impact studies demonstrating Intel's economic importance to Washington County, the Portland region, and the state as a whole (ECONorthwest 1998; 2003; Fruits 2005). One study noted that without the SIP, "Oregon will not be competitive for large capital investments by Intel or other companies, depriving Oregon and Oregonians of substantial economic benefits" (Fruits 2005, 3). Intel's public relations efforts were successful in 2005: the commissioners in Washington County and the Hillsboro City Council approved Intel's fourth request (which was advanced because the company had already reached the investment limit set in the 1999 agreement).

As a result of Intel's involvement in designing the tax break program, the SIP became popular across the Portland metropolitan region. Besides Washington County, other jurisdictions took advantage of it. Firms such as Integrated Device Technology, LSI Logic, Fujitsu Microelectronics, and Microchip have gained approval for the program from Multnomah County. Multnomah County is especially interested in attracting and retaining high-tech employers because it traditionally has been more of a "bedroom" community and has seen less economic growth in knowledge-based sectors than have other counties. However, some counties have rejected bids by firms. In 1995, for example, Yamhill County commissioners did not approve an application put forward by Japanese company Sumitomo Sitix because of concerns over increased growth and traffic (Hamilton and Barnett 1995). Sumitomo subsequently chose to locate in another state.

In 2005, the Oregon legislature changed the SIP to encourage investments in rural areas and in different kinds of industries that do not require large capital investments. The threshold for taxable investments in rural projects was lowered to $25 million, and the community service fee was reduced to 25 percent of the abated taxes, or $500,000 a year. Since these changes have taken place, three additional projects have been approved for SIP benefits. In 2006, Union County in Eastern Oregon approved benefits for a wind farm. Georgia-Pacific's Wauna Mill in Clatsop County on the Oregon coast received $193 million in benefits for paper-towel machinery. The third package was approved for Genentech, a San Francisco–based biotechnology firm in Washington County. Genentech qualifies for the lower rural threshold because the facility will be built on land originally zoned as rural that until recently had been located outside the urban growth boundary (Sickinger 2006b).

Intel became more deeply rooted in the Silicon Forest as a result of the SIP. The tax breaks that Intel received ensured continued expansion of the company's semiconductor manufacturing and R&D operations in the region. At the time of the first SIP agreement in 1994, Intel employed about 7,700 people; the total employment in the Silicon Forest high-tech industry was about 42,400. By 2006, Intel had more than 16,000 employees. (By contrast, the company employs about 5,300 in New Mexico and 10,000 in Arizona.) Intel operates seven campuses in the Portland metropolitan region.

Because R&D activities in the semiconductor field are very closely connected to the high-volume mass production process of chips, Intel's investments in the Portland region have ensured that the company continues not only its manufacturing operations but also its high-level innovation-oriented work. However, some critics argue that in recent years, Oregon has watered down the tax incentive program by allowing different kinds of industries that may have less of an impact on employment to take advantage of it.

Conclusion

This case study illustrates the ways in which high-tech firms can influence economic development policy decisions. In Oregon, firms like Intel and Tektronix have pressured policymakers to not only implement tax incentive programs but also focus on critical public goods such as higher education. Although cities and regions have not yet abandoned more traditional modes of economic development such as tax incentives, they are beginning to understand the increased importance that high-tech firms place on education and workforce development. In turn, they are adopting more "entrepreneurial" policy efforts (Clarke and Gaile 1998).

Until the latter part of the last century, local infrastructure for competing in a global knowledge economy did not exist in Portland. In partnering with state and local governments to formulate economic development policy, large corporations as well as other high-tech protagonists such as venture capitalists functioned as policy entrepreneurs (Atkinson 1991). Firms influenced policymakers and pushed for an economic development agenda that situated the region in a more favorable and competitive position. Atkinson (1991) describes this model of policy making as the active stewardship model, which is characterized by moderate-to-strong support from external interests such as businesses, a strong commitment to economic development by state leaders such as the governor, an executive style of policy making, and the strong influence of policy entrepreneurs. This notion of corporatism can lead to effective policies because organized interests are brought into the process as active, supportive partners.

The history of corporatist influence in the Portland region has to be interpreted from a perspective that takes into account not only changing dynamics in industry organization but also business self-interest. As entrepreneurship accelerated in the region and new high-tech firms were founded, the need for skilled labor increased, as did the complexity of operations. Since Portland did not have a strong higher education system sufficient to support innovative high-tech economies, firms began to form coalitions to address the problem. Researchers have noted that collaborative approaches wherein businesses serve as civic entrepreneurs to stimulate competitiveness can be important when other critical institutions in a region like universities are weak (Kanter 1995; Henton 2001; Markusen 1987). Kanter (2000, 173) notes that business coalitions "make most sense when 'public goods' are created that many businesses share, that are too costly for any one to fund alone or require the resources of many institutions, and that have longer-term time horizons and benefits. It is thus not surprising that coalitions focused on tax reductions, improved public services, economic development, or shared infrastructure (for example, airports) tend to be the most prevalent and effective. These efforts bring new shared benefits but do not ask anyone to give up anything. They also focus on concrete tangible projects with clear and measurable results."

Today, Portland is known as a vibrant albeit second-tier high-tech region. The region's high-tech firms that initially located in the region because of cost advantages attracted talented employees who contributed to entrepreneurship. The initial cost advantages of the region have decreased in importance over time because high-tech firms have begun to rely more heavily on activities that require innovation and knowledge creation. Thus, perhaps more so than typical economic incentives such as tax breaks, higher education infrastructure and work-force development have become critical. This case illustrates that when public and private entities collaborate, the interests of all may be served.

References

American Electronics Association. 1997. 1998. 1999. 2000. 2001. *Oregon technology benchmarks. State of the industry report*. Portland: American Electronics Association.

Atkinson, Robert D. 1991. Some states take the lead: Explaining the formation of state technology policies. *Economic Development Quarterly* 5:33–44.

Barlett, Donald, and James Steele. 1998. States at war. *Time*, November 8, 40.

Barnett, Jim. 1994. The two that got away. *The Oregonian*, May 22, K01.

Barnett, Jim, and Romel Hernandez. 1995. Higher education reforms. *The Oregonian*, November 11, E06.

Clarke, Susan E., and Gary L. Gaile. 1998. *Globalization and community*. Vol. 1 of *The work of cities*, ed. D. R. Judd. Minneapolis: University of Minnesota Press.

Colby, Richard. 1989. Goldschmidt promises to pick panel to review Portland college programs. *The Oregonian*, March 10, B06.

Cortright, Joseph, and Heike Mayer. 1999. *An overview of the Silicon Forest*. Portland: Institute of Portland Metropolitan Studies, Portland State University.

Dodds, Gordon B., and Craig E. Wollner. 1990. *The Silicon Forest: High tech in the Portland area*. Portland: Oregon Historical Society.

ECONorthwest. 1998. 2003. *Economic impacts of Intel's Oregon operations*. Portland: Intel Corporation. download.intel.com/community/oregon/downloads/ECONorthwest.pdf. Accessed April 16, 2007.

_____. 2005. *Comprehensive economic development strategy for the Portland-Vancouver metropolitan region*. Portland: Regional Partners for Business and the CEDS Strategy Committee.

Fruits, Eric. 2005. *Fiscal and economic impacts of Intel Oregon's potential future investments*. Portland: Intel Corporation. download.intel.com/community/oregon/downloads/IntelSIP2005.pdf. Accessed April 16, 2007.

Gorman, K. 2006. Genentech's ripple. *The Oregonian*, December 7, 18–20.

Hamilton, Don, and Jim Barnett. 1995. Yamhill County rejects tax break for plant. *The Oregonian*, May 25, A01.

Henton, Douglas. 2001. Lessons from Silicon Valley: Governance in a global-city region. In *Global city-regions: Trends, theory, policy*, ed. A. J. Scott. Oxford: Oxford University Press.

Hill, G. K. 2006. Windfall from wind farms drops. *The Oregonian*, November 17, D01.

Hill, Jim. 1989a. Idea of change has officials at PSU wary and watchful. *The Oregonian*, November 19, C01.

_____. 1989b. Industry panel calls for shutting PSU. *The Oregonian*, November 9, A01.

_____. 1990. Governor hails plan for urban higher education. *The Oregonian*, November 15, C03.

Intel Corporation, and Fiskum & McCormick Conkling. 2000. *Reputation at risk: Asking a community for tax incentives*. New York: Public Relations Society of America.

Kanter, Rosabeth Moss. 1995. *World class: Thriving locally in the global economy*. New York: Touchstone.

_____. 2000. Business coalitions as a force for regionalism. In *Reflections on regionalism*, ed. B. Katz. Washington DC: Brookings Institution Press.

Markusen, Ann R. 1987. Regions: *The economics and politics of territory*. Totowa, NJ: Rowman & Littlefield.

Mayer, Heike. 2003. Taking root in the Silicon Forest: The role of high technology firms as surrogate universities in Portland, Oregon. PhD diss., College of Urban and Public Affairs, Portland State University.

_____. 2005a. Planting high technology seeds: Tektronix role in the creation of Portland's Silicon Forest. *Oregon Historical Quarterly* 106:568–93.

_____. 2005b. Taking root in the Silicon Forest: The role of high technology firms as surrogate universities in Portland, Oregon. *Journal of the American Planning Association* 71:318–33.

National Science Foundation. 2002. WebCASPER. webcaspar.nsf.gov/index.jsp. Accessed August 15.

Oregon Business. 2004. *Research Oregon: A special report on college and university research programs*. Portland: Oregon Business.

Oregon Council for Knowledge and Economic Development. 2002. *Renewing Oregon's economy: Growing jobs and industries through innovation*. Portland: Oregon Council for Knowledge and Economic Development.

The Oregonian. 2000. Oregon's "quiet crisis." It's a shortage of qualified high-tech workers. October 1, G04.

Rogoway, Mike. 2005. Intel seeks to extend tax breaks to 2025. *The Oregonian*, February 23, A01.

Rojas Burke, Joe, and Steven Carter. 2000. Oregon Graduate Institute, OHSU want to merge. *The Oregonian*, July 26, A12.

Rubenstein, Sura. 1995. Hammered the battered history of Oregon higher education. *The Oregonian*, May 1, A01.

Saxenian, AnnaLee. 1994. *Regional advantage: Culture and competition in Silicon Valley and Route 128*. Cambridge: Harvard University Press.

Sickinger, Ted. 2006a. Georgia Pacific cutting 130 workers at Wauna Mill. *The Oregonian*, August 9, C01.

_____. 2006b. Tax break program reflects changing business climate. *The Oregonian*, August 2, D01.

Verhovek Howe, Sam. 1999. Fighting sprawl, Oregon County makes deal with Intel to limit job growth. *The New York Times*, June 8, A12.

Washington County. 2005. *Washington County and City of Hillsboro approve $25 billion Intel investment agreement*. Washington County, OR: County Administrative Office. www.co.washington.or.us/deptmts/cao/news/sipapp05.htm. Accessed April 6, 2007.

CHAPTER 5

Crossing State Borders: Utility-Led Interstate Economic Development Cooperation in New England

John R. Lombard

In 2000, a group of state business recruiters from throughout New England joined together to promote New England to corporate real estate and site selection consultants at the World Congress of Corenet Global (formerly known as the International Development Research Council) in New York City. At roughly the same time, the two metropolitan areas of Hartford, Connecticut, and Springfield, Massachusetts, formed the Hartford-Springfield Economic Partnership. These informal cross-state ventures represent a coalition of business, academic, political, and policy leaders whose intention is to foster and promote the combined regions' economic well-being. Although interstate cooperation is not new, what is remarkable in the former case (dubbed Team New England) is that six traditionally rivalrous New England states have cooperated in the area of business attraction—an economic development practice that has been and continues to be fiercely competitive at all levels of government. In the case of the Hartford-Springfield Economic Partnership, two metropolitan regions that share a state border have acted jointly in promoting their combined resources to facilitate business attraction as well as other economic development activities. Northeast Utilities Services Company, a gas and electric utility servicing three New England states (Connecticut, Massachusetts, and New Hampshire), has been instrumental in the development, funding, and evolution of these interstate cooperatives and has been the key convener in both instances.[1]

How is it that these states that pride themselves on independence and self-reliance have effectively collaborated to attract business investment? How have local and regional economic development organizations overcome historical competitiveness to develop a common economic development agenda? What role has Northeast Utilities played in orchestrating these ventures, and how are they faring today after seven years in operation? To what extent can lessons be drawn to inform other interstate cooperative efforts?

This case study seeks to answer these questions and others through interviews, field observations, and archived documents related to Northeast Utilities, Team New England, and the Hartford-Springfield Economic Partnership. In short, the purpose of this investigation is to identify the organizations, agents, and other key players involved in the formation of these cross-state economic development coalitions, highlight the issues surrounding their formation, and discuss their continued evolution as programs.

Intrastate Government Cooperation

Interjurisdictional or multijurisdictional local government cooperation has been the subject of much research. Affordable housing, transportation, workforce availability, and the environment are among the development-related issues local governments have addressed through cooperation on a regional basis. Chambers of commerce, councils of government, and regional planning agencies are familiar institutions on the economic development landscape that promote solutions to regional issues with local overtones.

Few studies have examined interjurisdictional or multijurisdictional cooperation in local economic development, and even fewer have done so in the context of cross-state local economic development collaboration. Among the research that has been conducted, Olberding (2002a) found that intrastate regional cooperation in economic development has been increasing since the mid-1980s: 80 percent of the 191 regional partnerships in economic development she examined were established after 1980. Her research also suggests that strong cooperative norms within business, government, and the community are related to the formation of regional partnerships, while economic need may drive partnerships in regions with weak cooperative norms. Holtkamp, Otto, and Mahmood (1997) evaluated the success of multicommunity development organizations in a rural setting. Using data on job retention and creation in Iowa, they found that successful multicommunity development organizations, when controlling for population difference, tended to have larger staffs and budgets and were in operation longer. Other literature mostly based on examinations of metropolitan or city-suburb intergovernmental agreements points to a number of factors contributing to the prevalence of regional economic development alliances, including increased global competitiveness, community fiscal stress, the impact of a major economic shock such as corporate relocation or downsizing, a tradition of regional activities within an area, and the presence of consolidated government (Olberding 2002a; 2002b; Barth 2001; Fitzgerald, Perry, and Jaffe 2002; Grossman 1998; Cole 1998; Heath and Henegar 1994).

The dynamics of intergovernmental cooperation and competition may be understood within the conceptual framework offered by Gordon (2007), which emphasizes the importance of political, organizational, and environmental cultures. One theme that emerged in the qualitative interviews he conducted in Illinois was the importance of "allies," defined as "entities that [are not] in competition with the community but have an active involvement in economic development" (Gordon 2007, 71). Similarly, Lackey, Freshwater, and Rupasingha (2002) reported that successful local collaboration necessitates some sort of "spark plug"; that is, a facilitator who plans and oversees the cooperative project. Utility-based economic development offices oftentimes fulfill this role. In the two examples of multijurisdictional cooperation discussed here, the economic and community development office of Northeast Utilities has functioned in this capacity.

Interstate Government Cooperation

Multistate cooperation in economic development is evident in organizations such as the Tennessee Valley Authority and the Appalachian Regional Commission. These regional bodies, developed through federal mandates and involvement, are geared toward serving particular multistate geographic areas deemed to be severely in need of economic growth and development. States have a history of cooperation in areas such as resource protection and remediation, higher education, drug prevention, and joint purchasing (Chi 1990), and there has been somewhat of a resurgence of state-initiated regionalism in economic development arenas. For example, the Southern Growth Policies Board, representing 13 states and the Commonwealth of Puerto Rico, has been successful in advancing "visionary economic development policies" (Southern Growth Policies Board 2007). The Western Governors Association initiated a regional approach to export trade marketing and promotion. The New England Governor's Conference has effectively addressed regional policy issues since the 1930s. However, these broad, multistate cooperative ventures avoid the more contentious and competitive activities associated with local or metropolitan economic development interaction in attracting capital investment and new jobs.

Most research has not examined interstate regional economic development efforts, likely because few examples of cross-state collaborations exist. (Cole's [1998] study of states coming together in response to the economic shock of a military base closure is a notable exception.) This case study attempts to redress the imbalance in the literature in order to understand the nature and scope of such activity. The findings indicate that of the 39 census-designated metropolitan areas that cross state borders, only 7 regional economic development organizations specifically mentioned in their mission statements or supporting demographic data that they served or represented jurisdictions from neighboring states.[2] Another 13 organizations mentioned serving other state jurisdictions but did not provide supporting demographic data indicative of neighboring representation. No mention of cross-state support was found for the remaining cross-state metropolitan areas.

Utility-Led Economic Development

Most large investor-owned electric utilities have functional economic development offices staffed at various levels. It has been estimated that American electric utilities invest more than $100 million annually in economic development programming (Ticknor and Pollina 2004). The adoption of this activity by electric utilities stems from the notion that they serve a fixed service territory, usually operating in a semiregulated environment.[3] Therefore, as populations increase and businesses grow and expand, utility revenue grows. Moreover, a utility is able to spread its fixed costs proportionately over its customer base. Aside from contributing to future revenues, economic development enhances government and public relations (Bacas 1991). Unlike lobbyists, economic development staffs work alongside state and local government officials on projects that often result in new jobs and investment, thereby increasing the political "goodwill" of the utility. In this semiregulated environment, utilities are able to offset the costs of their economic development operations by including those costs as part of the approved expenses in the base rate set by state regulators.[4]

The role of utility economic developers is much the same as that of local, regional, and state economic developers. They support and enhance other economic development efforts, act as business advocates, produce and maintain comprehensive economic development data, and help retain, expand, and recruit businesses. And like many localities, electric utilities often offer incentives that provide direct cost savings to new business. In short, they take on the role of lead facilitator and even function as intermediary, often promoting business interests in the site-selection process.

However, unlike local and state governments that operate within well-defined jurisdictional boundaries, utility territories often encompass multiple states. For example, Northeast Utilities operations extend across three New England states. While each state operating company of the utility conducts its own economic development activities, all activities are coordinated by central staff at Northeast Utilities headquarters. Other examples include American Electric Power, which operates across 11 states and provides a comprehensive listing of available buildings and sites across its service territory. The Southern Company coordinates economic development staff in Georgia, Alabama, Mississippi, and Florida. In essence, economic development within these large utilities transcends state boundaries, and information and best practices are able to be shared among operating units.

A primary role of economic development staff within a multistate utility, therefore, is advocating for regional solutions to economic development–related issues that may cross state borders. Utility economic development staffs are positioned to facilitate cross-border initiatives. The Inland Northwest Partnership, a coalition of eastern Washington and western Idaho communities organized by the Washington Water Company, is one example of an entity that promotes and fosters regional economic growth and development (Griffin and McCourt 1999). Northeast Utilities cross-border initiatives have focused on two of the most important economic development policy objectives: strategic industry cluster development and the attraction of new investment (McCarthy 2003). Deregulation has not impinged upon the economic development infrastructure of Northeast Utilities as it has upon that of other utilities.

Cross-Border Initiatives

Northeast Utilities is directly involved in two cross-border initiatives. The company was instrumental in bringing together two historically competitive regions, divided only by a state border, to form the Hartford-Springfield Economic Partnership. Representatives from the partnership attend monthly meetings hosted by the economic development staff of Northeast Utilities to work toward improving the region's social and physical infrastructure. The other initiative, Team New England, assembles the business recruitment directors of all six New England states in an informal cooperative. Its mandate is to attract global business to New England. Both groups jointly promote the region at international trade shows and appeal to corporate real estate executives. Thus, Northeast Utilities has brought together traditionally fierce rivals to attract mobile investments—a very competitive economic development strategy.

The Hartford-Springfield Economic Partnership

In February 1999, Northeast Utilities convened a meeting of the Connecticut Capitol Region Growth Council and the Economic

Development Council of Western Massachusetts, the two regional economic development bodies representing the greater metropolitan areas. Dialogue centered on the need for more cross-border cooperation on economic development issues, and an agreement was made to gauge the interest of other key local economic development organizations. In July 1999, Northeast Utilities convened a much larger group, including the regional economic development organizations as well as the respective regional chambers of commerce, planning commissions, the Bradley International Airport Commission, and the convention and visitors bureaus. Economic development representatives from the Universities of Massachusetts, Connecticut, and Hartford joined the group shortly thereafter. A total of 16 organizations throughout the region joined together "to position and advance the economic progress of the combined regions" (internal briefing document provided to author from Doug Fisher, Northeast Utilities Services Company, March 20, 2000). A public announcement heralding the collaborative effort was made in 2000 by the governors of both states.

The Hartford-Springfield Economic Partnership created a steering committee, the purpose of which was to (1) more effectively leverage the region's higher education assets; (2) create a brand identity for the cross-border effort to sell the concept to key stakeholders; (3) compile and distribute collateral material to define the region's demographic and economic strengths; (4) expand upon existing tourism promotion; (5) advocate regional transportation initiatives to promote the expansion of Bradley International Airport and the development of rail links between New Haven, Hartford, and Springfield; (6) promote international investment and trade for the region; and (7) support business retention, expansion, relocation, and workforce development (Hartford-Springfield Economic Partnership 2000). The steering committee existed without a formal charter, and Northeast Utilities staff provided support for the group as well as financial assistance.

The announcement of the cross-border collaboration was preceded by several instances of ad hoc joint venturing between the two regions. A major theme was transportation, particularly with regard to Bradley International Airport. The Pioneer Valley Planning Commission (Springfield) and the Capitol Region Council of Governments worked together to update the master plans for Bradley to develop ground transportation, expand air service, and attract new carriers. A second area of early and continued collaboration has been the promotion of an intelligent transportation system, cross-border commuting, major construction projects, and road maintenance along the I-91 corridor. Environmental improvements have been another focus of cross-border collaborations. The designation of the Connecticut River as one of only 10 American Heritage Rivers required the support of more than 50 sponsors (representing four states) as well as planning agencies, county governments, and chambers of commerce. These activities have fostered a regional mindset, the principle force behind which has been Northeast Utilities.

The New England "Knowledge Corridor" stretches from the Vermont border to Long Island Sound along I-91, linking Connecticut, Massachusetts, and Vermont, through which the Connecticut River flows. The area supported a once-bustling traditional machine-tooling and metal-working sector (Forrant and Flynn 1998). Together, the two metropolitan areas represent New England's second-largest population (behind metropolitan Boston). According to 2007 U.S. Census estimates, the combined region has approximately 1.86 million people, relative in size to the metropolitan areas of Orlando (Florida), Charlotte (North Carolina), and Columbus (Ohio). Human, economic, and educational resources have made the region attractive to businesses, site selection consultants, and mobile investors. The joining of these two regions has provided fodder for public relations campaigns and new advertisements touting the availability of business amenities.

Northeast Utilities has conferred other benefits. The company provided resources to Hartford-Springfield Economic Partnership to undertake a study of the regional economy and underwrote the costs of industry cluster studies for medical devices and plastics industry. Furthermore, it has been instrumental in marketing the Knowledge Corridor in conjunction with Team New England and has facilitated networking at venues such as marquee sporting events.

In addition to engaging in traditional business attraction activity, the Hartford-Springfield Economic Partnership has brought together workforce development boards to create a strategic alliance and has pursued federal grants. Hartford-Springfield Economic Partnership worked with the Bradley International Airport Commission to establish daily nonstop service to Amsterdam via Northwest Airlines. The partnership also conceived InternHere.com, a free, Web-based internship service that encourages students to live and work in the region and connects them with businesses. Currently, over 4,000 students are registered. Thus, through cross-border, informal collaboration among actors involved in economic development, planning, higher education, and the public and private sectors, Northeast Utilities has helped form a natural economic entity united by geography, transportation infrastructure, labor market, demographics, and culture (Connecticut River Valley 1999) (internal briefing document provided to author from Doug Fisher, Northeast Utilities Services Company, March 21, 2007).

Team New England

Team New England was the brainchild of Northeast Utilities. Several factors contributed to the evolution of the initiative. First, the broader manufacturing economy of the Northeast had been long suffering from changing industry dynamics and increased global competition. According to some, New England was "old and cold," having lost workforce talent, youth, and economic and political clout. Second, there was a general feeling among Northeast Utilities staff that the New England states were not participating in as many traditional economic development marketing events as other states. This lack of promotion stemmed from state budget crises that necessitated the elimination of even modest spending on marketing. In confidential interviews with the author, Northeast Utilities staff suggested that "traditional Yankee arrogance" had created a negative connotation associated with state "boosterism."

Backing the efforts of Team New England was another long-time business advocacy and policy organization: the New England Council. This 80-year-old bipartisan alliance of business, academic, health care, and public and private organizations provided some financial support for Team New England. Leadership from other New England regional organizations such as the New England Board of Higher Education, Discover New England (tourism), the New England Governors Conference, and the Federal Reserve Bank of Boston lent support to the initiative.

Since 1990, Team New England has engaged in very visible business recruitment activities, primarily the promotion of the region to the corporate real estate and site selection consulting industries. The coalition is associated with many of the larger business location, relocation, and expansion projects. Such consultant-led projects potentially can offer substantial employment opportunities and attract capital investment and publicity. It is imperative that as key players in the business mobility market, economic developers maintain networking relationships with these important industries. As one Northeast Utilities economic development manager commented, "It is not so important that you get to know the site selectors and the corporate real estate crowd but rather they get to know you."

Oftentimes, site selection consultants expect—even demand—special consideration for their client projects. These demands include immediate access to demographic and workforce data, confidential interviews with existing employers, site visits, access to senior government officials, and other time-consuming and resource-intensive requirements. As such, it is important that communities that are being considered for new investment maintain the capabilities to respond to consultant inquiries. Because many communities and even some states lack the staff, resources, and skills to deal effectively and efficiently with consultant requests, however, utility and regional economic development marketing organizations often assume this responsibility. As the primary facilitator of Team New England, the economic development staff members of Northeast Utilities perform this function.

Why did Northeast Utilities develop a coalition broader than its service territory, underwriting Team New England when only three of the six states are serviced by its operating companies? From a marketing perspective, it made sense to do so. As the head of the economic development office of Northeast Utilities noted: New England is a "brand." Tourism departments have been marketing New England jointly for more than a decade, and Northeast Utilities recognized the power of branding.

Second, the company's experience in working directly in competitor states suggested that a lot of duplication and overlap exist in state marketing messages and activities. Statewide nonprofit-based economic development marketing efforts often are not in sync with state marketing efforts. The company recognized that by creating Team New England, it would be better able to coordinate economic development efforts across its service territory, thereby leveraging its resources.

Third, Team New England provides a stable, nonpartisan marketing platform, which provides a way to cope with the turnover in state economic development staff that often occurs in conjunction with state governor election cycles. The downtime of staff training is effectively eliminated, and marketing efforts are professionalized. State business recruitment directors are undertaking joint promotion that maximizes limited marketing budgets and allows for New England to have a greater presence at more business mobility–related venues. Team New England is now a perennial participant at many trade shows, networking with businesses and hoping to attract future investments. Furthermore, there has been a sharing among states of best practices in economic development marketing.

In 2005, an outside consultant was hired to examine perceptions of the business climate of New England among executives involved in business mobility, the general population, and some international business executives (A. T. Kearney 2005). The report confirmed the consultant's suspicions that New England did not exhibit a strong brand presence and did very little economic development promotion compared with competing regions. As a follow up to the 2005 report, the Federal Reserve Bank of Boston and the New England Council commissioned a focus group study of branding (Browne 2006). To improve the region's reputation, Team New England is expanding traditional economic development marketing to international venues as well as networking with new client groups, such as real estate brokers.

Approach to Economic Development

State economic development policy has been classified as evolving through three phases, or waves, a concept that has been around since the 1900s (Eisinger 1988). The first phase emphasizes traditional business recruitment. The second is characterized by business retention and expansion. The third phase is typified by economic development networks, including the facilitation of strategic industry clusters as well as more trendy activities such as catering to the "creative class" and "economic gardening." As the emphasis within economic development policy has evolved, states as well as local economic development organizations still maintain very active and visible business attraction efforts.

Much of the academic research, however, points to the evils of business attraction, or "smokestack chasing." Loveridge (1996) provides a summary of the more substantive critical arguments for this apparent disconnect between economic development practice and academic research. One argument is that competition for footloose capital is a zero-sum game. Business relocation may benefit the winning community, but the national economy does not experience any net change. Another argument suggests that nonpolicy-controlled variables such as labor availability, quality, and costs or market accessibility are more important in the location calculus than community-provided financial incentives. A third argument points out that the odds of landing a substantial project are very low. On average, there are only a couple hundred major location projects a year, and there are some 15,000 or so local economic development organizations.

Moreover, communities may not have all the information they need to evaluate a project. Therefore, they tend to overbid for projects. Loveridge (1996) questions why business attraction remains such a popular economic development strategy. One hypothesis is that luring a business has immediate economic payoffs, unlike the gradual payoffs associated with investment in physical and human capital. Another reason may be that many communities derive a large share of their revenue from property taxes, so there exists a built-in motivation to capture as much physical capital within the taxing jurisdiction as possible. Likewise, successful business recruitment builds tremendous political capital. Those of us in economic development have no doubt witnessed the "politics of announcement" whereby elected politicians stand shoulder to shoulder with business executives to pronounce a victory for the community. Team New England and Northeast Utilities derive substantial goodwill with state governments and politicians given the kind of "win-win" they generate.

Nevertheless, Northeast Utilities has chosen to focus on business recruitment through cross-state collaboration. The New England states have employed certain methods to band together in this competitive area. Rather than merely delivering a proposal to attract business, New England states and competing jurisdictions such as Hartford and Springfield have actively pursued lead generation through trade shows, networking at corporate real estate conferences and with site selection consultants, and "cold calling." This selling of the region to potential businesses is an initial aspect of business attraction. Many major location projects come to the state either directly or through a site consultant.

There still remains the very sticky issue of lead sharing, however. When leads are developed, staff members assess the nature and scope of the lead for distribution to the appropriate state. Some leads are general in nature while others are specific in terms of geography. Northeast Utilities staff must constantly provide reassurances of neutrality. When questioned about this issue, the economic development staff of Northeast Utilities indicated that there was limited lead sharing across states. A large part of staff members' time is dedicated to reassuring state business recruiters that they act as a neutral or third party in adjudicating lead distribution.

Many of the events for Team New England and Hartford-Springfield Economic Partnership are specifically geared toward place promotion and stipulate specific guidelines and protocols for participation. CoreNet Gobal and the Industrial Asset Management Council are two such participating organizations. Membership in these organizations is made up of corporate real estate executives who enjoy privileged status as "active" members, while the bulk of "associate" members are from organizations that provide services to real estate corporations, including economic development agencies. The cost of exhibiting at these venues can be exorbitant, and typically only well-funded state economic organizations can afford an exhibit. By pooling resources, the New England states are able not only to maintain a visible and ongoing presence at these venues for very little cost but also to "smooth out the unevenness" of limited state budgets.[5] The economic development team plans, executes, and processes leads developed from these marketing venues. Various New England state representatives literally just have to show up at the venue and network. In short, Northeast Utilities provides a turnkey operation for participation at these important marketing venues.

Familiarization tours are another example of cooperative ventures to attract business. "Fam tours" usually are held in conjunction with high-visibility sporting events and are common tactics employed by many states and regions. Tours are geared toward particular representatives from site selection firms and corporate real estate executives and provide firsthand exposure to New England and its business climate. They are intensive efforts in coordination and necessitate dedicated resources to execute effectively. Fam tours provide captive audiences for targeted marketing and allow for the development of key networking relationships (Driver 2007).

Finally, it is important to note that these partnerships represent informal, somewhat loose coalitions that build upon existing organizations and relationships along the lines of the "ad hoc" regional alliances described by Barth (2001). The success of these modern-day partnerships is clearly linked to the role of Northeast Utilities staff as champions of cross-border collaboration in economic development.

Conclusion

The cross-border initiatives examined in this case study are reflective of the preconditions and success factors identified in previous examinations of intrastate government collaboration (see Cigler 1999). Evidence of these preconditions exists in both examples. Team New England and the Hartford-Springfield Economic Partnership initiatives emerged from the perceived stress of extreme manufacturing decline and regional depopulation. Although both initiatives had broad-based political constituencies and general support from key organizations, neither was awarded substantial financial resources.

Surprisingly absent from these examples was the early and continued support of elected local officials—usually a precondition for economic success. Rather, in both instances, these partnerships formed somewhat below the political radar, only relying on political endorsements when announcements were made. Neither were additional economic development resources required from participating governments. Northeast Utilities provided the necessary seed monies to ensure early and visible results.

Barth (2001) identified the characteristics of effective ad hoc regional organizations: they should be neutral conveners and facilitators; have no preordained mission, power structure, or rules; include voluntary participation; involve key decision makers; derive decisions by consensus; and start small and build upon successes. Effective regional ad hoc organizational characteristics exist in both initiatives presented in this case study. The role of Northeast Utilities economic development staff members cannot be underemphasized: their time, talent, commitment, and resources were the main factors contributing to the emergence of these initiatives. Northeast Utilities took on the role of key policy entrepreneur and neutral convener, building trust among competitors and facilitating nearly all the activities associated with both initiatives.

It should be noted that the apparent success of these initiatives did not occur overnight. They emerged from a regional identity fostered through hundreds of years of shared culture and have grown over the last six to seven years through the unwavering commitment and leadership of Northeast Utilities economic development staff. These examples attest to the fact that successful cross-state collaboration in economic development is indeed possible.

Notes

1. The author thanks the economic development staff members from Northeast Utilities for sharing their insights and information during this research. They were instrumental in arranging interviews with representatives of Team New England and the Hartford-Springfield Economic Partnership. The interviews took place on March 20 and 21, 2007, at Northeast Utilities headquarters. It should be noted that the author previously was employed as Director of Research and as a consultant for a national site selection firm and subsequently employed as Director of Business Recruitment for the State of Connecticut. These experiences have no doubt influenced interpretation of this case study.

2. Student researchers performed Web-based searches on every census-designated metropolitan area that crosses state borders to find a regional economic development organization that served that metropolitan area. Each site was examined for evidence of cross-state collaboration (i.e., specific mention within the mission statement and inclusion of demographic information tables and community contact data).

3. Northeast Utilities was deregulated in 1998. However, the rate that the utility is allowed to charge for delivering electricity to its customers is still regulated by the State of Connecticut Department of Public Utility Control. "Semiregulated" is used by the author to describe this business aspect of electric utility operation.

4. Utility rate structures, or tariffs, are typically set through legal proceedings as determined by each state's utility regulatory body. The base rate approved by the State of Connecticut Department of Public Utility Control includes administrative costs to do with economic development, marketing, customer service, employee salaries, and other expenses associated with utility operations.

5. State budgets for economic development in general and recruitment in particular vary. For the economic development department to plan a major recruitment event or trade show requires commitment very early in the planning process. By sharing in the costs for trade shows and events, state economic development organizations reduce their budget outlays.

References

A.T. Kearney Inc. 2005. *Sustainable prosperity: An agenda for New England.* www.newenglandcouncil.com/pdf/rep_webReports/rep_atKearney.pdf. Accessed June 27, 2007.

Bacas, Harry. 1991. Partners in promotion. *Nation's Business* 79:48–52.

Barth, Thomas. 2001. The role of ad hoc regional alliances in managing growth. *Public Works Management & Policy* 6:114–25.

Browne, Lynn. 2006. Developing a brand for New England: An update. Presentation to the John Laware Leadership Forum, Boston. www.tbf.org/tbfgen1. asp?id=3566. Accessed June 25, 2007.

Chi, Keon S. 1990. Interstate cooperation: Resurgence of multistate regionalism. *Journal of State Government* 63:59–63.

Cigler, Beverly A. 1999. Pre-conditions for the emergence of multicommunity collaborative organizations. *Policy Studies Review* 16:1.

Cole, Ben. 1998. The power of regional thinking: Surviving a Navy Base closure. *Economic Development Review* 16:4–8.

Connecticut River Valley Organizations. 1999. Highlights of collaboration. Unpublished internal document.

Driver, David C. 2007. The power of interstate collaboration. Presentation to EDA/IEDC/NARC Regional Economic Development Roundtable Symposium, Philadel-phia. www.iedconline.org/EDASymposia/Presentations/Driver.pdf. Accessed June 25.

Eisinger, P. K. 1988. *The rise of the entrepreneurial state: State and local economic development policy in the United States.* Madison: University of Wisconsin Press.

Fitzgerald, Joan, David Perry, and Martin Jaffe. 2002. *The new metropolitan alliances: Regional collaboration for economic development.* www.ceosforcities.org/rethink/research/files/Metro%20Report.pdf. Accessed June 25, 2007.

Forrant, Robert, and Erin Flynn. 1998. Seizing agglomeration's potential: The Greater Springfield Massachusetts metalworking sector in transition, 1986–1996. *Regional Studies* 32:209–22.

Gordon, Victoria. 2007. Partners or competitors? Perceptions of regional economic development cooperation in Illinois. *Economic Development Quarterly* 21:60–78.

Griffin, John, and Jeff McCourt. 1999. Economic development after deregulation: New roles for the electric power industry. *Economic Development Review* 16:13–20.

Grossman, Howard J. 1998. Regional economic development in the 21st century. *Economic Development Review* 16:9–13.

Hartford-Springfield Economic Partnership. 2000. *States launch new partnership.* www.hartfordspringfield.com/announcements.asp. Accessed June 25, 2007.

Heath, Mark D., and Edward G. Henegar. 1994. "Success story!" The Carolinas Partnership. *Economic Development Review* 12:80–84.

Holtkamp, Jan, Daniel Otto, and Nuzhat Mahmood. 1997. Economic development effectiveness of multicommunity development organizations. *Journal of the Community Development Society* 28:242–56.

Lackey, Steven B., David Freshwater, and Anil Rupasingha. 2002. Factors influencing local government cooperation in rural areas: Evidence from the Tennessee Valley. *Economic Development Quarterly* 16:138–54.

Loveridge, Scott. 1996. On the continuing popularity of industrial recruitment. *Economic Development Quarterly* 10:151–58.

McCarthy, Linda. 2003. The good of the many outweighs the good of the one. *Journal of Planning Education and Research* 23:140–52.

Olberding, Julie C. 2002a. Diving into the "third waves" of regional governance and economic development strategies: A study of regional partnerships for economic development in U.S. metropolitan areas. *Economic Development Quarterly* 16:251–72.

_____. 2002b. Does regionalism beget regionalism? The relationship between norms and regional partnerships for economic development. *Public Administrative Review* 62:480–91.

Southern Growth Policies Board. 2007. Mission statement. www.southern.org/about/about.shtml. Accessed July 8.

Ticknor, Tim, and Ronald R. Pollina. 2004. Grow it! *Electric Perspectives* (March–April). findarticles.com/p/articles/mi_qa3650/is_200403/ai_n9368407. Accessed July 18, 2007.

CHAPTER 6

Strategies for Small Town Success

Joe A. Sumners

Leaders in struggling rural communities and small towns often pin their hopes for economic prosperity on recruiting a large manufacturing plant to "save" their town. In Alabama, the recent success in attracting large automotive plants like Mercedes-Benz, Honda, and Hyundai, has fueled such a lust for industrial recruitment. In fact, several small towns have attracted first- and second-tier suppliers to these large automakers. These successes have further stoked the competitive fires and jealousies of other towns that are sure their big break is just around the corner, if only they can come up with the right financial incentives and recruitment strategy.

An unfortunate consequence of relying on strategies that focus exclusively on industrial recruitment is that many communities undervalue, or do not understand, the importance of other determinants of strong local economies. For example, business retention and expansion, small business and entrepreneurial development, tourism, and retiree attraction receive short shrift compared with industrial recruitment. More significantly, local leaders pay too little attention to building community and civic infrastructure.

Put another way, many small towns overemphasize marketing and sales (i.e., industrial recruiting) without adequate attention to product development (i.e., improving the quality of life in the community). Restoring health to struggling towns will require much more than just enticing a company to open a new plant in the local industrial park. Industry recruiters certainly play important roles in the economic development of their communities. But so do the high school principal, the hospital administrator, the plant manager, the city beautification council, the League of Women Voters, the church benevolence committee, and the citizen who organizes a town meeting. Prosperous small town economies are built upon the foundation of strong communities. And strong communities are characterized by diverse and collaborative leadership, engaged citizens, and a community mindset of pride and optimism. Prosperous communities also tend to have excellent schools, quality healthcare services, and amenities (e.g., arts and culture, recreation, dining, shopping, and entertainment) that contribute to a high quality of life. It is increasingly important in the 21st century knowledge economy that a community also have a modern telecommunications infrastructure. These community assets found in fully developed communities are "both a by-product of positive economic performance and a foundation for future prosperity" (North Carolina Manpower Development Corporation 2002, 1).[1]

Successful development strategies in small towns typically include the following objectives: (1) developing strong, diverse community leadership that is inclusive, collaborative, and connected; (2) identifying local assets and creating and carrying out a strategic plan based on these assets; and (3) joining with other jurisdictions to maximize economic resources.

The discussion that follows illustrates the value of each of these strategies based on the experiences of several communities in Alabama and Mississippi. They all have faced major economic challenges, and each has struggled for whatever success that has come its way. Although some of these communities continue to struggle, they all clearly understand that their success depends heavily upon leadership, planning, and partnerships.

Developing Inclusive and Connected Leadership

Successful communities all over the United States understand the importance of an expansive view of community leadership. The traditional notion of the community leader—often a mayor or other powerful "position holder"—as chief community problem solver has given way to a new, more dynamic model of the community leader as catalyst, connector, and consensus builder (Southern Growth Policies Board 2003).[2]

David Mathews, president of the Kettering Foundation, summarizes the foundation's research findings on community politics: "What stands out in the high-achieving community is not so much the characteristics of the leaders as their number, their location and, most of all, the way they interact with other citizens. The high-achieving community had ten times more people providing leadership than communities of comparable size. This [high-achieving] community is 'leaderful'; that is, nearly everyone provides some measure of initiative. And its leaders function not as gatekeepers but as door openers, bent on widening participation" (2003, 6).

This new model recognizes that leadership and community work are not confined to a few elected officials or business leaders. Rather, successful leadership requires mobilizing the talents of every segment of the community. This model acknowledges that everyone has something to offer—unique knowledge, perspectives, and talents. Today's successful communities tend to be full of leaders.

The following stories from Tupelo, Mississippi, and the Alabama communities of Uniontown and Demopolis illustrate how citizen leaders have taken the initiative in turning around struggling communities.[3]

Tupelo, Mississippi

In 1940, Lee County, Mississippi, was one of the poorest counties in the nation. Grisham (1999) describes how strong community leadership provided the foundation for an economic revival that took place in Tupelo during the second half of the 20th century (see Grisham and Gurwitt 1999). During this period, Tupelo and Lee County rose from poverty to become a model for community and economic development success.

It was the editor of the *Tupelo Daily Journal*, George McLean, who provided the vision and leadership that sparked Tupelo's transformation. He wrote editorials, cajoled, badgered, and eventually convinced local businessmen and farmers that, if they worked together, Tupelo and Lee County would grow and prosper. McLean told them, "There is no limit to what an organized community can do if it wants to" (Grisham 1999, 3).

In the early stages of community development, George McLean was the champion, or catalyst, who pushed the effort forward. But he understood that even the best ideas would fail if they were not connected to, informed by, and "owned" by a larger body of participants.

McLean persuaded local businessmen that it was in their interest to help the region's farmers. The more prosperous the farmers, he reasoned, the more money they could spend in Tupelo stores. Tupelo's businessmen agreed to invest in the local dairy industry. Tupelo merchants funded one of the first artificial insemination programs in the country, which upgraded the quality of milk cows and consequently filled the town's cash registers. The dramatic and highly visible success of the dairy program reinvigorated Tupelo and erased any doubts that a grassroots economic development project could work.

McLean and other Tupelo leaders realized that in order to sustain and expand the success of the dairy program, they needed to establish community-based organizations dedicated to long-term development. In 1946, Tupelo leaders created rural community development councils to provide a structure for involving farmers in development of their own communities. The council meetings worked much like New England town meetings; they provided a forum for members of the communities in northeastern Mississippi to come together and determine their shared priorities and strategies.

Tupelo leaders next decided the city needed a new vehicle for the community to invest in itself on a continual basis. In 1948, 88 of Tupelo's leaders formed the Community Development Foundation (CDF). Anyone willing to pay the dues (set on a sliding scale according to income) could join. The CDF embraced the philosophy that Tupelo's citizens were responsible for creating their own future. The CDF also recognized from the beginning, however, that neither it nor the community as a whole held all the answers. When necessary, it sought outside advice and assistance.

The CDF cultivated a network of community organizations that have shaped community life in Lee County—especially the rural community development councils. They have given ordinary citizens a way to influence community decisions. With each new success, the community has gained momentum to help it meet the next challenge. This model of citizen leadership continues today, with impressive results.

Today, Lee County is the second-wealthiest county in the state and is home to more than 200 highly diversified manufacturers, including 18 Fortune 500 companies. Tupelo, with a population of just under 35,000, serves as the industrial and commercial hub for northeastern Mississippi. In 2007, Toyota Motor Manufacturing selected Tupelo as the site for its newest automotive manufacturing plant. This plant represents an investment of $1.3 billion and will eventually employ more than 2,000 people. Tupelo is also home to a 650-bed hospital, the largest nonmetropolitan hospital in the nation and the hub of a 22-county health care system with more than 430 physicians. Its public school system is recognized as one of the best in the state and is a two-time recipient of the U.S. Department of Education's Excellence in Education Award (in 1984 and 2000).

The Tupelo experience shows that as the attitudes of people within the community change, the attitudes of people outside the community also change. Tupelo has been successful in attracting new business and industry because people see it as a place worth investing in. Community development—the ability of citizens to work together on issues of common concern—made Tupelo's success in economic development possible.

Uniontown, Alabama

Uniontown, a community of less than 2,000, is located in the heart of the Alabama Black Belt, a region named for a deposit of dark, fertile soil extending from Mississippi's border through the heart of Alabama. Once the backbone of the state's agricultural economy, this region now suffers from pervasive poverty and economic stagnation. An area of urgent need, the region faces a declining population, an inadequate health care system, substandard schools, and weak business development. Uniontown is one of the poorest of the many poor communities in the Alabama Black Belt.

Uniontown has had several aggressive mayors who attracted assistance to the community through federal grants and the help of outside experts, and Auburn University and the University of Alabama have made significant outreach efforts. Citizens, however, were mostly inactive. The few citizens who attended public meetings often were passive and appeared reluctant to express their viewpoints. They tended to look to a leader (the mayor or outside experts) for answers to community problems.

In fall 2000, Auburn University began an outreach project in Uniontown based on a different approach. The focus was less explicitly on solving problems and much more on facilitating dialogue, listening, and responding to the needs of Uniontown citizens as they defined them. Instead of working through the city's mayor, Auburn University leaders decided to engage ordinary citizens.

To do so, Auburn recruited about 25 individuals representing all segments of the community to participate in a focus group. This biracial group of citizens representing a wide range of age groups, income levels, and occupations continues to meet biweekly. In order to create a sense of shared identity, the citizens gave their group the name Uniontown Cares.

Since the creation of Uniontown Cares, citizens have taken advantage of the new public space to deliberate community issues, identify and take ownership of community problems, and connect with one another and with other members of their community. As they discussed local problems, they began to realize their capacity for doing something about them. Talk became action. And these actions led to results, such as cleanups of parks and cemeteries, the creation of an Alcoholics Anonymous chapter, and the development of an Adopt-a-Park program.

In 2006, Uniontown Cares sponsored a community design charrette, conducted by the Auburn University Center for Architecture and Urban Studies. About 75 residents attended, and the results inspired a new plan for Uniontown's downtown. Uniontown Cares also leads a community coalition (the Uniontown Fatherhood and Family Initiative) to educate youth on the costs of teenage pregnancy, the benefits of responsible fatherhood and strong family relationships, and alternative options and career paths for their futures. The project aims to provide male role models, mentors, and a peer support network to male youth in the community, many of whom have never witnessed positive models of fatherhood or a healthy relationship between two parents.

Uniontown Cares is making a difference, and others in the community are beginning to notice. More and more members of the community have joined the group. In fact, the group outgrew its original city hall meeting room and moved to space in a new public library, which Uniontown Cares members helped renovate and stock with new books and computers.

The enormous problems of the Alabama Black Belt persist. But for the people participating in Uniontown Cares, things are looking better. Despite many setbacks and struggles, they have come to see themselves as citizens instead of victims, as public actors instead of clients of services. They see that they can control many things about their lives and community. They understand that they have a long way to go, but this group of Uniontown citizens continues to work and struggle to make more of their community. And from that struggle comes hope, a commodity that has been in short supply.

The Uniontown experience demonstrates that government alone cannot solve the problems facing economically challenged communities. Dealing with these problems requires a collaborative approach by government, citizens, other community institutions, and external resources. Relying solely on government or outside experts can relegate people to the sidelines and stifle the community-building process.

Demopolis, Alabama

Demopolis, Alabama (population 7,135), just 20 miles down the road from Uniontown, has seemed to avoid many of the problems of its Black Belt neighbors. In the late 1960s, when Alabama schools finally desegregated, Demopolis leaders— white and black—decided to work together to support an integrated city school system. In most other Black Belt communities, white residents essentially abandoned the public schools, choosing instead to create a dual school system by establishing all-white private academies. Today, almost every Alabama Black Belt community maintains a segregated school system, with blacks attending public schools and whites attending private academies.

Demopolis citizens, however, speak with pride of their excellent schools and commitment to a racially diverse public school system. A socially and economically vibrant community, Demopolis was one of the initial eight communities selected to participate in the Alabama Communities of Excellence program.[4] While other Black Belt communities were coming apart, the Demopolis community chose to come together—and that made all the difference.

According to Demopolis Mayor Cecil Williamson (interview with the author, April 25, 2007), "Leaders need to be representative of the makeup of the community. You have to be intentional when putting together boards, commissions, and task forces. You need to be sure that everyone who should be at the table is at the table. You need to be inclusive as far as gender, race, and age."

Tupelo's experience was similar. While most of Mississippi was torn apart by racial division during the civil rights struggle, the Tupelo community held together. As early as 1961, Tupelo's recreation department began refusing to allow any of the sports teams it sponsored to compete against communities that maintained segregationist policies. In 1965, it became the second community in the state to sign a school antidiscrimination agreement and desegregated its schools the next school year without incident.

Demopolis and Tupelo illustrate that economic progress requires the resources of the entire community. Communities that are divided—whether racially, politically, or socially—face nearly insurmountable barriers to economic advancement.

Identifying Community Assets and Creating a Strategic Plan

Strategic Planning Considerations

As the old saying goes, "If you don't know where you're going, any road will take you there." Citizen leaders and stakeholders in high-achieving communities know where they are going. They understand that an environment of rapid social, cultural, and technological change requires a proactive approach to addressing current and future problems. They engage in a strategic planning process to identify what makes their place special and decide how to cultivate and promote their unique assets, be it a river, lake, mountain, or rich history. The result is a strategic plan that identifies community priorities and outlines specific strategies to make best use of available assets and address local challenges. It becomes a road map for the future and a benchmark to measure community progress.

In addition to the actual product of strategic planning, one of the most beneficial aspects is the process itself. A successful strategic planning process brings together a diverse group of stakeholders who address basic questions for the community: "Where are we now?" "Where do we want to go?" and "How do we get there?" There are few other occasions when representatives from throughout the community come together for an extended period to discuss shared hopes, dreams, knowledge, perspectives, ideas, and concerns. Broad-based strategic planning is a "mega-crossroad" and one of the best tools available for building and strengthening community connections.

The key to the success of any strategic plan is to align the community so that it can take full advantage of its assets. For Eufaula, Alabama (population 13,350), the greatest local assets include its abundant natural resources and beautiful environment. With Lake Eufaula and miles of shoreline along the Chattahoochee River, the city is a bass fishing paradise. The Eufaula National Wildlife Refuge hosts nearly 300 species of birds and 40 different types of mammals including deer, bobcats, coyotes, and foxes.

Protecting these treasured environmental assets for future generations was the primary goal of the community's 2002 strategic planning process. In fact, the Eufaula 2020 plan is the first community-wide strategic plan in Alabama—and perhaps the first in the nation—to be based explicitly on the principles of "sustainability." The strategic planning committee decided that every aspect of the plan—from economic development to transportation to education—must take environmental impacts into account.

More than 120 Eufaula citizens, representing a broad cross-section of the community, participated in the strategic planning process. They produced the following vision statement:

> Eufaula, Alabama, is a sustainable community committed to building its future while preserving its treasured assets. It is a family-oriented community that values its beauty, natural resources, and rich history. Eufaula is friendly, progressive, and inclusive. It is characterized by excellent schools, safe and attractive neighborhoods, diverse cultural, recreational, and employment opportunities, quality public services, a strong infrastructure, a vibrant economy, and active involvement of all citizens.

To make this vision a reality, Eufaula 2020 outlines six strategic issues: preserving the natural environment; empowering citizens; building a sustainable economy; building a strong community; preserving history, beauty, and aesthetics; and delivering quality government. For each of these issues, the plan outlines broad goals and specific objectives and includes a detailed action plan for each objective.

The community has received national recognition for its efforts. Audubon International named Eufaula the first Audubon Cooperative Sanctuary community in the United States, and CNN covered the community meeting in which Eufaula 2020 was unveiled. More importantly, Eufaula now knows where it is going, and it has a plan for getting there.

From Planning to Action

If the Eufaula story ended with the creation of a strategic plan, it would resemble most other community planning efforts. The result would be a plan that looks good on paper but ends up collecting dust on a shelf. That did not happen in Eufaula, however, because leaders created a mechanism—the Eufaula 2020 Executive Committee—to take responsibility for implementing the major objectives in the plan. This group, which includes representatives from government, business, education, and faith-based institutions, meets monthly to monitor the community's progress on the plan and make needed modifications to ensure that the plan remains relevant to community priorities and needs. Six years after the plan's creation, citizen committees are still working to implement its objectives. In fact, Eufaula has already achieved or made significant progress on 130 of the 175 specific objectives contained in the original plan.

The value of the group is not just that it checks items off the list of community objectives. It serves as an important community "crossroads," giving key stakeholders the opportunity to think, work, and act together. Instead of focusing narrowly on the interests of "my school," "my church," "my business," or "my government," stakeholders see how each part of the community can work with the others to accomplish shared objectives.

This strategy is rarely used, but it is powerful. Sadly, a nearly universal observation of many who work in community development is how seldom they see coordinated effort. Most communities have many excellent people, programs, and projects. All communities have at least some institutional assets—city government, churches, schools, civic clubs, and chambers of commerce. But far too often, individuals and organizations work independently rather than in concert with one another. Like Eufaula, the truly high-achieving communities create crossroads where leaders from various organizations and institutions come together to address community issues in a comprehensive way.

In its report, *The New Architecture of Rural Prosperity: 2005 Report on the Future of the South*, the Southern Growth Policies Board recommends that regions and communities be more proactive in creating such connections among stakeholders. It also recommends the creation of Regional Prosperity Alliances, networks of stakeholders from government, business, education, faith-based groups, and others that meet and work together to improve the region (or community). The alliances would serve as organizations within the region that aim high and envision major sustained improvement. An alliance would convene, coordinate, plan, fund, and measure (based on established benchmarks and targets for success). It would not need to replace or compete with existing organizations, and it might even be housed and administered by an existing organization (e.g., chamber of commerce). Its purpose would be to ensure that existing resources are fully utilized and enhanced.

One community that is putting this strategy to work is Headland (population 3,715), a small, rural community in southeastern Alabama, about 12 miles north of Dothan. Key leaders from government, business, and education, among others, have joined to create a group called Renaissance Headland. The group, which meets monthly, has created four committees charged with developing and implementing comprehensive strategies for leadership and citizen engagement, community planning, economic development, and improving the quality of life, especially in terms of education, health care, and community aesthetics.

Forming Regional Partnerships

Many important issues facing rural areas and small towns transcend the governmental boundary lines established in the 19th century to meet the needs of people who went to town in a mule and wagon. Because these areas are sparsely populated, they lack a critical mass of taxpayers, leadership, financial capacity, infrastructure, and skilled labor. If small towns are to survive, they must join forces and work together. Small towns must learn to see their neighboring communities as competitors only for the Friday night football game.

Attracting new businesses should be one aspect of a holistic approach to economic development. But small towns rarely possess adequate resources to be effective in the increasingly competitive arena of economic development. Hiring a professional economic developer is an impossible dream for most small communities—that is, unless they partner with their neighbors.

Many Alabama communities already understand the value of multijurisdictional and regional alliances for economic development. For example, in 2004, three counties in southwestern Alabama (Conecuh, Escambia, and Monroe) joined forces to create the Coastal Gateway Economic Development Authority (CGEDA). In 2007, the CGEDA expanded to five counties when Choctaw and Clarke Counties joined the alliance. Headed by a professional economic developer, the CGEDA markets these counties to prospective industry and businesses and serves as a clearinghouse for existing industrial parks and sites in the region. The CGEDA has initiated a regional asset mapping and strategic planning process, established regional priorities, and initiated a successful fund-raising campaign to support collaborative marketing efforts, entrepreneurship, and regional networking opportunities. An early priority of the organization was to secure additional property so that the counties would have more available industrial sites.

Coastal Gateway has attracted an impressive number of new businesses to the region, adding hundreds of new higher-paying jobs. The CGEDA president has also focused on civic improvements within each community through leadership development, planning, and quality-of-life enhancements in addition to the economic development initiatives.[5] Six of the communities within this region have been selected by the Alabama Communities of Excellence program as model communities—almost a third of the 19 total Alabama towns to receive the recognition. According to the CGEDA president, Wiley Blankenship (interview with the author, February 27, 2008), "We're trying to build communities. It's a slow process, but it's something we're dedicated to doing. Community development must precede industrial recruitment, especially in rural areas."

The need for a regional approach to community and economic development is clear, considering that the largest municipality in this region has just over 7,000 people. The 26 municipalities in these five counties have a total 45,546 people—collectively still less than one-fourth the size of the City of Mobile, a regional neighbor. It's simply unreasonable to expect a single small community to compete on an equal footing with a community of 50,000 or 100,000 residents.

Conclusion

As these stories illustrate, both small towns and larger jurisdictions are best served by a holistic approach to economic development. Industrial development may be one good strategy, especially if done in partnership with regional neighbors. But it should not be the *only* strategy, nor will it usually be the most effective. Small towns need to cultivate strong and diverse community leadership that is inclusive, collaborative, and connected. They need to identify their unique assets, create and implement a strategic plan, and establish partnerships among community stakeholders and with other jurisdictions. And they need to be proactive in creating community and regional crossroads—organizations and structures that allow leaders to connect regularly and assess, plan, and work together. In the words of Tupelo's George McLean (Grisham 1999, 3), "There is no limit to what an organized community can do if it wants to."

Many city dwellers long for what people in small towns already have and often take for granted: a slower pace of life, friendly people who know their neighbors, attractive open spaces, beautiful scenery, quaint shops, historic homes and buildings, parades, festivals, and streets that are safe and free of traffic congestion. Many of our small towns still possess a sense of authenticity and charm that cannot be replicated in bigger cities.

These inherent quality-of-life advantages—enhanced by leadership, planning, and partnerships—ultimately make small communities more attractive to both existing and potential residents and employers. In other words, investments in product development make the community much easier to market and sell. The irony is that strategies emphasizing community development (over industrial recruitment) ultimately make small towns much more attractive in the competition for those large manufacturing plants they covet.

Notes

1. North Carolina Manpower Development Corporation (a private, nonprofit organization in Chapel Hill, North Carolina) has spent 35 years publishing research and developing policies and programs to strengthen the workforce, foster economic development, and remove the barriers between people and jobs in the rural South. In "The Building Blocks of Community Development" (October 2001), the corporation identified six interrelated fundamental components of a community's economic prosperity business development, workforce development, physical infrastructure, social infrastructure, cultural and environmental stewardship, and civic infrastructure.

2. The Southern Growth Policies Board adopted the following objective in its report: "Build the civic capacity of Southern communities to respond to emerging opportunities and challenges with new models of leadership, engagement and social capital."

3. The observations here are based on the author's experience working with Uniontown officials and citizens from 1999 to 2007 on outreach projects related to strategic planning, civic engagement, and other community improvements.

4. Alabama Communities of Excellence (ACE) is a nonprofit program that uses the collective expertise of its partner public and private organizations to assist Alabama's communities with populations of between 2,000 and 12,000 as they attempt to become communities of excellence. In order to be selected, a city must have both the capacity and commitment to become a community of excellence. These communities are guided through three stages of assistance, including an inventory of community assets (Phase I), creation of a leadership development program and strategic plan (Phase II), and help with comprehensive planning, industrial attraction and retention, commercial and business development, tourism, education enhancement, health and human services, recreation, and general quality-of-life improvements (Phase III). Upon comple-

tion of the third phase, the community is declared a community of excellence. The program takes a minimum of two years to complete. An ACE team created for each community consists of representatives of the ACE partner organizations. The ACE team works closely with local stakeholders as the community progresses through the three stages of the program. For more information, visit the Web site at www.alabama communitiesofexcellence.org.

5. The CGEDA is committed to ensuring that the entire region meets the ACE program's Criteria of an Excellent Community in the areas of leadership development, planning, economic development, and quality of life. The characteristics of an ACE Community can be found at www.alabamacommunitiesof excellence.org.

References

Grisham, Vaughn. 1999. *Tupelo: Evolution of a community*. Dayton, OH: Kettering Foundation Press.

Grisham, Vaughn, and Bob Gurwitt. 1999. *Hand in hand: Community and economic development in Tupelo*. Washington, DC: Aspen Institute.

Mathews, David. 2003. The little republics of American democracy. *Connections* 13:6.

North Carolina Manpower Development Corporation. 2002. *The building blocks of community development*. Chapel Hill, NC: MDC Inc.

Southern Growth Policies Board. 2003. *Reinventing the wheel: Report on the future of the South 2003*. Raleigh, NC: Southern Growth Policies Board.

_____. 2005. *The new architecture of rural prosperity: 2005 report on the future of the South*. Raleigh, NC: Southern Growth Policies Board.

CHAPTER 7

The "Shrinking" Strategy of Youngstown, Ohio

Wendy L. Hassett

Youngstown, Ohio, has taken a unique approach toward facing its future—one that questions the long-held assumption that "bigger is better." The city's newly adopted philosophy runs counter to the one embraced by the mainstream, which equates growth with prosperity. Instead, Youngstown's municipal leaders and residents have adopted an approach to "shrink" the city in the hope that downsizing the city will spur positive physical and economic transformations throughout the community. What happens in Youngstown in the years to come will hold powerful lessons for all American cities facing economic stagnation and population decline.

One of the key cities in the state of Ohio, Youngstown is located in the northeastern region of the state, just 10 miles from the border of Pennsylvania. The city is midway between New York City and Chicago, about 60 miles southeast of Cleveland, and some 62 miles northwest of Pittsburgh. According to the U.S. Census Bureau, the city had a population of 82,026 in 2000, a drop of 14 percent from 1990 (Swope 2006). By 2003, the city's population had dropped again to 79,271.

Youngstown was named for John Young, who first settled there after purchasing more than 15,000 acres from the Western Reserve Land Company in 1797. When coal was discovered there in the early 1800s, the Youngstown area was made part of the Erie Canal network. The railroad followed in the mid-1850s. Both the canals and the railroad then connected the Mahoning Valley, through which the Mahoning River flows to the Ohio River, to the rest of the country. Because of the area's rich deposits of coal and iron, Youngstown soon developed a flourishing steel industry. The area's first steel mill began operations in Youngstown in 1892.

In following years, miles of steel plants were established in the Mahoning Valley. As a result, the Steel Valley soon became recognized as one of the largest manufacturing regions in the United States. Increasingly, European immigrants settled in the area to work in the industries. By 1920, Youngstown was the 50th-largest U.S. city by population and ranked just behind nearby Pittsburgh in its production of steel. During World War II, the region served as a major industrial hub for steel production and continued to grow in population and wealth.

From the early 1900s to the mid-1970s, Youngstown also served as a vibrant retail center in the Mahoning Valley. Downtown Youngstown boasted modern theaters, department stores, and upscale shops. The city's economic vibrancy declined in the second half of the 20th century as its manufacturing base began to wane due to foreign competition, business costs, industry consolidation, and modernization issues. As a result, local businesses suffered. Meanwhile, the city faced a troubling reputation for corruption; in the late 1950s and early 1960s, Youngstown was nicknamed Bomb City for its identification with Mafia-related car bomb incidents. In the early 1970s, two newly constructed shopping malls challenged the viability of the downtown retail shops and were ultimately blamed as a major cause for their downturn.

On September 19, 1977, which became known as Black Monday, the Youngstown Sheet and Tube Company, headquartered in Youngstown and one of the nation's most important steel producers, announced its pending closure. Because Youngstown never became as economically diversified as other larger industrial cities such as Pittsburgh, Chicago, and Cleveland, the closing of the steel plants in the 1970s came close to destroying the city's economy. Increasingly, Youngstown residents left in search of new employment opportunities. The collapse of the city's steel industry continued to affect Youngstown, its remaining residents, and business owners decades later.

The city is still home to a few steel and metal-working companies, but there are far fewer now than during the height of steel production in the early 1900s. Many of the buildings and neighborhoods that were once bustling with activity have become abandoned and dilapidated. Today, Youngstown's largest employer is Youngstown State University, the primary institution of higher learning in the Youngstown-Warren metropolitan area, with an enrollment of about 13,000 students.

The 2000 U.S. Census reported the city's total population as 82,026—less than half of the 170,002 recorded by the 1930 census. The Census reported 32,177 households in the city. The racial makeup of the city was roughly 51 percent white, 44 percent African-American, and 5 percent Hispanic (Puerto Ricans make up the dominant Spanish-speaking group). The median household income was $24,201, and the median family income was $30,701. Approximately 25 percent of the population was below the poverty line.

Most cities facing decline focus on regaining the city's former glory. Youngstown, however, has taken a very different approach. It has embraced its smaller size and is positioning itself for a new future as a smaller city. Youngstown's leadership approaches the disappearance of the once-predominant steel industry as an opportunity to enhance greenspace and quality of life. The city is identifying and redesigning declining neighborhoods with the help of residents. In other abandoned areas, the city is providing incentives for people to move out (El Nasser 2006). Mayor Jay Williams said it this way: "It was unrealistic to think we'll be a 100,000 [population] city. But why not be an attractive city of 80,000 or 85,000 that offers a quality of life that competes with other cities across the state and across the country?" (Swope 2006).

"Shrinking" Cities

Cities that have shrunken in population contradict the commonly held image of success as a large city with constant economic and demographic growth. This common assumption may be changing, however. The U.S. population has reached more than 300 million and is expected to continue growing. At the same time, some of the most populous cities in 1950 have fewer residents today. Many experts point to the suburban ring around cities as a main cause of those declines.

When a city shrinks instead of grows, municipal leaders and residents are forced to reconsider the city's future and revisit the notion that "growth" is good and "shrinking" is not. The drastic demographic changes in shrinking cities present a host of challenges, the most predominant and powerful of which is economic. Social and cultural challenges, however, are also significant.

One example of this notion of shrinking on a grand scale is Germany in the early 1990s. The fall of the Berlin Wall in 1989 greatly transformed Germany economically and demographically. In an incredibly short time, nearly one million people moved from East Germany to West Germany, vacating more than one million housing units and abandoning countless industrial parks. This rapid decline led Germany's Federal Cultural Foundation to initiate the Shrinking Cities project aimed at assisting Eastern Germany in analyzing and managing the large-scale changes it encountered and continues to face. The challenges of shrinking cities are not restricted to Germany or even the United

States. Countries across Europe and Asia facing low fertility rates and aging populations are also interested in how cities can shrink gracefully.

In his study of "growth without growth," Gottlieb (2002) placed Youngstown in a category with Buffalo, New York; Toledo, Ohio; and Scranton-Wilkes Barre, Pennsylvania. The challenge for these places, he states, "is to think about policies that might encourage slower population growth without restricting the mobility of people or capital. More specifically, local officials may want to avoid economic policies that target job growth as their primary objective, and instead enact policies that boost per-capita income. Per-capita income growth is the best proxy for the local policy maker's true goal, which is to improve the economic welfare of current constituents" (2002, 8).

In their study of communities that experienced extended periods of economic growth based on one dominant industry or company that then closed or suffered dramatic decline, Mayer and Greenberg (2001) found that the community's reaction was usually delayed by at least a decade. During that time, economic stagnation and decline led to other unfortunate community problems such as high unemployment. Once a plan was in place to diversify the community's employment base, however, civic leadership and a shared community vision were the critical factors to facilitate recovery.

The findings of both Gottlieb (2002) and Mayer and Greenberg (2001) speak to the situation in Youngstown. In particular, they are reflected in the centerpiece of the city's strategy to move Youngstown forward: *Youngstown 2010*.

Youngstown 2010

The city's current mayor is Youngstown native Jay Williams.[1] Williams is the city's first African-American mayor and its first independent mayor since 1922, and when elected at age 34, he was its youngest mayor. Williams's election as Youngstown's mayor has been considered a watershed event in the changing political landscape of the community. Prior to serving as mayor, Williams spent five years as director of the city's Community Development Agency. In that capacity, Williams played a leading role in the city's ambitious urban renewal planning initiative, *Youngstown 2010*.

The City of Youngstown, in partnership with Youngstown State University and community volunteers, organized the initiative in 2005 to create a revitalization plan and a common vision for the future of Youngstown. At the time of this undertaking, the city was operating under a comprehensive plan that was created in the early 1950s and updated in the mid-1970s. This outdated plan was based on an inaccurate projected population of more than 200,000.

The initiative evolved over the course of a series of public meetings that involved substantial input from citizens who expressed hope that Youngstown could experience revitalization and once again enjoy a measure of economic success. The ultimate goal of the 2010 plan was that Youngstown would be a "safe, clean, enjoyable, sustainable, attractive city."

The *Youngstown 2010* Plan Web site (www.youngstown2010.com) describes the plan:

> The *Youngstown 2010* Plan is based on a new vision for the new reality that accepts we are a smaller city that will stabilize at 80,000 people.
>
> Linear population projections produced by the Ohio Department of Development and analyzed by Youngstown's metropolitan planning organization, Eastgate Regional Council of Governments, indicate that by 2030 Youngstown's population will fall to 54,000. Linear projections may be accurate if there is no change in the status quo. *Youngstown 2010* is a chance to change the status quo and alter the slope of the projected trend line.
>
> The City of Youngstown is positioned to become a competitive city once again. Keeping *Youngstown 2010* a viable movement and not just another plan on the shelf will take the continued involvement of the community who helped bring the process to fruition. The City of Youngstown cannot, on its own, do everything that is called for in the plan. It will be the energy of each neighborhood and each community member that makes this plan work. It is you that will make this plan work.
>
> *Youngstown 2010* is a guide for the community and future city administrations to follow and implement. Although change is inevitable, this document is intended to provide a solid foundation for a cleaner, greener, and more efficient city.

The *Youngstown 2010* process has resulted in much attention focused on improving the city's quality of life and addressing its declining tax base. Youngstown's city officials have responded by directing its municipal investments to where they will have the greatest impact. Housing, neighborhoods, abandoned buildings, and unused or underused infrastructure top the list of issues that need immediate attention.

Many of the strategies of the city's new policy aim to address Youngstown's widespread abandoned and dilapidated buildings. As of 2006, Youngstown had approximately 14,000 vacant lots with 1,000 rundown houses and commercial structures on them. The city made more than $1 million available to tear down 300 to 400 of these properties in 2006. The city is also attempting to tackle the large number of delinquent property tax bills so that these properties can be returned to "productive use" (Swope 2006).

Past city planner and current director of the Center for Urban and Regional Studies at Youngstown State University, Hunter Morrison, commented on Youngtown's efforts (Swope 2006):

> In parts of Youngstown where [there is] vacant property on land that is hard to drain, [the plan suggests] that's one area where you don't sell off the land.... There [may be a street] with one house on it, where you have water and sewer and electricity and you plow the street when it snows.... [T]he policy ought to be to close [that type of street] down and perhaps reassemble that property and look at ways in which property that is wet might be converted to formal wetlands. The fact that you're shrinking means you have more land to work with. And you can create greater value in the land you do keep for redevelopment. But you don't want to have an unrealistic goal of building back to what [you] once were.
>
> We have to be a more attractive right-sized, mid-size city.... [N]ot every building is worth saving or can be saved. A simple concrete building that is standing open and vacant and vandalized is not helpful. So to preserve what remains, you have to cull. Sometimes it's better to have a vacant lot.... [A]rson and theft and abandonment are tearing down more houses than any act of the city.

The city has adopted a twofold strategy to address Youngstown's housing stock and neighborhoods. First, residents are encouraged to move out of neighborhoods that simply cannot be revitalized. Second, programs are being implemented to improve the housing stock and otherwise stabilize transitional and middle-class neighborhoods. New development is being encouraged where people want to live.

In a similar vein, the city is taking a hard look at the costs of providing public services to semi-abandoned areas of the city and reducing nonessential infrastructure in increasingly unpopulated neighborhoods. Mayor Williams stated, "[I]n terms of resource allocation and the city's capital expenditures—we have to provide police and fire [fighting services] for every citizen in this city. And it's strategically easier to provide police and fire [in] densely populated areas of the city, as opposed to [areas] in the furthest reach of the city where there were once 1,000 people but now there are 100" (Swope 2006).

A *New York Times* article speculated on a possible long-term outcome for the city: "Instead of trying to recapture its industrial past, Youngstown hopes to capitalize on its high vacancy rates and underused public spaces; it could become a culturally rich bedroom community serving Cleveland and Pittsburgh, both of which are 70 miles away" (Lanks 2006a). University of Toronto professor Charles Waldheim further commented, "To the extent that northeastern Ohio has a market for housing, it seems that Youngstown's future is making itself available for the garden living of the suburb" (Lanks 2006b).

Clearly, the city intends to reposition itself for a future different from the one it once imagined. Today's vision of a sustainable smaller city centers on a much more diverse economy than the steel industry of its past. Youngstown is focused on enhancing its quality of life by attacking the urban decay entrenched for so many decades. One key to doing so is making the most of its unique civic treasures.

Cultural Amenities

One advantage of having once been a much larger and wealthier city is that the vestiges of those prosperous years remain. Youngstown's outstanding amenities exist only because of its former days of prosperity. In fact, today even the wealthiest communities would be hard-pressed to replicate the remarkable parks and facilities currently present in Youngstown (Swope 2006).

For example, Youngstown's Mill Creek Park is the second-largest municipal park in the country, behind New York's Central Park. This five-mile-long stretch of natural wooded landscapes, flowering gardens, and recreational activities is located in the heart of the city. Park visitors may explore nature trails, the Davis Education and Recreation Center, a restored 19th-century mill, dramatic rock formations, and a small museum showcasing the history of the park and honoring Volney Rogers, the Youngstown attorney who set aside the park property years ago. Also downtown is the Children's Museum of the Valley, which provides regional opportunities for hands-on learning. Activities and exhibits explore the culture, art, drama, construction, science, and natural history associated with the Mahoning Valley.

On the edge of Youngstown State University's campus and just north of downtown is Youngstown's most widely known museum, the Butler Institute of American Art. It was the first museum in the country dedicated solely to American art. The original building, dedicated in 1919 and widely considered an architectural masterpiece, is listed on the National Register of Historic Places.

On the historic north side of the city is Wick Park, a smaller municipal recreation area. The periphery of Wick Park is lined with early 20th-century mansions built during the city's glory days by industrialists, business leaders, and professionals. Another remnant of the past is Powers Auditorium (formerly the Warner Brothers' theater), which serves as the city's primary music hall and home of the Youngstown Symphony Orchestra.

Crime and Housing

In spite of the optimistic *Youngstown 2010* plan and the city's impressive cultural amenities, one of the most pressing problems that plagues the community is crime. In fact, Mayor Williams identified fighting crime as his first and largest priority for 2007. Thirty-five murders were recorded in 2005, and just slightly fewer in 2006 (Skolnick 2007b). *CNN Money* reported that violent crime in Youngstown rose 10 percent in 2005, and property crimes (including burglary and arson) increased more than 20 percent from the prior year (Cox 2007).

One of the Youngstown Community Watch representatives commented to a reporter that residents of her area try to get all of their activities done during daylight hours and do not regularly attend weeknight church services because they are afraid to be outside after dark. She stated, "Once it gets dark, if they don't have to be out, they're not out" (Gorman 2007).

The connection between deindustrialized cities and crime has received some attention. Matthews, Maume, and Miller (2001) examined 85 midsized municipalities in the Rust Belt that had experienced economic deterioration. These authors found that unemployment and population change are either directly or indirectly (via socioeconomic deprivation) associated with homicide rates in these cities.

It is not surprising, then, that the housing market is reacting. At a time when the national median price is $225,000 (Cox 2007), buyers can purchase a home in Youngstown for significantly less. It is not uncommon to find four-bedroom, two-bath homes on the market for less than $50,000 and three-bedroom, two-bath homes with upgrades listed for $65,000 or less. On the positive side, the plentiful and affordable housing market may lure new investors to Youngstown. Commenting on the pool of interested purchasers, the owner of Youngstown's ERA Tri-Sun Real Estate said, "The bulk of my buyers are investors who come from all over the country, primarily from California. They see the potential to purchase a home at a greatly reduced price, so they are persuaded more on price per square foot versus what the crime rate is. They have no intentions of living here. The crime rate isn't a factor to them personally" (Cox 2007).

Chevrolet Centre

The city-owned Chevrolet Centre (www.chevroletcentre.com) is another fiscal challenge for the city. This multipurpose arena, built for approximately $42 million on the site of a former steel mill, opened in October 2005. The cost was significantly offset by a $26 million HUD redevelopment grant. The Chevrolet Centre is home to a local hockey team that is a member of the Central Hockey League. The roughly 169,000-square-foot facility boasts a seating capacity of up to 7,000 seats and 400 on-site parking spaces. It also offers more than 500 "club seats" and 26 "luxury suites."

Although this venue has the potential to serve the city well by attracting visitors and positive publicity, it has struggled to make a profit. The 2005–6 fiscal year resulted in a financial loss for the facility of $23,653 (Skolnick 2007a), and reports on the 2006–7 do not look much better. In early 2007, a local news article reported (Skolnick 2007c),

> The Chevrolet Centre's profit for the final three months of 2006 is about one-quarter the amount it made during the same period in 2005. Also, the profit for its first quarter of its fiscal year 2007, October through December 2006, was 40 percent of what the company managing the facility predicted. Global Entertainment Corp., the Phoenix-based company operating the city-owned facility, estimated a profit of $356,446 for October through December of 2006. But figures for that time frame, released Monday, show the center's profit for those three months at $144,323. In comparison, the center made a $545,469 profit from October to December 2005.

In spite of the disappointing financial picture, officials working with the Chevrolet Centre are optimistic that hockey attendance will increase over time and that events will draw large crowds. The number of events booked in 2006–7 met and exceeded the projected goal (Skolnick 2007a).

Downtown Development Efforts

Increasingly in recent years, downtown Youngstown has seen modest levels of new construction. A number of dilapidated buildings in the downtown area have been razed or restored. In 2004, Arlington Heights, a new residential development, began construction at the site where run-down public housing once stood. Soon thereafter, Federal Street, one of the main downtown corridors that had been closed to traffic to create a pedestrian-only area, was reopened to automobiles. A nonprofit organization called Wick Neighbors is planning a large-scale revitalization project for an area on the edge of downtown dubbed Smoky Hollow. The plan calls for hundreds of mixed-use and mixed-income residential units, greenspace, and commercial space.

Governments at all levels are also playing a role in improving downtown Youngstown. New additions to the area include two federal courthouses and the George Voinovich Government Center, a state office complex. The City of Youngstown is also playing a key role in 20 Federal Place, the Youngstown Business Incubator, and the Taft Technology Center—all of which are located in downtown Youngstown.

20 Federal Place

Now-bankrupt Phar-Mor, which once operated a successful chain of discount drugstores, had its corporate headquarters in downtown Youngstown at 20 Federal Plaza West from the late 1980s to the late 1990s. At that time, the downtown building was called The Phar-Mor Centre. The company closed all its stores in 2002 and ceased its operations. The building has since been renamed 20 Federal Place and is now owned by the City of Youngstown. The city has attracted a number of new tenants to the building, including law firms, eateries, and a catering business.

Youngstown Business Incubator

One of the area's more successful economic development ventures in recent years has been the Youngstown Business Incubator (YBI). Located in a former downtown department store, the incubator houses a number of start-up technology companies that are given access to office space, furnishings, and utilities. It fosters these fledgling companies in the hopes that they will develop and eventually become self-sufficient and profitable cutting-edge companies.

The YBI began its operations in November 1995 with a mixed group of tenants working primarily in light manufacturing. Although it had had many successes, the YBI adopted a new strategy in January 2000 that focused on technology-based firms. The YBI Web site (www.ybi.org) states that its current mission is "to accelerate the startup and growth rates of scalable technology-based businesses in the greater Mahoning Valley. Although the YBI will work with firms possessing a broad range of proprietary technologies, its current focus is on developing B2B (business-to-business) software application companies."

According to the YBI Web site, this particular technology niche was identified and selected for several reasons: "First, there is sufficient local talent to found, and subsequently staff, new B2B software firms. Second, B2B are relatively inexpensive to start. Third, B2B software companies are fast to market. And fourth, a substantial number of vertical markets are underserved, or are not yet served, with quality B2B software applications."

To attract and support its fledgling B2B companies, the YBI provides, at no cost or at deferred cost, resources typically unavailable or unaffordable to start-up companies. For example, resources provided to tenants at no cost include office space, office furniture, telephone hardware, utilities, high-speed Internet connectivity, and early-stage legal and accounting services. Tenants also have access to video and teleconferencing systems, multimedia conference centers, presentation equipment, trade show booths, and research databases.

In December 2006, the YBI's eight companies employed about 165 people at an average salary of $58,000 and generated $38 million in income (Skolnick 2006). In fact, many of the companies have benefited so much from the nurturing environment of the incubator that some are beginning to outgrow their current space. In an effort to keep these companies operating in the downtown, the incubator secured approval to demolish a row of vacant buildings nearby to allow space for expansion. And in September 2006, the U.S. Economic Development Administration officially presented a grant of $2 million to expand the YBI. The approval of this grant was largely based on the fit between the incubator and administration's mission of assisting in changing distressed areas into vibrant economies (Shilling 2006). The incubator, which currently boasts more than a dozen business tenants, will soon begin construction on a multimillion-dollar downtown technology center, where some of its largest firms will relocate.

Taft Technology Center

The $5.9 million Taft Technology Center will eventually sit next to the YBI on West Federal (Skolnick 2007b). The center is named in honor of Bob Taft, who served as governor for eight years. During his tenure as governor, the state approved $3.5 million for this project. In November 2006, five buildings were torn down to make way for the new building, which is expected to be three stories tall and about 30,000 square feet. This new facility is intended to house some of the graduates of the YBI in hopes that they will make Youngstown their permanent home, thereby maintaining and strengthening the existing employment base.

Joint Economic Development Districts

One of Mayor Williams's new economic development strategies is the joint economic development district (JEDD) initiative. This regional approach to economic development, which the mayor promotes in many of his speeches, would partner the City of Youngstown with other communities (Dick 2007). The Ohio Department of Development Web site (www.odod.state.oh.us) describes a JEDD as providing "a mechanism by which municipalities and townships can cooperate to foster development activities without modifications to jurisdiction boundaries."

A JEDD is essentially an economic development tool available to Ohio cities that wish to join forces with a township to cooperatively encourage commercial or industrial growth and development on township land. Benefits can be enjoyed by both of the partnering entities. The benefit to the host city is that it receives a portion of the tax revenue generated within the district without actually annexing the land. The benefit to the township is that it does not lose its prime land and thereby continues to collect property taxes from it.

To create a JEDD, the municipality and township enter into a contract that specifies details of the cooperative venture. The contract spells out each party's amount and type of contribution, lists all the services and other improvements to be provided, annexation prohibitions, and the powers of the board of directors, including whether the board has the power to levy an income tax. The communities must approve the contract for the JEDD to be created. The result is a quasi-governmental organization governed by a board of directors. The JEDD is supported by the income tax generated within the district. These revenues are typically reinvested in the district to facilitate the creation of new business opportunities and possibly new infrastructure.

Although the intended purpose of a JEDD is to promote economic development and to create and preserve jobs, the issue of annexation is naturally intertwined with the proposal and is hotly debated. As a result, the city's JEDD initiative has attracted quite a bit of attention in terms of what JEDD agreements could mean for Youngstown's ability to annex the outlying townships. This debate has continued in spite of Mayor Williams's constant message that annexing outlying areas is not what he is proposing (Skolnick 2007a).

The discussion is largely rooted in a legal case that involved the City of Perrysburg. In a recent Ohio Supreme Court ruling, the court concluded that a city could base the provision of utilities outside its boundaries on the condition to annex (*Bakies v. Perrysburg*, 108 Ohio St. 3d 361; 2006 Ohio 1190; 843 N.E.2d 1182; 2006 Ohio LEXIS 696 [2006]). Specifically, the court held that ordinances requiring customers located outside city limits to annex in exchange for continued utility services is a "valid exercise of the police power" of a city. Further, the court found that the City of Perrysburg proved a valid basis for requiring annexation by arguing that issues surrounding tax revenue, the proximity to the city limits, and increasing the size of its tax base were not arbitrary or capricious (Mentel 2006). This legal decision clearly states that municipalities that supply utility services to neighboring townships have the ability to annex them, or the townships may face termination of their utility service (as long as there is not a contractual obligation to the contrary). This powerful option, which is apparently available to JEDD host cities, could be used to force these areas to annex—a possibility that is garnering much attention from those who are staunchly opposed to annexation.

JEDDs could offer an additional benefit by lowering Youngstown's income tax rate, which is currently 2.75 percent. Youngstown's high income tax is one of the negative factors businesses and individuals consider when contemplating a move to Youngstown. Mayor Williams has stated that through the JEDD proposal, the city's tax rate could be reduced to as low as 2 percent (Skolnick 2007a). While Youngstown has not yet adopted the JEDD approach, the city hopes to employ it as a part of its overall strategy of positioning itself for a new and very different future.

Conclusion

Youngstown has rejected the notion that "bigger is better." Through the *Youngstown 2010* process, a plan that has gained national recognition, the city has engaged in an honest self-examination and has come to realize that it will never again be what it once was. The *Youngstown 2010* plan is intended to serve as the city's road map as it faces complex issues through a new approach of shrinking the city while building on its existing strengths and providing better control over its urban challenges: enhancing safety, increasing quality development, and improving quality of life. These are laudable goals, but the solutions to the existing municipal problems identified in the 2010 plan require funding. In order for the city to make significant improvements, it must secure adequate funding to make the improvements. Mayor Williams's efforts in the area of JEDDs are the cornerstone of the city's plan in that regard.

The city's recognition that it will never again require the infra-structure and services that it did during the height of steel production has been another significant paradigm shift. As a result, the city has adopted a unique approach to development by scaling down un-needed infrastructure and removing abandoned houses and vacant steel plants and replacing them with greenspace, mixed-use housing, and new office buildings.

The story of Youngstown raises a larger question, however: how long can an ever-expanding municipal economy, with a growing population and increasing demand for infrastructure and services, guarantee a stable and fiscally healthy future for the city and its residents? Youngstown's "leaner" approach is, at the least, disarming to those who work in or study local government because it is such a dramatic shift from the long-held notion that success equals growth.

Only time will tell if Youngstown's strategy will pay off. Com-munity supporters suggest that when greenspace increasingly appears where boarded-up houses once stood and wildlife areas are enjoyed where abandoned warehouses used to sit, Youngstown's seemingly coun-terintuitive approach will start to make sense to its skeptics, and the city government and its residents will reap the rewards of a local economy that is vibrant and healthy once again.

Note

1. Adopted in 1924, Youngstown's Home Rule Charter established the founda-tion for the city's governmental operations. Youngstown has a mayor-council form of government. The mayor appoints many of the key positions within the city government, including the department heads, and serves as the head of the executive branch of the municipality. The mayoral term is four years with a limit of two consecutive terms. Eligibility for reelection is only possible after an intervening term. The mayor is allowed to participate in all council discussions but does not have voting privileges. The mayor's duties as chief executive officer include overseeing the city's administration, recommending legislative action to the city council, advising the council on financial matters, preparing any reports requested by the council, and appointing or removing directors of all municipal departments and members of the city's boards and commissions. The city council consists of eight members: a council president and representatives of the city's seven wards. When the mayor is out of town or otherwise unable to perform his or her duties, the council president is the acting mayor. The council heads the legislative branch of the city and appoints the city clerk.

References

Cox, Jeff. 2007. Some boomtowns face rising crime. *CNN Money*, January 5. money.cnn.com/2007/01/04/real_estate/real_estate_crime/index.htm. Accessed January 10.

Dick, Denise. 2007. At annual event, mayor reviews past, looks ahead. *The Vindicator*, January 7. www4.vindy.com/content/local_regional/324392244423082. php. Accessed January 10.

El Nasser, Haya. 2006. As older cities shrink, others reinvent themselves. *USA Today*, December 26. www.usatoday.com/news/nation/2006-12-26-shrinking-cities-cover_x.htm. Accessed January 1, 2007.

Gorman, Joe. 2007. Police gearing IP for weed & seed. *Tribune-Chronicle*. January 10. www.tribune-chronicle.com/news/articles.asp?articleID=12974. Accessed January 10.

Gottlieb, Paul D. 2002. Growth without growth: An alternative economic development goal for metropolitan areas. Discussion paper. Brookings Institution Center on Urban and Metropolitan Policy.

Lanks, Belinda. 2006a. Creative shrinkage. *New York Times*, December 10. www.nytimes.com/2006/12/10/magazine/10section1B.t-3.html. Accessed March, 15, 2008.

—————. 2006b. The incredible shrinking city. *Metropolis Magazine*, April 17. www.metropolismag.com/cda/story.php?artid=1907. Accessed January 1, 2007.

Matthews, Rick A., Michael O. Maume, and William J. Miller. 2001. Deindustrialization, economic distress, and homicide rates in midsized Rustbelt cities. *Homicide Studies* 5:83–113.

Mayer, Henry J., and Michael R. Greenberg. 2001. Coming back from economic despair: Case studies of small- and medium-size American cities. *Economic Development Quarterly* 8:203–16.

Mentel, Sean A. 2006. Supreme Court allows conditions for the continued provision of municipal services and allows required sewer connections. *Finley's Ohio Municipal Service*. www.bricker.com/publications/articles/979.pdf. Accessed March 15, 2008.

Shilling, Don. 2006. EDA offers Youngstown incubator help in future. *The Vindicator*, September 9. www4.vindy.com/content/local_regional/330778624066979. php. Accessed January 15, 2007.

Skolnick, David. 2006. Governor, various officials attend naming ceremony. *The Vindicator*, December 22. www4.vindy.com/content/local_regional/287787200979267.php. Accessed January 10, 2007.

—————. 2007a. Facility's figures frustrate city officials. *The Vindicator*, May 17. www4.vindy.com/content/local_regional/307868208998383.php. Accessed May 23.

_____. 2007b. Mayor: Good outweighs bad in city; the best is yet to come. *The Vindicator*, January 1. www4.vindy.com/content/local_regional/321608982702579.php. Accessed May 23.

_____. 2007c. Profits fail to meet official predictions. *The Vindicator*, February 6. www4.vindy.com/content/local_regional/311904395082632.php. Accessed May 23.

Swope, Christopher. 2006. Shrinking cities Q & A. *Governing*, November. www.governing.com/articles/11citiqal.htm. Accessed January 1, 2007.

CHAPTER 8

Keeping up with the Joneses: Town Centers as Economic Development Tools

Robert Sharp and John Lombard

Town centers, or urban villages, are designed to give suburban communities unique identities and to attract young professionals, dual-income households, empty nesters and any other demographic with disposable income. The model is not new; it is a return to a centuries-old pattern of people settling in clusters where they live, work, and socialize. Town centers are, in effect, a modern, high-tech interpretation of pre–World War II community life. They are a product of new urbanism, a backlash against urban sprawl aimed at recreating pedestrian friendly, mixed-use communities (see Leccese and McCormick 2000).

This chapter presents case studies of two neighboring cities that developed suburban town centers and evaluates these developments in terms of interjurisdictional competition theory. Interjurisdictional competition "entails competition between governments having comparable powers in the federal system" (Kenyon and Kincaid 1991, 2)—in other words, competition among governments at the state or local level. State and local governments rely on business investment to generate tax revenue that pays for public goods and services. The American governmental system is composed of multiple jurisdictions, each with a great deal of policy responsibility and autonomy. Naturally, each jurisdiction chooses policies that will allow it to compete with its neighbors.

Competition is beneficial to the extent that it encourages governments to improve the quality and efficiency of their services. It can, however, also emphasize short-term gains at the expense of long-term success. There are three general categories of interjurisdictional competition: active rivalry, implicit competition, and yardstick competition.

Each type of competition affects state and local economic development policies (Kenyon 1997).

Active rivalry often occurs at the prospect of new investment. For example, when a major manufacturer announces plans to build a new facility, oftentimes governments bid against one another in an attempt to lure the investment. States and communities usually offer an increasing level of inducements that combine tax and financial incentives, training assistance, and infrastructure investments.

Implicit competition occurs when states or communities adjust their policies in an attempt to provide a more attractive location for business investment than other states or communities. Sometimes the focus is on improving the quality of services or infrastructure, such as schools or roads. In these cases, the effect on business investment is often only one justification among many for whatever new spending is proposed. Other times, the focus is on improving the business climate by lowering the cost of doing business in a state or community. The cost reduction can be accomplished by tax or nontax policies.

Yardstick competition occurs when citizens use information about policies in other jurisdictions to evaluate their own governmental policies. They compare the taxes they pay and the goods and services they receive with those of neighboring states and communities. If they find their own jurisdiction lacking, they apply pressure to elected officials, who presumably will respond out of a desire for reelection. Yardstick competition is likely to result in many of the same policies as implicit competition (Kenyon 1997). The distinction between implicit and yardstick competition can be subtle; it relies on the difference in motivations of the policymakers. Implicit competition is related to concern about the location decisions of businesses—that is, businesses "voting with their feet." Yardstick competition, on the other hand, is concerned with citizens voting at the ballot box. In short, as the following two case studies indicate, yardstick competition is a likely motivation for establishing town center developments.

The Rising Popularity of Town Centers

Over the last 40 years, American suburbs have become highly developed at the expense of downtowns. Thanks to the expanding network of roads and highways, shopping centers, office and industrial parks, and public buildings, suburban residents can find a wide variety of goods, services, and recreational opportunities within short driving distance of their homes. But in many areas, suburban sprawl has become problematic. Suburban sprawl is characterized by low-density development spread over large areas and segregated into single-use zones

(Ewing 1997; Gordon and Richardson 1997). Increasingly, people are required to take to the highway for every activity. That "short driving distance" has become longer, more congested, and more stressful. Business and community leaders see sprawl as a hindrance to their ability to compete with other jurisdictions. They are looking for an alternative that establishes an identity for the community and offers a place for residents and visitors to come together. Residents are also voicing concern over the need for a community focal point, something that lends character to a community (Duerksen and Dale 1999).

In recent years, town center developments have emerged as one answer to suburban sprawl. They have attracted the interest of the development community as promising new forms of real estate investment. Town center developments are appealing mixed-use areas resembling the cozy "Main Street" shopping districts of earlier times. They typically feature an open-air design with fountains, benches, restaurants, bookstores, upscale clothing shops, and a variety of other merchants. Parking is convenient and designed to blend in with the architecture. There is a welcoming sense of place that encourages visitors to stay longer, come back more often, and ultimately, spend more money. The ambience makes them popular; the retail makes them profitable.

The idea has caught on. The number of mixed-use projects of 15 acres or more increased 28 percent a year from 1996 to 2003 (Steuteville 2004). In 2004, there were 650 projects at various stages of completion throughout the United States (Hart 2006). The investment is paying off. Shoppers spend $84 per hour in a town center's stores, compared with $57.50 per hour in a traditional enclosed mall (Urban Land Institute 2006). Additionally, according to the International Council for Shopping Centers, town center sales average $298 per square foot compared with the traditional mall's $242 per square foot (Grant 2004).

Two neighboring cities in southeast Virginia—Newport News and Hampton—decided on this approach, relying on town centers as tools for economic development. The City of Newport News developed a town center in an existing business park with a large area of underutilized land. The City of Hampton replaced an aging mall in an otherwise vital and highly developed part of town with a vibrant town center. Newport News's primary goal was to diversify its tax base and tap into an increasingly affluent surrounding population. Hampton hoped to increase its tax base and take advantage of a larger, citywide redevelopment initiative.

Characteristics of the Region

Hampton and Newport News are both part of the Chesapeake Bay area in the southeastern corner of Virginia, 200 miles south of

Washington, D.C., and 100 miles south of Richmond, the state capital. The two cities sit at the tip of the Virginia Peninsula and share a common city limit. Neither city has room to expand its city limits, but Newport News, with undeveloped land in the Oyster Point area in the northern part of the city, is the more elastic of the two (see Rusk 1995).

Hampton and Newport News's economic role in the region has changed significantly over the past 30 years. Prior to the interstate system, the Hampton Roads region comprised individual cities and towns within counties: Hampton, Newport News, Williamsburg, Poquoson, and York County on the Peninsula and Norfolk, Portsmouth, Suffolk, Chesapeake, and Virginia Beach on the Southside. These communities were relatively self-contained and only marginally connected. With the building of Interstate 64 and a tunnel connecting the Peninsula to the Southside in the 1960s and 1970s, regional mobility increased (City of Hampton 2004). The interstate system, local government annexation and consolidation, and suburban expansion set the stage for the region's growth in the upcoming decades.

The expanding economy in the 1970s and 1980s united those cities and towns into a single economic region. I-64 was the primary regional transportation link to Richmond and the rest of the state. Located at the edge of the region and with excellent interstate access, Hampton and Newport News were well situated for suburban growth. During this time, their populations increased and developed land expanded, and the area experienced its most prosperous years (Callaham 1998).

In the 1990s, the regional interstate loop (I-664) was completed, including a second alternative tunnel connection. The regional frontiers of growth expanded north up the Peninsula and west across the James River (Callaham 1998). The two cites were no longer on the edge of a fast-growth area but at the center of a stable region. The competitive advantages they once enjoyed—inexpensive land and proximity to new growth—were now gone (City of Hampton 2004).

Because of their proximity and similarities in size and demographics, the two cities are in economic competition with each other as well as the rest of the region. Table 1 compares Newport News and Hampton using 2006 information. In light of these changing economic and social conditions, both cities have implemented aggressive economic development programs, including town centers.

Table 2 shows the retail square footage for Newport News, Hampton, and the Virginia Peninsula from 2003 through 2007. The two cities supported a similar amount of retail space during this period. Aside from some slight fluctuations, the amounts have remained mostly

Table 1: Demographic Comparisons of Newport News and Hampton, Virginia, 2006

City	Population	Size (square miles)	Median household income[a]	Per capita income[b]
Newport News	182,000	68	$36,597	$17,843
Hampton	146,000	52	$39,700	$19,774

Source: quickfacts.census.gov/qfd.states/51000 (accessed March 1, 2007).
[a]State of Virginia median household income = $50,028.
[b]State of Virginia per capita income = $23,975.

Table 2: Retail Square Footage in Newport News, Hampton, and the Virginia Peninsula, 2003–7

Year	Newport News		Hampton		Peninsula total[a]
	(N)	(percent)	(N)	(percent)	
2003	5,177,358	33	5,863,884	38	15,546,085
2004	5,233,859	33	6,069,455	38	16,094,161
2005	5,210,919	33	5,677,930	36	15,799,778
2006	5,561,835	34	5,876,444	36	16,337,458
2007	5,826,670	35	5,922,222	35	16,895,155

Source: E. V. Williams Center for Real Estate and Economic Development (2003–7).
[a]Includes Newport News, Hampton, Poquoson, Williamsburg, and York County.

stable. Additionally, the percentage of retail space in each city compared with the total Virginia Peninsula has remained relatively constant.

Newport News: City Center at Oyster Point

The Plan

Newport News is the largest city on the Virginia Peninsula. It covers 68 square miles and has a population exceeding 180,000. The city's generally stable economy is anchored by Northrop Grumman Newport News (Newport News Shipbuilding). The shipbuilding industry has been the backbone of the economy in Newport News since the late 1800s. The Shipyards, as they are called locally, employ about 18,850 people, down from about 30,000 in the 1970s and 1980s. The company occupies much of the city's traditional downtown along the James River. The Shipyards, builders of U.S. Navy ships, are dependent on government contracts (Callaham 1998).

Another important economic force is the considerable military presence, primarily the Fort Eustis Army and Langley Air Force Base installations. The military employs about 18,300 locally, and the military members stationed there are major consumers of housing and spend millions of dollars a year in the local economy. Altogether, the defense sector and related support industries account for about 33 percent of the region's employment (Virginia Employment Commission 2007). As a result, the Newport News economy is particularly vulnerable to changes in national defense spending.

Over the last 20 years, however, Newport News has made some progress in diversifying its economic base. The technology sector is one of the fastest-growing new directions. The nearby NASA Langley Research Center and the Thomas Jefferson National Accelerator Facility are two major high-tech drawing cards. Firms such as Canon, Siemens VDO Automotive, Symantec, and Allied Aerospace produce electronic automotive components, precision machinery and instrumentation, nuclear components, precision engineering models, and other technologically advanced products (Newport News Department of Development 2006). In the interest of further diversifying the retail portion of their economic base, city officials decided to invest in a city center development.

City Center at Oyster Point is a 40-acre mixed-use development within the 700-acre Oyster Point business park in Newport News, near the intersection of I-64 and two major thoroughfares. Construction began in 2001, and when completed the project will contain one million square feet of office space, plus more than 300 apartments, 225,000 square feet of retail and entertainment space, a full-service hotel and conference center, and parking space for 4,500 cars. The centerpiece will be a five-acre fountain.

The City of Newport News and its Economic Development Authority assisted Newport News City Center LLC in developing this city center. The project is expected to result in $70 million to $80 million in private investment in Oyster Point (Newport News Economic Development Authority 2004). The city also anticipates an increase in density and the creation of thousands of well-paying jobs. From the outset, Newport News city leadership believed City Center would reduce the city's vulnerability to the ebb and flow of its traditional economic drivers: shipbuilding and military installations (Batts 2005).

Altogether, City Center at Oyster Point is an estimated $300 million development. It is the largest concentration of Class A urban scale development on the Peninsula (Newport News Department of Development 2005). Class A refers to top-of-the-line, professionally managed space in a desirable location. While the developer has paid for most of the new project, the city is picking up some of the expenses, including costs for four parking garages, roads, and other improvements. Over 25 years, city officials expect to spend about $40 million on the development, but they expect to recoup about $60 million of that investment, mostly from taxes on meals and property (Snider 2002a).

Background and Development

In the 1960s, Oyster Point was a swampland dotted with military munitions storage sheds. The city obtained the land from the federal government and regional economic authority in 1973 for about $1.8 million. The area was first developed as an industrial park, but in time it took on more of a commercial quality, as banks, law firms, business and finance offices, and medical practices moved into the area.

Demographic studies indicated that Newport News and the surrounding area had the households necessary to support upscale shopping and development, and the upper-middle-income portion of the population was increasing (Snider 2002a). Within a 20-minute radius of Oyster Point, 70 percent of the households had incomes of at least $50,000. Also within that drive time were 60 percent of the Virginia Peninsula households that earn $100,000 or more (Snider 2002a). In addition to those affluent households, there was a large population of affluent white-collar workers within a three- to five-mile radius of Oyster Point. These workers clustered in the area of the Thomas Jefferson National Accelerator Facility, various medical communities nearby, and the Oyster Point Business Park. Banking on the area's growing influence, city officials decided to develop a mixed-used area on the property (Glynn 1998).

In 1999, NAI Harvey Lindsay Commercial Real Estate and local investors partnered with Riverside Health Care to form the Newport News Town Center LLC (Batts 2005). The LLC teamed with the city's economic development authority to begin the project, originally called the Oyster Point Town Center. Construction began in April 2001 with the Fountain Plaza I office tower, a 10-story, 110,000-square-foot office building with a five-level parking deck. (Snider 2001a). Eventually, Fountain Plaza II, III, and IV were built. Also in 2002, Merchants Walk One, the first retail building in City Center was erected (Snider 2002b). In February 2003, developers changed the name to City Center at Oyster Point in an effort to distinguish it from other new mixed-use projects taking shape in nearby communities. The president of HL Development Services LLC said, "With several other 'Town Center' developments popping up across the region and nation, we want to find a name that more aptly describes the unique, city-life atmosphere we're creating here at Oyster Point" (Snider 2003).

In Spring 2004, NASA announced plans to open an office at City Center. NASA's move brought in 500 jobs with an average annual salary of $60,000 each. This announcement prompted Red Star Tavern, an upscale, contemporary restaurant, to open a location at City Center. Following Red Star Tavern's lead, several other "sit-down" restaurants opened in City Center (Snider 2004).

Later, developers of City Center admitted that selling their projects to retailers, particularly those outside the region, was not always easy. Some had outdated perceptions about Hampton Roads. It was seen as an unsophisticated area of mostly military families with low incomes and blue-collar tastes. Developers of City Center also had to persuade stores to locate off the main thoroughfares of I-64 and Jefferson Avenue and onto a stretch of land originally designed as an industrial park. Although visibility is a key factor for retailers, in this case, the city's strong political and financial support for the project, the mix of other businesses and services, and the increasingly affluent population served as incentives (Shapiro 2006).

In September 2004, the city council voted to expand the business park. The expansion cost the city an additional $45 million (above the $36 million of city money already committed to the project) for a $26 million conference center and $15 million parking garage. The city's spending triggered another $85 million in private spending, including a $32 million hotel and $52 million for about a dozen other buildings to house offices, shops, and condominiums.

There was some local opposition. Other Newport News hotel and tourism-related businesses objected to using public money for funding competition to their existing businesses. Some council members questioned whether Newport News could actually draw enough visitors who could afford the $120 per night room rate for the new Marriott Hotel. But the city manager stood behind the decision, saying, "If we don't capitalize on something like this, we're just going to fall by the wayside" (Carroll 2004).

After that decision, several well-known retailers signed on. Talbots, a high-end women's clothing retailer, was one of the first to arrive. Along with Talbots, a parade of national retailers opened shops at City Center: Ann Taylor Loft, Chico's, J. Jill, Coldwater Creek, Jos. A. Bank, and Ten Thousand Villages. They joined several locally owned jewelry and gift shops that had grabbed some of the first spots along City Center's streets. Additionally, about a half-dozen more stores and a day spa opened in a central marketplace. Developers seemed to have overcome the dated, blue-collar image of Newport News (Shapiro 2006).

City Center developers had to prepare large enough retail space to accommodate shops in groups, not one at a time. According to the development team, retailers are like teenagers: they generally travel in packs and fear venturing alone, preferring the company of likeminded peers with similar interests. Talbots's move to Newport News paved the way for Ann Taylor, Coldwater Creek, J. Jill, and the others (Snider 2005d).

With the success of the Newport News project, national entities took notice. In March 2005, Northwest Mutual, a Milwaukee-based insurance company, became an equity partner in the development with a $42 million investment (Batts 2005). Northwest is one of the nation's largest institutional real estate investors. That investment came less than two weeks after the ground breaking for the Marriott, which was developed through a partnership between Armada Hoffler, Crestline Hotels and Resorts Inc., and Hampton University. The university provided the financing, Armada Hoffler was the developer, and Crestline operates the hotel (Lynch 2006c).

The Marriott Newport News is a 12-story hotel featuring 112 rooms and suites catering to tourists and business travelers, 25,000 square feet of conference space, and a front entranceway facing the five-acre fountain that is the centerpiece of the development (Lynch 2006a). "It's the key element to the whole live, work and play environment," said a member of the development's architectural team. "It's the one element that has the ingredients that will attract more businesses to the area because it's a centerpiece for people" (Snider 2002b).

As of this writing, City Center at Oyster is at about 85 percent completion. Most of the retail space is filled, and the office buildings are at 90 percent capacity. City officials and the development team are currently developing mass transportation links between City Center and other parts of Newport News.

Hampton: The Peninsula Town Center

The Plan

The City of Hampton is somewhat smaller than Newport News. Hampton has successfully diversified its economy with a healthy blend of industry, technology, and business. In 2005 and 2006 alone, companies invested more than $100 million in Hampton and created more than 2,400 new jobs ("Growth and Development" 2006).

Strategically designed industry clusters have created growth for well-established industries in the area such as aerospace, modeling and simulation, homeland security and defense, and communications and communications equipment. These clusters have also helped emerging sectors like health care and medical device manufacturing. These clusters are driven by local assets, including NASA Langley Research

Center, Langley Air Force Base, Hampton University, the Langley Full Scale Wind Tunnel, and the National Institute of Aerospace. Hampton is also home to several state-of-the-art business parks. Hampton Roads Center North Campus, the newest business park, is home to the Air Force Command and Control, Intelligence, Surveillance and Reconnaissance Center and the Virginia Peninsula Association of Realtors headquarters (City of Hampton 2006).

Hampton has been aggressively developing (and redeveloping) its urban retail, entertainment, and upscale residential areas with a focus on the Coliseum Central District. Coliseum Central's identity stems from its location at the intersection of I-64, I-664, and Hampton's main thoroughfare, Mercury Boulevard, and from its major regional attractions such as the Hampton Coliseum and Coliseum Mall. The district also includes a diverse assortment of residential neighborhoods, businesses, schools, churches, hospitals, and parks.

The Coliseum Central District draws shoppers from all over the Virginia Peninsula. The city's strategic plan recognizes the area as one of the most important economic engines within the region. Taxes generated in this area make up a significant annual revenue stream for the City of Hampton (City of Hampton 2004). In recent years, Coliseum Central has experienced both large-scale public and private investments. A new Hampton Roads Convention Center, interstate interchange, commercial development, housing starts, and hospital complex represent more than $250 million in new investments. At the same time, however, the area has suffered significant disinvestment in some of its largest and most visible properties. Commercial vacancies have increased, leaving more than 600,000 square feet of empty retail space in the district (City of Hampton 2004). The City of Hampton and real estate developers viewed these vacancies as both a warning and an opportunity for the district to redefine itself.

The new Peninsula Town Center is a complete, ground-up redevelopment. Once completed, it will cover more than 900,000 square feet. It is intended to be "a synergistic mix of retail, office, residential and recreational space" (Shearin 2005, 25). Town Center will feature both open-air and enclosed spaces, tree-lined walks, fountains, and parks. The plan is to replace most of the existing structure with several smaller buildings interspersed with streets and walkways to create an urban town center. The changes will cost city taxpayers about $30 million from 2005 through 2010. While the plan calls for Town Center to be open for business in 2008, it may take up to 20 years to fully complete the project (Snider 2005a).

Background and Development

Historically, the Coliseum Mall played an important role in the Central District. Built in 1973, the mall sat on 75 acres and was for many years a vibrant shopping area. But by 2006, its sales numbers had declined, and the mall owners decided it was time to "reinvent their property" ("Mall No Longer Profitable" 2006). The city was looking for development that would support a new convention center and hotels in the district. The Peninsula Town Center Development Team's goal was the best long-term use of the mall property in terms of both usability and profit. According to spokespersons for the development team, the idea of building a modern, mixed-use district with multiple centers was welcomed (interview with Raymond Tripp, Peninsula Town Center general manager, Hampton, VA, May 8, 2007).

The city contracted with Steiner & Associates, a firm from Columbus, Ohio, to head the project. Steiner & Associates was chosen for their experience in developing urban town centers in Dayton, Kansas City, Milwaukee, and Arlington (Steiner 2006b). Construction on the Peninsula Town Center began in August 2006 with the demolition of the old Dillard's location, which made room for the new J.C. Penney's store. The new Penney's is one of the first based on the chain's new prototype (Steiner 2006a). The parking structure features state-of-the-art speed ramps designed to get shoppers in and out quickly. Digital signs posted on streets around the parking structure will tell shoppers which floors have open parking spaces as well as how many are open. Eventually, the parking structure will be surrounded by upscale town homes and serve as a dynamic entry point to the Town Center (City of Hampton 2006). The Town Center will offer retail, restaurant, entertainment, office, and residential space. In addition to J.C. Penney's, Hecht's, and Barnes & Noble, a wide variety of specialty shops and restaurants will be featured (Shearin 2005).

The City of Hampton will benefit from redevelopment of an underperforming area and a potential increase in the city's tax base. The estimated cost of the project is $207.5 million. The developer will contribute about $142 million, and the City of Hampton Community Development Authority will provide the remaining $65.5 million ("Council Approves New Peninsula Town Center" 2006). The city's investment is capped, and the city should receive approximately 50 percent of additional tax revenues generated by the new development (Newport News Department of Development 2006). The project, including demolition and new construction, could potentially bring jobs and increased consumer spending into the coliseum area ("Council Approves New Peninsula Town Center" 2006). Based on projections of the Hampton market, nondepartment store sales at the Town Center are likely to exceed $200 million by 2009 (Shearin 2005).

Discussion

From the developer's perspective, agreeing to take on the project was a purely economic move that could result in a significant return on its investment over time. But city leaders in Hampton and Newport News felt the pressure to keep up with the town center developments in nearby Virginia Beach, Chesapeake, and Williamsburg and to provide a similar (or better) retail environment for their own constituents (interview with Mitch Salmon, leasing director for Mall Properties, and Joel Rubin, president of Rubin Communication Group, Hampton, VA, May 8, 2007). In this case, then, local governments were not bidding against one another to entice a particular investor or adjusting business policies to create a more attractive business environment. What seems more likely is that Hampton and Newport News were responding to peer pressure from neighboring communities. By developing town centers in their own areas, city leaders could demonstrate that they are concerned with the economic well-being and quality of life of their constituency, who they hope will in turn support them at election time.

The yardstick model gets it name from the idea of citizens comparing their city with nearby cities, using their neighbors as a standard by which to measure their own situation. It is the only one of the three models that focuses on voice and the "politics within the governmental unit itself" (Kenyon 1997, 14). The residents of the two cities might have compared their situations not only with each other but with other cities in the region. For example, nearby Virginia Beach had been planning a major redevelopment of one of its prime retail areas—Pembroke—since the mid-1980s (Mizal-Archer 2002). Virginia Beach's plans for a town center were included in its 2000 economic development strategy (Point 2000). Chesapeake and Williamsburg had similar plans in the works. When the citizens and policymakers of Hampton and Newport News looked around the region, they saw their neighbors—their economic competitors—benefiting from increased business taxes brought in with city center–type developments.

In addition to wanting to please their constituents, policymakers in Newport News and Hampton might have realized that their cities were directly affected by the changing regional economy. Newport News needed to diversify its tax base and reduce the city's dependency on the Shipyards and military installations, both of which were highly susceptible to changes in national defense spending. Further, maintaining Hampton's aging, underproducing mall would be out of synch with the city's greater economic development goals. Diversifying and expanding the cities' business tax base would serve to reduce personal income taxes without affecting services. The developments promised new jobs for residents and spurred economic growth without increasing taxes. The tax relief and job opportunities might encourage residents to support elected officials and choose to stay in their current cities.

Newport News City Center at Oyster Point

For Newport News, developing a city center meant taking advantage of the latest trend in retail and convincing regional businesses to establish headquarters in its new development. It also offered voters visible evidence that city leaders were working for the area's economic benefit.

Newport News took advantage of available open space in the 700-acre Oyster Point business park to provide a location for businesses that might otherwise have had to operate out of Norfolk or Virginia Beach, 30 to 50 traffic-congested miles away. The dense traffic patterns around Oyster Point made it easier to market the area to retailers and other businesses and to overcome the working class reputation of Newport News. The Newport News City Mayor commented, "For too long Newport News had been thought of as a blue collar community capable of only small things, but today we set the standard for our city. . . . [I]t changes the quality of offerings for space in upscale apartments, office and retail. . . . [I]t changes how people live, work, shop, eat and exercise because everything is within walking distance" (Snider 2001b).

These qualities appealed to businesses like Riverside Healthcare and professional firms such as the Williams Mullen Law firm, which had headquarters on the south side (across the Chesapeake Bay). They wanted a presence on the Virginia Peninsula: "There was a need to be here because we tap the entire Peninsula market from Oyster Point," said a partner in the Mullins firm (Batts 2005). It is more efficient for these organizations to open an office on the Peninsula to alleviate the travel time from South Hampton Roads and to have better access to customers and clients. Additionally, the Peninsula is seen as a high-tech, government contract–oriented area that appeals to those involved in high-technology, intellectual property, and government contract law (Callaham 1998).

Early indications are that the Town Center at Oyster Point will be a success. Office space was 90 percent leased within 18 months of completion (Snider 2001a), and City Center shop owners are optimistic. For example, owners of The Lunch Bell said, "We see new faces in here every day," and they have expanded their hours. The C & F Bank president commented that the bank's location in City Center "has exceeded expectations" and "there's been more foot traffic with each and every building that's gone up" (Carroll 2004). Developers and investors feel they have made the right decision. "It'll be the place to go, and I think the Peninsula lacked that centrality," said the president of the commercial real estate company developing City Center. "There was an organizational element that I think we hit on that people responded to" (Shapiro 2006).

There are some negative consequences, however. Some critics accused Newport News of turning its back on its traditional downtown by developing Oyster Point and City Center, which are about eight miles north. City officials worked to counter the charge by keeping the bulk of the city offices based downtown and opening only satellite offices at City Center. City officials acknowledged, however, that it is a challenge to keep offices in both areas (Newport News Department of Development 2005).

Also, Newport News will spend at least $1.54 million per year in expenses directly related to City Center—costs that did not exist in the city budget before the project began. Most of the money goes to leasing office space, maintaining the city-owned parking garages, and marketing. City officials say the spending is needed to build interest in City Center. But others question the city's priorities. Some city councilors are upset about the marketing and event planning money. "It's a real burr in my saddle," one said. "Just give me a million bucks, and let me put in some sidewalks. What our Public Works people could do with a million dollars!" (Lynch 2006b)

Hampton's Peninsula Town Center

For Hampton, the primary benefit was the promise of renewed retail interest in its Coliseum District. Unlike Newport News, Hampton did not have the benefit of a large area of available, undeveloped land. In order to develop, it first had to demolish existing infrastructure. Because the Peninsula Town Center is still in its early stages, there are few measures of success or failure. Hampton hedged its bets, however, by first doing its homework. Before beginning, the city conducted an extensive market analysis that considered the entire Central District. The Town Center was incorporated into a master economic development plan (City of Hampton 2004). Once the decision was made to proceed, the city hired a proven, award-winning urban center developer, Steiner & Associates, to head the project. Additionally, local developers met with city leaders and community members directly affected by the development's life cycle (interview with Raymond Tripp, May 8, 2007).

Developers and the city officials recognized and exploited one of the area's key strengths: its location at one of the major crossroads (I-64 and I-664) on the Virginia Peninsula. They capitalized on residents and visitors traveling around the heavily populated region. More than 550,000 people live in the Peninsula region, and more than 880,000 are within 30 minutes of the development location (City of Hampton 2004). Additionally, the parties adopted a finance plan that reduced the impact on taxpayers. Although the changes will cost the city approximately $30 million from 2005 to 2010, there were no upfront investments on taxpayers' part (interview with Raymond Tripp, May 8, 2007; Snider 2005b).

Hampton's leadership faces one negative consequence during part of the development process: most of the existing 1,250 Coliseum Mall jobs will be lost. While Hampton's director of economic development has claimed that there will eventually be even greater employment opportunities with the retailers brought in through redevelopment (Snider 2005c), in the short term, there may be some dissatisfaction concerning jobs.

Conclusion

As Kenyon and Kincaid (1991, 1) have noted, "Competition among governments can be defined as rivalrous behavior in which each government attempts to win some scarce beneficial resource or to avoid a particular cost." Of the three general categories of interjurisdictional competition introduced earlier—active rivalry, implicit competition, and yardstick competition—the yardstick model best describes the Newport News and Hampton cases. The differences between yardstick competition and implicit competition have to do with the motivations of the policymakers involved. Are policymakers more concerned with businesses leaving the area (implicit) or gaining the confidence of their voting constituency (yardstick)? In this case, Hampton and Newport News policymakers probably were responding to development patterns in the surrounding communities. Supporting town center developments in their own cities provided highly visible evidence of their commitment to their communities' economic well-being. The assumption was that by comparing what was happening at home with what was happening in the surrounding areas, voters would gain confidence in their leaders and be more likely to support them at the polls.

In what could be interpreted as an effort to "measure up" to other cities in the region, Newport News and Hampton turned to town center developments. In doing so, they took a long-term approach to economic development and may have avoided some of the pitfalls associated with short-term options such as tax breaks or other concessions to attract business and industry. The city leaders weighed the economic and political costs against potential long-term benefits. By investing time, money, and political capital into town center projects, the civic leaders and developers of these projects have demonstrated an ambition to create unique places with lasting value rather than standardized developments to be quickly built and sold.

References

Batts, Battinto. 2005. City Center at the heart of Newport News growth. *Virginian-Pilot*, May 2. www.global.factiva.com.proxy.lib.odu/ha/default.aspx. Accessed January 11, 2007.

Callaham, Frank. 1998. *Hampton Roads, gateway to America's East Coast*. Montgomery, AL: Community Communications, Inc.

Carroll, Fred. 2004. Newport News, Va., plans massive expansion of business park. *Daily Press*, September 24. www.global.factiva.com.proxy.lib.odu/ha/default.aspx. Accessed January 11, 2007.

City of Hampton. 2004. *Coliseum Central master plan: Hampton, Virginia*. www.hampton.gov/ed/plans/coliseum.html. Accessed February 18, 2007.

_____. 2006. *Master plans*. www.hampton.gov/ed/plans/index.html. Accessed February 3, 2007.

"Council approves new Peninsula Town Center." 2006. *Daily Press*, March 8. www.hampton.va.us/ed/releases/towncenter.html. Accessed December 8.

Duerksen, Christopher, and Gregory Dale. 1999. Creating city centers. *The Commissioner*. www.planning.org/thecommissioner/summer99. Accessed December 4, 2006.

E. V. Williams Center for Real Estate and Economic Development. 2003–7. *Market survey*. Norfolk, VA: E. V. Williams Center for Real Estate and Economic Development, Old Dominion University.

Ewing, Reid. 1997. Counterpoint: Is Los Angeles-style sprawl desirable? *Journal of the American Planning Association* 63:107–26.

Glynn, Matt. 1998. Newport News, Va., seeks developers' ideas for Oyster Point site. *Daily Press*, April 27. www.global.factiva.com.proxy.odu/ha/default.aspx. Accessed January 11, 2007.

Gordon, Peter, and Harry Richardson. 1997. Point: Are compact cities a desirable planning goal? *Journal of the American Planning Association* 63:95–106.

Grant, Lorrie. 2004. Shopping in the great outdoors. *USA Today*, August 4. www.steiner.com/?page=newsarticlesandpressreleases. Accessed December 8, 2006.

"Growth and development." 2006. *Virginia Business Magazine*, May 6. www.virginiabusiness.com/edit/magazine/yr2006/may06/region1.shtml. Accessed January 23, 2007.

Hart, Kim. 2006. The trend: Building urban villages, remade city centers find mass appeal. *Washington Post*, November 13, 1.

Kenyon, Daphne. 1997. Theories of interjurisdictional competition. *New England Economic Review* (March–April): 13–27.

Kenyon, Daphne, and John Kincaid, eds. 1991. *Competition among states and local governments: Efficiency and equity in American federalism*. Washington, DC: Urban Institute Press.

Leccese, Michael, and Kathleen McCormick, eds. 2000. *Charter of the new urbanism*. New York: McGraw-Hill.

Lynch, Patrick. 2006a. Center of attention: Marriott opening in Newport News. *Daily Press*, June 15. www.global.factiva.com.proxy.odu/ha/default.aspx. Accessed January 11, 2007.

_____. 2006b. NN to spend at least $1.54M directly on project this year: For that money, the city will receive marketing, maintenance, event planning and more. *Daily Press*, October 22. www.global.factiva.com.proxy.odu/ha/default. aspx. Accessed January 11, 2007.

_____. 2006c. On the waterfront: The man who helped guide Baltimore's Inner Harbor redevelopment has a new piece of property—facing the fountain at City Center. *Daily Press*, June 23. www.global.factiva.com.proxy.odu/ha/default.aspx. Accessed January 11, 2007.

"Mall no longer profitable." 2006. *Daily Press*, August 26. www.global.factiva.com.proxy.odu/ha/default.aspx. Accessed January 11, 2007.

Mizal-Archer, Michelle. 2002. Investors promise town center will transform beach. *Virginian-Pilot*, February 3, 20.

Newport News Department of Development. 2005. *The City Center at Oyster Point*. www.nngov.com/development/resources/ccop. Accessed December 8, 2006.

_____. 2006. *A review of the economy*. www.nngov.com/development/resources/rec2006. Accessed December 8.

Newport News Economic Development Authority. 2004. *City Center at Oyster Point*. www.newportnewsva.com/site_selection/economy/econews.htm. Accessed December 5, 2006.

Point, Thomas. 2000. *Final report economic development strategy: 2000. Virginia Beach*. www.vbgov.com/print.aspx?vgnextoid=ce7bede97. Accessed December 8, 2006.

Rusk, David. 1995. *Cities without suburbs*. 2nd ed. Washington, DC: Woodrow Wilson Center Press.

Shapiro, Carolyn. 2006. Mixed-use developments proving to be magnets for retail. *Virginia Pilot*, April 9. www.global.factiva.com.proxy.odu/ha/default.aspx. Accessed December 8.

Shearin, Randall. 2005. Steiner redevelops center for Hampton Roads. *Shopping Business Center* (December): 24–25.

Snider, Jody. 2001a. Development company slates construction on Newport News, Va., office tower. *Daily Press*, March 30. www.global.factiva.com.proxy. odu/ha/default.aspx. Accessed January 11, 2007.

_____. 2001b. Tenants commit to Newport News, Va., office complex. *Daily Press*, June 13. www.global.factiva.com.proxy.odu/ha/default.aspx. Accessed January 11, 2007.

_____. 2002a. Newport News, Va., development might get $1.5 million boost from city. *Daily Press*, November 10. www.global.factiva.com.proxy.odu/ ha/default.aspx. Accessed January 11, 2007.

_____. 2002b. Newport News, Va., Town Center developer says mix of people, business is key. *Daily Press*, November 10. www.global.factiva.com.proxy. odu/ha/default.aspx. Accessed January 11, 2007.

_____. 2003. Mixed-use development in Newport News, Va., gets name change. *Daily Press*, February 27. www.global.factiva.com.proxy.odu/ha/default. aspx. Accessed January 11, 2007.

_____. 2004. Upscale restaurant is coming to Newport News, Va., along with retailers. *Daily Press*, May 21. www.global.factiva.com.proxy.odu/ha/default. aspx. Accessed January 11, 2007.

_____. 2005a. Coliseum makeover could take 20 years. *Daily Press*, February 24. www.global.factiva.com.proxy.odu/ha/default.aspx. Accessed January 12, 2007.

_____. 2005b. Firm to give update on mall. *Daily Press*, February 23. www.global.factiva.com.proxy.odu/ha/default.aspx. Accessed January 12, 2007.

_____. 2005c. Re-imagining Coliseum Mall as a town center. *Daily Press*, April 27. www.global.factiva.com.proxy.lib.odu.edu/ha/default.aspx. Accessed January 12, 2007.

_____. 2005d. Talbots coming to City Center in Newport News, Va. *Daily Press*, April 12. www.global.factiva.com.proxy.lib.odu.edu/ha/default.aspx. Accessed January 11, 2007.

Steiner. 2006a. *The Peninsula Town Center continues development plans.* www.steiner.com/?page=peninsulanews. Accessed December 8.

_____. 2006b. *Who Is Steiner and Associates?* www.steiner.com/?page=steiner associatesarticles. Accessed December 8.

Steuteville, Robert. 2004. The new urbanism: An alternative to modern, automobile-oriented planning and development. *New Urban News 5.* www.newurban news.com. Accessed December 8, 2006.

Urban Land Institute. 2006. *A choice of lifestyles.* www.uli.org/am/template.cfm7 section=october10&template=1members. Accessed February 11.

Virginia Employment Commission. 2007. *Hampton Roads statistical digest.* www.gatewayva.com/biz/virginiabusiness/research/digests/hampton/06. Accessed January 30.

CHAPTER 9

Transit-Oriented Development:
The Euclid Corridor Transportation Project and the Greater Cleveland Regional Transit Authority

Floun'say R. Caver and Grace Gallucci

Confronted with the realities of job losses in the manufacturing sector, increasing inner-city poverty, and population decline, Cleveland and Northeast Ohio have recognized the need for new economic development strategies. Among these strategies, transit-oriented development is proving to be an important component. The Euclid Corridor Transportation Project stands as the city and region's largest such project, and it is being credited with the rebirth of the city's major employment, education, arts, and entertainment corridor.[1]

Cleveland, the second-largest city in Ohio, is located in Northeast Ohio on the Lake Erie shore. The city is situated in Cuyahoga County, the largest in the state, and is part of the Cleveland-Elyria-Mentor metropolitan area. According to the U.S. Census Bureau (2006), the city's population is 53.2 percent African American, 38.3 percent white, and 8.1 percent Hispanic or Latino. The median family income in Cleveland is $33,477, and 22.2 percent of families live below the poverty level (the national average is 9.8 percent).

Historically, the city's economy had been strongly linked to its manufacturing base. As it has in many other industrial regions, the decline in American manufacturing has adversely affected the central city as well as the region. Over the past 55 years, the city's population has shrunk by 51 percent, from a high of 915,000 in 1950 to 574,000 in 1980 and 452,000 in 2005 (U.S. Census Bureau 1960; 2007). The economic strife that accompanied the decline received national exposure in 1978, when the City of Cleveland defaulted on $15.5 million in short-term loans. Despite the economic hardships, in the mid-1990s the city gained positive national attention as the "Comeback City" for its downtown redevelopment work. More recently, however, the economic hardships returned to the forefront when the U.S. Census Bureau identified Cleveland as the poorest large city in America in 2004 and 2006 (U.S. Census Bureau 2003; Webster and Bishaw 2006).

This case study examines a transit-oriented development (TOD) project in Cleveland, Ohio—specifically, the Euclid Corridor Transportation Project. TOD is development near or oriented toward transit facilities. The benefits of such projects include more efficient transportation allocations, new development in declining neighborhoods, energized downtowns, increased rents, and job growth. Examples of TOD can be seen today in San Francisco, Baltimore, Chicago, Dallas, and Washington D.C., among other major cities.

At its height in the late 19th and early 20th centuries, Cleveland's Euclid Avenue, known then as Millionaires' Row, was the epicenter of American industrial power and promise. It was home to such luminaries as John D. Rockefeller, Charles F. Brush, John Hay, and Amasa Stone. Its guests included Presidents Rutherford B. Hays and James A. Garfield and the industrialists William K. Vanderbilt, Andrew Carnegie, and J. P. Morgan. The victory parades, St. Patrick's Day parades, and other festivities that have taken place along Euclid Avenue over the decades have helped to define the Cleveland experience—this street holds a special place in Clevelanders' hearts. Between the 1980s and 1990s, however, the street lost its luster as the city's fortunes declined. With the Euclid Corridor Transportation Project, the Greater Cleveland Regional Transit Authority (RTA) has provided an important vehicle for its restoration as a premier avenue in America.

Transit-Oriented Development

TOD is an elusive concept, part of a potent mix of principles that characterize sustainable urban development: sustainability, smart growth, mixed use, location efficiency, new urbanism, regionalism, and economic development. TOD both encompasses these concepts and is itself another buzzword. Herein lies the problem. Exactly what is TOD, and how does it work? How does it fit into the mix of urban development and sustainability? What role can it play in the choices regarding future growth of American cities, both economic and geographic? How do we make it a reality?

The *Transportation Demand Management Encyclopedia* (Victoria Transport Policy Institute 2007) defines TOD as "residential and commercial areas designed to maximize access by transit and non-motorized transportation, and with other features to encourage transit ridership." It also outlines TOD density requirements as 7 residential units and 25 employees per acre as part of residential and commercial centers, respectively. Bernick and Cervero (1997, xi) further define TOD, or the "transit-village" concept, as "an organizing principle for creating places—built environments, social environments, and economic environments—that embrace and evolve around mass transit systems." The Transportation Research Board (1999, 4) identifies five characteristics of TODs: sufficient density, which promotes public transit use; residences, jobs, and retail destinations that are located within proximity of public transit; mixed uses; a grid transportation network; and urban design features that support a pedestrian orientation.

Transit agencies across the country are advocating TOD. They are pursuing it as a way to increase ridership and revenue and address environmental, social justice, and overall economic issues. Creating high-density development in an area immediately surrounding a transit facility promotes joint development opportunities, which in turn facilitate the other goals, including economic development. Transit agencies have embraced TOD in their capital improvement and strategic operational plans. Further, the federal government has encouraged TOD through its policies and financial assistance.

Intrinsic in this mix, however, are land-use policies. Since transportation is a critical component of any community's infrastructure, it has a significant influence on land use and growth patterns. TOD is believed to be the answer to many parts of the urban sustainability question, particularly the consequences of urban sprawl, including disinvestment in central cities. Transportation policies and practices clearly affect urban sprawl and urban economic decline. Ironically, urban sprawl is a direct consequence of federal actions that were intended as solutions to urban problems. Within 50 years after World War II, the U.S. Department of Transportation spent five times more money on roads and highways than on city-oriented mass transit (Rusk 1995, 105). It encouraged automobile transportation and, by extension, suburban development—all of which contributed to urban decline.

The federal government has attempted to reverse the effects of its earlier transportation policies by, for example, enacting the Intermodal Surface Transportation Equity Act (ISTEA) in 1991. The programs and policies of ISTEA encouraged a "systems approach" to transportation policy and its subsequent investments (Camph 1997). It attempted to mitigate some of the negative consequences related to urban sprawl by promoting "smart growth." TOD was a specific part of that promotion, and economic development a specific outcome of TOD, along with increased transit ridership and transit revenues. In the context of smart growth, this emphasis means increasing population densities and encouraging mass transit as the transportation mode of choice over the private automobile (O'Toole 2001, 1).

TOD has also been recognized and supported for addressing social justice issues through economic development. Because of its promotion of public transit, TOD has been shown to enable individuals and households to build wealth and to help eradicate poverty. Communities benefit from outright financial investment in communities with TOD, as well as its multiplier effects, and the mixed uses of TOD result in more efficient places to live and work. Less competition for space, time, and money leads to increased community assets, which lead to increased home ownership, which results in better neighborhoods, schools, and quality of life (Bernstein 2001, 1–2).

Many communities across the country have recognized the benefits of TOD and have implemented policies to support such efforts. Some have already successfully executed TODs, while others are just breaking ground—both figuratively and literally—as is the case in the Greater Cleveland area. The region has begun discussions about TOD, and the Greater Cleveland RTA and many other local stakeholders have taken the initiative to create the environment necessary for TOD. The RTA is developing a Bus Rapid Transit (BRT) corridor as a part of its major transportation infrastructure. BRT models itself after the light rail mode of transportation, but it uses bus-like vehicles to produce a more cost-effective and flexible system. BRT is an excellent example of a transportation investment that applies TOD concepts to improving the transit system and generating economic development in the immediate area.

Cleveland's Grand Avenue

Euclid Avenue began as an obscure road that served travelers to and from Buffalo, New York, with small businesses, lodges, and restaurants (Cigliano 1991). At that time, Superior Street was the business avenue, and Ontario Street was the residential street of choice. As time passed, however, Euclid Avenue grew in prominence and grandeur and came to symbolize the city's industrial wealth and status.

Between 1850 and 1910, Euclid Avenue was called the most beautiful street in the world (Cigliano 1991). Its list of residents, their mansions, and their well-manicured estates rivaled those of New York's Fifth Avenue, New Orleans's St. Charles Avenue, and Prairie Avenue in Chicago. The residents of Euclid Avenue represented a "Who's Who" of industrial captains, lawyers, politicians, and inventors. These men built fortunes on both their individual talents and Cleveland's natural strategic location. The city's location enabled its status in the railroad, shipping, steel, oil refining, and banking industries. The city served as an important point for connecting goods from the East Coast and South to places such as Chicago, Detroit, and Canada.

Euclid Avenue's most internationally known resident was John D. Rockefeller, whose first residence on the street was 3920 Euclid Avenue. Rockefeller began his oil business with the Rockefeller and Andrews Refining Company (1865) and later founded the oil empire Standard Oil in 1870 (Cigliano 1991). In addition to his 3920 Euclid residence, Rockefeller and his partners built the Standard Block at East 4th and Euclid Avenue. This site served as the Standard Oil Company's headquarters until 1907 (Gregor 2006). In 1877, Rockefeller moved to his Forest Hill Estate in East Cleveland, which overlooked Euclid Avenue, and its gatehouse address was 13652 Euclid Avenue. The new BRT will travel this corridor every day.

Another famous resident of the avenue was Charles F. Brush, whose residence was 3725 Euclid Avenue. Brush is famous for his dynamo and arc light inventions, which brought electric lights to America's city streets. In 1879, when Brush unveiled his invention to the world by lighting Cleveland's Public Square, it brought him instant fame and riches. He then created Brush Electric Light and Power Company in order to build central power stations in New York, Philadelphia, and Boston, among other major cities (Cigliano 1991). Brush's company eventually merged with the Thompson Houston Company and the Edison Electric Company to form the General Electric Company.

Between the 1920s and 1970s, Euclid Avenue shifted away from its residential roots and became the city's shopping and entertainment home. It housed department stores (e.g., Halle Brothers, Higbees, and the May Company), theaters (e.g., Allen Theatre and Keith's Palace Theater), and banks (e.g., Cleveland Trust). During this period, its vibrancy compared with that of Chicago's Michigan Avenue.

By the 1970s, the shopping along Euclid Avenue had given way to suburban shopping centers and malls in outlying areas, as it did in many urban centers. The avenue's final descent was signaled in 1982, when Halle Brothers Co. department store closed its doors for good. Revitalization along the avenue is beginning, however, and the Euclid Corridor Transportation Project is a major catalyst.

The Euclid Corridor Transportation Project

The ECTP Concept

The Euclid Corridor Transportation Project (ECTP) is a major transit improvement currently under construction in Cleveland. At a cost of nearly $200 million, the project features a BRT designed to improve service along one of Cleveland's primary public corridors. To qualify as a BRT, a project must have several major elements, including exclusive transit lanes, fewer stops along the route, special boarding facilities, prepaid fare collection system, traffic signal prioritization, and unique vehicles. It also must generate travel time savings, be reliable, have a branded identity separate from the general bus system, improve safety and security, and increase bus capacity. Benefits for the transit authority and community include increased ridership compared with the existing bus line, transit-supportive land use, enhanced environmental quality, capital cost-effectiveness, operating efficiency, and flexibility (Federal Transit Administration 2004).

BRT is aligned with the Federal Transportation Administration's strategic plan of providing accessibility and improving mobility through an efficient transportation system, with the ultimate goal of reducing traffic congestion and air pollution and addressing other problems such as urban sprawl and central city decline that are attributed to the automobile and the highway system. The federal government currently sponsors 10 demonstration projects in the United States that are exploring the feasibility of BRT as an alternative to light rail. The BRT demonstration projects are funded and closely monitored by the Federal Transit Administration. They were selected by a competitive process through the same funding mechanism as light rail. Justification for the project is based on the proposed benefits in areas such as mobility improvements, environmental benefits, operating efficiencies, cost-effectiveness, and land use.

The ECTP is one of the BRT demonstration projects. The goals of the ECTP are to improve service to RTA customers by increasing transit system efficiency, promote long-term economic and community development and growth in and adjacent to the Euclid Avenue Corridor, and improve quality of life for those living, working, or visiting the corridor. The transit project will provide a convenient link between the central business district of downtown (the region's largest employment center), the University Circle area (the region's second-largest employment center and its principal cultural, medical, and educational hub), and the City of East Cleveland (a first-ring suburb and location of the last and one of the busiest rapid transit stations on the Red Line East) through a series of transportation roadway construction and improvement projects covering 9.4 miles along Euclid Avenue.

The logistics of the project include construction of a center median lane, designation of exclusive lanes with signal preemption for ECTP vehicles, development of unique vehicles, installation of attractive streetscape and landscape improvements and public art, and construction of bike lanes. Specialized stations with platforms and docking equipment will be built to offload passengers quickly. A new fare collection system will expedite payment by having passengers pay prior to boarding. And electronic and audible signage will be developed to communicate the arrivals and departures of the vehicles in real time.

ECTP Benefits

The project is funded by a partnership including the U.S. Department of Transportation, the State of Ohio Department of Transportation, the regional metropolitan planning organization, the City of Cleveland, and the RTA. As part of the justification for the funding, economic development was used as the basis of the financial plan. The case was made that it would be more prudent to invest in the corridor because to do nothing would increase the likelihood that future revenues would decline as the corridor declined. Passenger fares and sales taxes are the two largest revenue sources for the RTA's operating budget, both of which are reliant on a healthy economy. Without the project, ridership and fare revenues would likely continue to erode, and the city would lose its opportunity to realize the corridor's direct impact on sales tax revenue.

The economic development benefits of the ECTP are expected to fall into three categories: short term, long term, and intangible. Both the short-term and long-term benefits represent quantifiable factors, such as the translation of the developmental impacts into tax revenue. The benefits were compared with a "no-build" scenario and on a 20-year forecasting model. This analysis justified the project from a cost/benefit perspective. But as with most governmental projects, the financial analysis is augmented with nonquantifiable factors, some of which have financial components but cannot be defined, and some of which can be deemed quality-of-life benefits.

In the short term, some "one-time" incremental benefits are anticipated with the construction activity of the ECTP project itself, along with the construction activity of projects spurred within the corridor. The estimate prepared as part of the grant application process stated that construction costs along the corridor would total $1.9 billion. This investment would result in $6.3 million in sales tax revenue and $14 million in income tax revenue, mostly generated by individuals working on the projects within the corridor.

To date, the project is surpassing its original construction and TOD projections. The RTA estimates that $2.7 billion has been invested in education, health, entertainment, the arts, and housing. Table 1 presents TOD projects that are currently proposed or under way both along and adjacent to the Euclid Corridor as of February 2008.

The Cleveland Plain Dealer has attributed an even more impressive economic development impact to the Euclid Corridor project. One reporter wrote, "Amid all the bad news about Cleveland's economy,

Table 1: Euclid Corridor TOD Projects

Project	Amount
Cleveland Clinic Foundation Heart Center complex	$506,000,000
Cleveland Museum of Art	$225,000,000
VA hospital complex	$250,000,000
VA office complex	$120,000,000
Ameritrust complex	$200,000,000
University hospitals	$500,000,000
University arts and retail district	$120,000,000
Cleveland Institute of Art	$40,000,000
University Circle streetscape plan	$7,000,000
Hawken School	$3,500,000
Mandel Center for Nonprofit Organizations	$11,600,000
Victory Lofts	$10,000,000
Baker Motor Car Company building	$6,000,000
Charter One initiative	$150,000,000
Avenue district	$250,000,000
4600 Euclid	$10,000,000
Cleveland State University master plan	$180,000,000
Museum of Contemporary Art	$25,000,000
1021 Euclid	$45,000,000
2010 and 2020 Euclid	$9,200,000
Hanna Theatre renovation	$14,700,000
668 Euclid (Atrium office building)	$65,000,000
Total	$2,748,000,000

Source: Greater Cleveland Regional Transit Authority (2008).

one big, positive number is sure to impress all but the most hardened cynics: $4.3 billion. That's how much fresh investment—conservatively speaking—is being poured into [Euclid Avenue]" (Litt 2008, A8). His observations were based on information from private developers and analyses of projects completed since 2000, those that are currently under way, and those that are scheduled to commence within the next five years.

The long-term economic benefits of the ECTP are viewed as annual incremental benefits assessed through population growth, job growth, and property value increases. It is expected that more than 5,000 residential dwellings will be built along the corridor in response to the demand generated by the improvements to the corridor, bringing nearly 12,000 new inhabitants to the area. This permanent residential housing growth in turn may generate $2.5 to $7 million in income tax revenue annually over the 20-year forecast period. In addition, an expected significant increase in visitors to the corridor for employment and recreational purposes would generate $1.75 million annually in sales tax revenue. Other revenue, including "sin" taxes and parking taxes, is also anticipated as a result of the visitor activity. Increased employment opportunities from businesses and retail along the corridor could result in 29,000 new jobs. This predicted growth could lead to $17.4 million annually in new personal income tax revenue, in addition to corporate and excise taxes.

The redevelopment with the ECTP also brings the likelihood of increased property values. It is expected that 6.1 million square feet of commercial and retail space added to the 5,000 new residential units will generate $38.3 million in real property taxes that will support the school district, city, county, and library and parks systems. Furthermore, the redevelopment will result in a decrease in uncollected property taxes and an increase in tangible personal property taxes as housing characteristics improve and owner-occupied housing increases. Overall, the region's financial condition should strengthen as the economic and tax base increases.

Among the intangible benefits from the economic development associated with the ECTP, most evident is the improvement of the image of the city and region. This large, permanent infrastructure investment will help to define Cleveland as a first-class city. It will positively affect others' views of Cleveland as well as Clevelanders' views of themselves. The quality of life of the region will also improve as the corridor becomes more attractive, more vibrant, and safer. And as the mobility through the corridors improves, travel will become faster, more reliable, and more pleasant.

TOD Best Practices and Strengths

In order to maximize the use of TOD projects within its planning and infrastructure investments, the RTA has developed best practices (see Box 1). The RTA's 2007 *Transit Oriented Development Best Practices* study synthesized the best TOD practices from the Bay Area Rapid Transit, Santa Clara County Valley Transportation Authority, Dallas Area Rapid Transit, Massachusetts Bay Transportation Authority (Boston), Metro (Baltimore), Metro (St. Louis), Tri-Met (Portland, Oregon), and the Washington Metropolitan Area Transit Authority. The case studies highlighted and analyzed TOD successes such as Dallas's Mockingbird Station, Portland's Center Commons, and the D.C. area's Bethesda Row projects. Evaluations of these and other experiences were summarized in a manual. Best practices are grouped into three general categories: establishing roles, developing the development, and playing to the region's strengths. These lessons coalesce around the importance

Box 1: TOD Best Practices

<table>
<tr>
<td rowspan="1">Establishing Roles</td>
<td>

1. While a city planning agency's role is more frequently "passive" (i.e., the agency zones land but cannot choose who develops it), a transit agency has the opportunity to more actively direct the land development and most important, to ensure that the land uses reinforce transit and vice versa.

2. TOD is a team effort. The most successful projects involve municipal leadership that invested time, money, and political capital to achieve TOD. . . . Coordination between stakeholders must start early and occur often throughout the length of the planning process.

3. A significant role of leadership is helping to make projects work financially. This should include implementation of TOD policy by creating zoning that allows for more density and mixed-use, making infrastructure improvements, and providing predictability and transparency in the form of plans, guidelines, and permissible uses and densities.
</td>
</tr>
<tr>
<td>Developing the Development</td>
<td>

1. Pay more attention to the program aspect of the project to ensure success of the retail and community uses. For example, identify local businesses that would be particularly appropriate for the project and then offer them reduced rent for a period of time to assist them in getting established.

2. Expand the retail customer base to the surrounding area. Place small retail spaces along the street, rather than at a single, somewhat isolated node at the station. Design pathways to provide direct access to nearby neighborhoods.

3. Retailing follows rooftops, even in a transit-intense setting. While it is often an attractive component of a TOD, retailers and developers look to the amount and mix of housing nearby, more so than the transit connections, to evaluate feasibility. Most developers insist that retail spending far exceed that delivered through a transit connection alone. Encouraging housing along a transit corridor helps support additional retail, regardless of how the shoppers get there.

4. Even a very small lot size can promote TOD concepts. The promotion of TOD on urban infill parcels creates an important opportunity for the revitalization of older communities and neighborhoods.
</td>
</tr>
<tr>
<td>Play to the Region's Strengths</td>
<td>

1. Even in suburban communities, TOD can serve as an important tool to achieve a broader community strategy of creating a sense of place. TOD neighborhoods provide gathering places, open spaces, and community resources frequently lacking in traditional suburban developments.

2. TOD is an excellent opportunity for communities to expand their supply of affordable housing. With significant transit options within close proximity, households may not need a car (or may be able to eliminate second and third cars).

3. Design housing for the target market.

4. Some of the best TOD opportunities are on parking lots originally built for commuters.
</td>
</tr>
</table>

Source: Greater Cleveland Regional Transit Authority (2007a, 58–59).

of "project stakeholders, the project design, and the community for which the project is proposed" (RTA 2007a, 57). The results of these studies may be helpful to other communities interested in TOD.

The RTA (2007b) also developed a document to communicate to communities, developers, and citizens its dedication to TOD, its goals and strategies, and its guidelines. The RTA has presented the findings in various forums to address TOD in its service area. Box 2 shows the intended goals of the TOD initiatives and the RTA's strategies to achieve the goals.

Conclusion

As demonstrated in Cleveland, TOD is a valuable component of a region's economic development strategy. The ECTP is credited with

Box 2: TOD Policy

Goals of Initiatives	1. High quality private or public development that is sensitive to the existing built environment 2. Development that promotes and enhances transit ridership by planning uses that are "transit-oriented" and that provide maximum linkages between transit stations and the development for transit patrons, pedestrians, and bicycles 3. Reduction in auto use and congestion through encouragement of transit-linked development 4. Value to RTA based on a fair market return on public investment, future revenue streams, additional taxes, and reduction in the cost of the site construction for RTA 5. Development that maximizes the highest and best use of the real estate based on land use and economic development goals of the surrounding community and conforming to local and regional development plans 6. Value to the neighborhood, the developer, and RTA through intensive, high quality development
Strategies to Achieve Goals	1. Work collaboratively with the stakeholders and local jurisdictions as appropriate adjacent to its transit facilities to proactively promote and develop locations, plans and designs that maximize the benefits of the transit linkage 2. Solicit proposals for transit-oriented joint development through a competitive selection process where feasible in terms of the market and availability of land 3. Accept proposals for joint development projects as received 4. Request funding for joint development activities as part of RTA's capital program as appropriate 5. Complete an assessment for RTA owned facilities to maximize development opportunities through adjacent development activities and leasehold interests within RTA facilities. RTA real estate will be viewed as the asset it is in facilitating the [TOD goals]

Source: Greater Cleveland Regional Transit Authority (2007b, 15–17).

creating between $2.7 billion and $4.3 billion in new investment in Cleveland. But what is the future of TOD? Four trends appear to have emerged at the beginning of this century. First, there has been renewed interest and investment in downtowns. The second trend is the continued growth of the American suburb. Third is the continued increase in the price of fuel. And fourth is a more open-minded perspective regarding public transit and transit investment (Belzer and Autler 2002). All of these trends suggest that there exists an environment conducive to TOD.

TOD is an ideal part of a policy set to curb urban sprawl, move toward more sustainable communities, and reduce American oil dependency and fuel consumption. Its attributes—including density, mixed uses, and pedestrian orientations—encourage increased transit ridership, higher tax revenues, lower development risks, and more viable residential and retail spaces. TOD likely will realize its full potential if it recreates development rather than only presents marginal improvements. A paradigm shift in the development concept is needed. But as Beltzer and Autler (2002, 7) warn, "TOD cannot be and should not be a utopian vision: It must operate within the constraints of the market and realistic expectations of behavior and lifestyle patterns."

The ECTP exhibits a tangible example of TOD. The project brings two of Cleveland's major employment, cultural, and educational hubs closer by way of BRT and better transportation service. The visible commitment signaled by the exclusive center lane dedicated to the BRT, the attractive streetscape, specialized stations, and signal preemption will stabilize the development environment and allow developers to make substantial investments along the corridor. Moreover, ridership may increase as a result of this attractive transportation option along Euclid Avenue. University students, employees, tourist, business persons, conference attendees, new condominium owners, and current residents along the corridor may find it a convenient way to access Euclid Avenue.

For a street that was recently devoid of life, the new vibrancy and excitement reinforced by the ECTP is a welcome change. The project will be completed in December 2008. In addition to its technical merits, the project has benefited greatly from cooperation among political, nonprofit, and business leaders. Such cooperation is imperative to the success of this specific project and TOD in general.

Note

1. See the following multimedia Web sites for the project video and photographs: euclidtransit.org/euclid_corridor_project/video.asp, euclidtransit. org/project_update/default.asp, and euclidtransit.org/upblic_art/default.asp.

References

Belzer, Dena, and Autler, Gerald. 2002. *Transit oriented development: Moving from rhetoric to reality*. Washington, DC: The Brookings Institution and the Great American Station Foundation.

Bernick, Michael, and Robert Cervero. 1997. *Transit villages in the 21st century*. New York: McGraw-Hill.

Bernstein, Scott. 2001. *The benefits of transit-oreinted development—why bother?* Chicago: Center for Neighborhood Technology.

Camph, Donald H. 1997. *Dollars and sense: The economic case for public transportation in America*. Washington, DC: The Campaign for Efficient Passenger Transportation.

Cigliano, Jan. 1991. *Showplace of America: Cleveland's Euclid Avenue, 1850–1910*. Kent, OH: Kent State University Press.

Federal Transit Administration. 2004. *Characteristics of Bus Rapid Transit for decision making*. trb.org/news/blurb_detail.asp?id=4213. Accessed June 3, 2007.

Greater Cleveland Regional Transit Authority. 2007a. *Transit oriented development best practices*. Cleveland: Greater Cleveland Regional Transit Authority Programming and Planning Department.

_____. 2007b. *Transit oriented development guidelines*. Cleveland: Greater Cleveland Regional Transit Authority Programming and Planning Department.

_____. 2008. *Euclid Corridor transportation project progress report no. 113*. Cleveland: Greater Cleveland Regional Transit Authority Programming and Planning Department.

Gregor, Sharon E. 2006. *Images of America: Forest Hill, The Rockefeller Estate*. Chicago: Arcadia Publishing.

Litt, Steven. 2008. The rebirth: Euclid Corridor Project has already brought $4.3 billion in new investment to the city. *Cleveland Plain Dealer*, February 10, A1, A8.

O'Toole, Randal. 2001. The folly of "smart growth." *Regulation Magazine*. www.cato.org/pubs/regulation/regv24n3/otoole.pdf. Accessed June 4, 2007.

Rusk, David. 1995. *Cities without suburbs*. Washington, DC: Woodrow Wilson Center Press.

Transportation Research Board. 1999. The zoning and real estate implications of transit oriented development. *Legal Research Digest* 12:4.

U.S. Census Bureau. 1960. 2007. *Statistical abstract of the United States*. Washington, DC: U.S. Government Printing Office.

_____. 2003. *American Community Survey 2003 data set*. www.census.gov/acs/www/products. Accessed March 12, 2008.

_____. 2006. *American Community Survey 2006 data set*. factfinder.census.gov. Accessed March 11, 2008.

Victoria Transport Policy Institute. 2007. Transit oriented development: Using public transit to create more accessible and livable neighborhoods. In *Transportation demand management encyclopedia*. www.vtpi.org/tdm/tdm45.htm. Accessed June 4.

Webster, Bruce H., Jr., and Alemayehu Bishaw. 2006. *U.S. Census Bureau, American Community Survey Reports: ACS-02, income, earnings, and poverty data from the 2005 American Community Survey*. Washington, DC: U.S. Government Printing Office.

CHAPTER 10

Tragedy of the Crescent City:
State and Local Economic Development in New Orleans after Hurricane Katrina

R. Paul Battaglio

The disaster to the Gulf Coast region brought about by Hurricanes Katrina and Rita in 2005 was unprecedented. The damage to the region was exacerbated by a number of missteps at the federal, state, and local levels that have produced a host of scholarly debates on government's response to national disasters (Jurkiewicz 2007). While much has been discussed concerning government responsiveness, there is still much to be gained from examining the economic impact of the storms on the region and its implications for future recovery efforts. By exploring the economic recovery of Louisiana, scholars and practitioners may learn from the mistakes made at the state and local levels, and their insights can be applied to future collaborative recovery efforts in the wake of other national catastrophes.

Not only is the New Orleans metropolitan statistical area (MSA) a key economic center for the state of Louisiana but the city is also a vital economic conduit for the region and nation. The overall economic impact of the devastating hurricane season of 2005 has been felt far beyond the New Orleans metro area. For the region, economic development in the wake of Hurricanes Katrina and Rita presents both opportunities and challenges (Kiel and Watson 2006; Waugh and Smith 2006; Chang 1984; Skidmore and Toya 2002; Webb, Tierney, and Dahlhamer 2002). This chapter highlights federal, state, and local economic development initiatives in Louisiana since 2005, especially in light of the difficulties facing both the New Orleans area and the state. These initiatives are part of a major effort to redevelop and encourage economic growth in the region after the devastation.

An Overview of Economic Recovery

The Housing Market

Recent reports on the recovery efforts in the New Orleans MSA have emphasized the importance of the housing market in moving toward a full economic recovery (Richardson 2006; Scott 2007; Brookings Institution Metropolitan Policy Program 2006). Key indicators in economic analyses of the recovery include housing rehabilitation and demolition, home sales, and rent and home prices. A review of those indicators demonstrates that there has been some momentum since the hurricane, but housing affordability remains an issue.

Housing development and demolition remain priorities for the New Orleans MSA, especially the need to create housing for much-needed workers for restoring area businesses. Without essential renovations, businesses will find it difficult to remain operational, further hampering the sustainability of the area's economy. Demolition activity and issuance of permits in 2006 (up 117 percent) indicated that the once-stagnant recovery effort was gaining some ground, but some signs of slowing development in recent months have emerged (Scott 2007; Brookings Institution Metropolitan Policy Program 2006; 2007).

Initially, home prices took a tumble, with the homes in the parishes most affected by Hurricane Katrina being hardest hit. Although lack of available housing contributed to the decline in prices, a bifurcated housing market more readily explained the decline in home values. Scott (2007) asserts that the price of undamaged homes exceeded that of damaged homes; those in the latter category saw a 65 percent drop from October 2005 to February 2007. In 2007, consumer confidence appeared to be bouncing back, with values of undamaged single-family homes in the New Orleans MSA peaking (Brookings Institution Metropolitan Policy Program 2007). However, Louisiana now appears to be feeling the crunch from the nationwide slowdown as a result of the recent mortgage crisis (Brookings Institution Metropolitan Policy Program 2008).

Although much-needed federal assistance for rebuilding is finally arriving, several complications have hindered its distribution. To be eligible for certain federal funds, residents who wish to build must comply with the new flood elevation levels. This requirement adds to the estimated 50 percent increase over the pre-flood value of homes to rebuild and renovate (Scott 2007). Due to political wrangling, large construction efforts scheduled for the area involving billions in federal funding and insurance dollars have only recently begun. It was not until final passage through Congress in June 2006 that the state agreed upon a program, dubbed the Road Home Program, for allocating funds.

At the end of January 2007, only 258 Road Home checks had been distributed (Scott 2007).

Income Levels

Personal income for MSAs in the United States is another indicator of the economic impact of both Hurricane Katrina and Hurricane Rita on Louisiana. Preliminary data for 361 MSAs from 2003 through 2005 provide a snapshot of the extent to which the natural disasters of 2005 depressed personal wealth in two key MSAs in Louisiana, New Orleans and Lake Charles, which were in the direct paths of Hurricanes Katrina and Rita, respectively (Bureau of Economic Analysis 2006). New Orleans and Lake Charles were two out of the five shown in Table 1 as having experienced negative percent changes during this period.

As the country experienced 5 percent growth in personal income, the New Orleans and Lake Charles MSAs incurred a reduction of 33 percent and 8.5 percent, respectively. The consequences of such declines in personal wealth reverberate in the economies of the two MSAs, further hampering progress in the area. By the end of 2006, however, personal income in Louisiana had rebounded with total growth of 19.4 percent compared with the previous year. This growth was fueled primarily by rising salaries in the oil, natural gas, and construction industries (Brookings Institution Metropolitan Policy Program 2007). Personal income growth rates in Louisiana fell to 0.9 percent in the third and fourth quarters of 2007—lower than the national growth rate of 1.3 percent and 1 percent, respectively, in the final two quarters (Associated Press 2008). Economists attributed the initial spike in growth in the first

Table 1: Personal Income and Per Capita Personal Income by Metropolitan Area, 2003–5

Metro area	Personal income[a]			Percent change	Per capita personal income[b]		
	2003	2004	2005	2004–5	2003	2004	2005
Metropolitan portion of the United States	7,978,326	8,458,879	8,885,062	5.0	33,047	34,668	36,048
New Orleans MSA	38,591	40,889	27,340	−33.1	29,342	31,024	20,722
Lake Charles, LA MSA	4,906	5,134	4,695	−8.6	25,323	26,427	24,078
Flint, MI MSA	12,509	12,475	12,361	−0.9	28,277	28,130	27,847
Champaign-Urbana, IL MSA	6,786	6,204	6,166	–0.6	31,643	28,858	28,579
Kokomo, IN MSA	3,190	3,159	3,154	−0.2	31,478	31,236	31,115

Source: U.S. Bureau of Economic Analysis (2006).
[a] In millions of dollars.
[b] In dollars.

two quarters to the Road Home Program. The state's personal income growth (compared with pre-Katrina levels) has been cited as being a result of low-wage earners leaving Louisiana after the storm. The state's actual personal income (as opposed to the personal growth rate) remains in the median among the 50 states (Associated Press 2008).

Labor Force

By February 2007, nonfarm employment in the New Orleans MSA still lagged far behind pre-Katrina levels. The MSA was still 163,100 jobs short of its pre-hurricane level (Scott 2007, 10). Although the number of jobs in the MSA has been growing at a rate of 3,700 per month, the recovery appears to be languishing in other measures. Table 2 gives a snapshot of the gap in employment that remains. Several factors have prevented these sectors from rebounding. Typically, private insurance monies and federal assistance flow rapidly into disaster areas, creating a boom in construction-related sectors and driving the economy back to pre-disaster levels or better (Scott 2007). Unfortunately, however, standing floodwaters have drastically altered private insurance coverage; without flood insurance, regular homeowner's insurance does not cover flood-related damage.[1] The result, as Scott (2007, 10) states, is that monies are not flowing into the New Orleans MSA at a pace commensurate with the level of housing destruction, flood insurance payments have not adequately covered the costs of rebuilding, and planning and funds for housing development have been slow to materialize (Table 2).

Table 2: Change in Nonfarm Employment in New Orleans MSA, December 2004–December 2006

Sector	Change in employment	Percent change
Natural resources and mining	1,600	18.8
Construction	−7,600	−25.3
Manufacturing	−9,600	−25.0
Trade, transportation, and utilities	−34,300	−27.1
Information	−3,300	−30.6
Financial activities	−7,600	−22.2
Professional and business services	−23,900	−32.6
Education	−8,500	−43.1
Healthcare	−23,500	−38.2
Leisure and hospitality	−26,300	−30.8
Other services	−11,700	−13.2
Government	−13,900	−13.2
Total	−68,900	−27.4

Source: Scott (2007).

There is positive news in terms of jobs for New Orleans. The rise in gas prices and increase in construction and infrastructure rebuilding in the area seem to have had a moderately positive impact on metro-area jobs. The 18 percent gain in employment in natural resources, mining, and construction demonstrates that the industry is on pace to meet pre-Katrina levels of production (Table 2; see also Scott 2007, 116). The casino industry, which suffered significant losses and damages, is also showing signs of significant recovery. Brisk business has been reported by three reopened casinos: Harrah's, the Boomtown, and the Treasure Chest. Although some staffing issues persist, the casinos appear to be committed to reviving the local economy with new development marked by the opening of Harrah's brand-new 26-story, 450-room hotel in September 2006 (Scott 2007, 37). Job creation in the leisure and hospitality industry is an additional sign of progress. Recent estimates place hotel business and visitor travel to the region at roughly 75 percent of pre-Katrina levels (Brookings Institution Metropolitan Policy Program 2006; Scott 2007, 37). At the Louis Armstrong airport, passenger levels are just 20 percent shy of pre-storm levels. This increase in visitors to the city is evident in the number of hotels that have reopened. International flights have yet to return to the airport, but domestic flights should be expanded with the addition of ExpressJet (Scott 2007). This news means the city's cultural and economic life is recovering to pre-hurricane levels.

While hotels have returned to New Orleans, however, restaurants and other food establishments are still struggling. According to Scott (2007, 40), more than 50 percent of the city's eateries closed after the hurricane. There were initial signs of recovery, but the restaurant industry's employment has slowed significantly. If more restaurants do not come back, the positive tourist trends the city has recently encountered may reverse. Also troubling is the drop in convention business, which is significantly related to the hotel and restaurant industries. Scott (2007, 37) states that this decline halted planned expansions to the Convention Center and discouraged future developers. Moreover, while many of the businesses before Katrina catered to tourists, others slow to rebound, including grocery and convenience stores, are needed to meet the needs of local residents.

Current Recovery Strategies

The Louisiana Recovery Authority (LRA), coordinating primarily with the Federal Emergency Management Administration and the Department of Housing and Urban Development, is the chief body responsible for planning and implementing recovery efforts for the state and regional authorities. The 33-member board recommends short- and long-term policies and services for the recovery effort, coordinating federal, state, and local economic planning and resource allocation (LRA 2007). Although New Orleans has assigned recovery efforts to its own respective committees (the Bring Back New Orleans Commission), Mayor Ray Nagin has committed to ultimately reporting to and coordinating with the LRA (Whelan 2006). The LRA, then, plays a key role in economic development tied to major policy, regulatory, and legislative initiatives (Whelan 2006).

Federal Economic Development Policies

Federal assistance comes primarily through two important pieces of legislation: the Gulf Opportunity Zone Act (GO Zone Act) and the Katrina Emergency Tax Relief Act, both of 2005. The GO Zone Act in particular represents one of the more ambitious business incentive packages in U.S. history (Louisiana Economic Development [LED] 2006a; 2006c; see also Box 1). The financial incentives are intended to sustain local businesses. Another aim of the act is to further economic development in a way that promotes investment by the private sector rather than solely by public financing of infrastructure (LED 2006c). The GO Zone Act addresses three critical concerns for economic development in local areas eligible for the programs: existing business support and rehabilitation and new development.[2]

The GO Zone Act affords existing businesses a number of incentive packages for rebuilding and revitalization. There is an enhanced net operating loss carryback, which provides for a portion of net operating losses to be leveraged for tax refunds over the previous five years. It offers an expanded ability to write off business expenses of up to 50 percent of demolition and cleanup costs, and it extended the deadline for writing off business expenses through December 31, 2007, for remediation and certain environmental cleanup costs. The act also provides tax credits for employee retention and work development (LED 2006a; 2006c). For individuals, the act waived limitations for personal casualty losses as a result of the hurricanes through October 15, 2006, to encourage home repairs.

Several GO Zone Act programs also aid new development and rehabilitation of existing businesses. Tax-exempt bond financing ($7.9 billion in GO Zone Bonds) is available for a limited time to private businesses for office buildings, warehouses, rental housing, manufacturing facilities, shopping centers, retail stores, and many other private-sector projects (LED 2006a).[3] A 50 percent bonus depreciation is available for new development, along with an increase in Section 179 (of the IRS Code) deductions (up to $200,000 of expenditures) for depreciation of new and used personal property in a trade or business, along with

Box 1: The Gulf Opportunity Zone Act at a Glance

- Increases Rehabilitation Tax Credit to help restore commercial building
- Allows employer-provided housing incentives
- Expands the availability of below-market mortgages in the disaster areas
- Allows 50 percent bonus depreciation within the GO Zone
- Provides enhanced Section 179 (IRS Code) expensing for small businesses
- Extends net operating loss carryback
- Provides for expensing of cleanup costs
- Provides relief for small timber owners
- Expands the Employee Retention Tax Credit
- Increases New Markets Tax Credits
- Increases available tax credits for qualified tuition and related expenses for the HOPE Scholarship and Lifetime Learning Credits
- Provides additional bonding authority
- Allows Louisiana and municipalities to reduce costs by restructuring outstanding debt
- Authorizes Gulf Tax Credit debt service bonds
- Makes Gulf Coast Recovery Bonds available to private business owners and corporations to borrow capital at very favorable tax-exempt rates

Source: Louisiana Economic Development (2006a).

certain other eligible property (LED 2006a). The act also provides for expensing up to 50 percent of cleanup costs. (GO Zone Act 2005). Additional tax credits are also available for restoring commercial buildings, employee retention, and new markets (LED 2006a; 2006e).

Because housing factors into economic recovery and development efforts, the GO Zone Act includes several incentives for growth in this sector. For the initial six months of employment, employers may take a 30 percent tax credit for the cost of providing housing for employees, up to $600 per month per employee (LED 2006a). The act also expands the availability of below-market mortgage rates for first-time homebuyers who meet certain income and purchase price limits in the disaster zones, with part of the mortgage proceeds being used for repair.

Another essential factor in economic recovery is stimulating growth in personal income. The Katrina Emergency Tax Relief Act of 2005 offers charitable giving incentives and tax relief for families affected by Hurricane Katrina, including a waiver of the 10 percent penalty for early distributions of pensions and IRAs for taxpayers suffering an economic loss due to the hurricanes (LED 2006a). A number of deductions are also available to corporations through the Katrina Emergency Tax Relief Act for charitable cash contributions and individual casualty losses in the designated zone areas.

State Economic Development Policies

With the influx of federal funding for recovery efforts in the region, economic development has also been a top priority for the state. Louisiana offers a number of incentives to cultivate and sustain business and industry, some specifically deployed for post-Katrina recovery. The LED Board of Commerce and Industry administers traditional economic development incentives, while the Louisiana Recovery Authority (LRA) is responsible for coordinating hurricane disaster–related economic recovery efforts. Traditional programs include Enterprise Zones, Quality Jobs, and a variety of tax incentives for businesses meeting qualifications. In addition, the Louisiana Economic Development Corporation offers a number of loan packages combining public, private, and nonprofit assistance for starting up and expanding small businesses (LED 2006d).

The state Enterprise Zone program aims to create jobs by providing income and franchise tax credits to businesses employing a minimum number of net new jobs. Enterprise Zones are areas with high unemployment, low income, or a high percentage of residents receiving some form of public assistance. To qualify for the program, 35 percent of these net new employees must meet one of four job certification criteria. The creation of jobs may result in a sales/use tax rebate on materials, furniture, fixtures, machinery, and equipment purchased and used exclusively on the Enterprise Zone site. In addition, a one-time tax credit of $2,500 may be earned for each certified net new job created, and certain aerospace or automobile parts manufacturers may qualify for as much as $5,000 for each net new job. The Board of Commerce and Industry is responsible for approving these applications, and the LED's Business Incentives Services administers this program (LED 2007).

The Quality Jobs program provides cash rebates to targeted businesses that locate in Louisiana, create quality jobs, and promote economic development. The annual rebate may be as much as 6 percent of the gross payroll for new direct jobs. In order to qualify for the Quality Jobs program, these new direct jobs must come from businesses in the state's Vision 2020 plan designated as a seed and traditional cluster industry. These industries include but are not limited to biotechnology and biomedical; micromanufacturing; software, Internet, and telecommunications; environmental technology; food technology; and advanced materials. The Quality Jobs program also offers the same sales/use tax rebate as the Enterprise Zone program (LED 2006e).

Several tax incentives also provide economic development assistance for business and industry. The Restoration Tax Abatement offers a five-year deferment of the ad valorem property taxes on renovations and improvements in existing development districts in municipal and local areas. An industrial tax exemption is offered to manufacturers equivalent to up to 10 years of local property taxes (ad valorem) on a manufacturer's new investment and annual capitalized additions. Firms may also take advantage of a research and development tax credit claim against state income and corporation franchise taxes for up to 8 percent of the state's apportioned share of increased research and development expenses or 25 percent of its apportioned share of federal research credit claimed. The goal is to encourage existing businesses with operating facilities in Louisiana to establish or continue research and development activities within the state (LED 2003; 2006b; 2006d). The Headquarter Growth Program eliminates the taxes on interest and dividends for firms with headquarters in Louisiana and, as it does in other states, apportions income from capital gains. An early-stage "angel" investment incentive provides accredited Louisiana investors with a 50 percent tax credit divided into portions of 10 percent over five years on income or corporate franchise taxes owed to the state for "early-stage investments" and startups (LED 2006d).

Incentive packages target specific industries for development in the state as well. The Louisiana Film Tax Incentive Program provides a flat 25 percent tax credit for investments totaling $300,000 or more. The film industry incentive also provides a 10 percent credit for aggregate payroll in Louisiana and a 15 percent credit for infrastructure investments (e.g., new production facilities or studios) (LED 2006d). The Digital Media Tax Incentive Program targets developers in the video game industry with a 20 percent tax credit against expenditures for production and long-term infrastructure in the state (LED 2006d). These programs are part of the state's efforts to diversify the economy from traditional industries such as oil, gas, and petrochemicals.

There are also two corporate assistance programs available to qualified participants that target exemptions for a number of state and local sales, corporate, and franchise taxes, as well as other taxes when applicable. The Industry Assistance Program provides a tax exemption for manufacturers and their contractors that give preference to Louisiana manufacturers, suppliers, engineers, contractors, and labor, with special consideration for purchase and contract for machinery, supplies, and equipment manufactured and sold in Louisiana and used by the proposed tax-exempt facilities. The Industry Assistance Program is available to existing businesses with operating facilities in Louisiana that can demonstrate a commitment to maintaining current employment levels and making significant investment. The Tax Equalization Program helps attract and retain as well as encourage the expansion of manufacturing establishments, headquarters, and warehousing and distribution establishments that might not otherwise locate in Louisiana. The program eliminates the difference between the overall taxes for a Louisiana site and a competing site in another state. The sites under consideration must be valid and viable for the proposed operations, and the competing site must offer comparative advantages equal to or greater than those at the Louisiana site (LED 2006d).

Additionally, a number of policies associated with state economic development are linked to hurricane recovery efforts. The LRA has recently developed plans and received legislative approval for the bulk of the $10.4 billion in funding that Congress appropriated for Louisiana's recovery (LRA 2007). This funding includes programs for homeowner assistance (e.g., the Road Home Program), infrastructure redevelopment, and economic recovery. Legislative approval and federal authorization have facilitated implementation of many of these programs. According to recent reports (LRA 2006), approximately $350 million of the nearly $10.4 billion has been dedicated to economic development. Table 3 details the approved programs for economic development using Community Development Block Grants from the Department of Housing and Urban Development.

The first of these programs, the Bridge Loan Program, was intended to give businesses short-term financing while they awaited insurance payments or Small Business Association loans. This program was implemented in three phases beginning in fall 2005 and concluding in October 2006 (LRA 2006). When the Bridge Loan Program ended, the governor's office, along with the LRA and LED, reallocated $100 million of economic development disaster recovery funds to create a pilot program that would provide grants of up to $20,000 to approximately 3,400 small businesses (White 2007). The pilot program, the Business Recovery Grant and Loan Program (Box 1), affords grants

Table 3: LRA Economic Development Programs Budgets

Approved program	Community Development Block Grants
Louisiana Recovery Bridge Loan Program	95.0
Long Term Recovery Loan Guarantee Program	95.0
Louisiana Tourism Marketing Program	28.5
Technical Assistance to Small Firms Program	9.5
Business Recovery Grant and Loan Program	38.0
Recovery Workforce Training Program	38.0
Higher Education Research and Education Program	28.5
Administrative costs	17.5

Source: Louisiana Recovery Authority (2006).
Note: Amounts are expressed in millions of dollars.

and no-interest loans to help restart and sustain small and independent businesses in areas affected by the hurricanes. The pilot program began in January 2007, and disbursements took place in early April (White 2007). The Business Recovery Grant and Loan Program is managed by LED through a request for proposal (RFP) process similar to that implemented in New York City after September 11, 2001.

Additional funding for technical assistance in long-term recovery efforts is also available to firms. The Technical Assistance to Small Firms program provides such aid to entrepreneurs, small firms, and non-profits in the form of hands-on training. Also modeled after a New York City program, this program has a budget of $9.5 million and is managed by LED through an RFP process (LRA 2006). For firms affected by the hurricanes that are unable to obtain conventional loans due to risk or revenue problems, there is the Long Term Recovery Loan Program. The $95 million budgeted for the program guarantees low-interest loans or tax-exempt bonds, and it leverages approximately $550 million. Loans are underwritten and approved by local banks with a maximum of $1.5 million per loan for fixed assets, equipment, and working capital (LRA 2006).

The LRA has also emphasized revitalizing the tourism industry—the second-largest industry prior to the hurricane—as a key component of economic recovery (Kiel and Watson 2006; LRA 2006). In particular, the plan targets development of the once-vibrant leisure and convention tourism industries in the New Orleans area. The Department of Culture, Recreation, and Tourism manages $28.5 million for initiating a marketing and advertising campaign for the fastest-growing industry before Katrina. In addition, Community Development Block Grants are being used for the Tourism Recovery Program in regional areas and key agencies in New Orleans.

Funding workforce training and educational enhancement are additional priorities for the state's economic development plan. The Recovery Workforce Training Program anticipates training and placement needs for key economic sectors vital to recovery. Managed by the Louisiana Workforce Commission through RFPs, the program targets the needs of firms in industries such as construction, health care, advanced manufacturing, transportation, oil, gas, and tourism (LRA 2006). Funding is also a priority for the research capacities of universities adversely affected by the hurricanes. The Research Recovery and Educational Enhancement Program seeks to attract research talent and transfer the resulting technology to Louisiana businesses in affected areas (LRA 2006). Public- and private-sector cooperation has resulted in a strategic plan for the program administered through the state Board of Regents by an RFP process.

Finally, housing will be a key component of economic recovery for the state and affected areas, particularly New Orleans. The Road Home Program applies to residents impacted by the hurricanes, with policies encouraging repair and rebuilding of affordable rental units and development of mixed-income housing (LRA 2006). The governor, state legislature, and federal agencies have approved over $9 billion for Community Development Block Grants and the Hazard Mitigation Grant Program for homeowner assistance, workforce development and affordable housing, developer incentives, code enforcement, homeless shelter infrastructure and services, and other costs (LRA 2006). The infusion of such a large amount of funding will also affect industries related to housing construction.[4]

In view of the corruption in past state practices, careful attention has been paid to ensuring transparency and accountability in the recovery and rebuilding effort. The LRA has an audit committee that coordinates and disseminates information from the various units that monitor recovery spending. The Anti-Fraud Task Force, comprising federal and state agencies, is charged with auditing consumer, contractor/subcontractor, and application fraud (LRA 2006). The Legislative Auditor's Office is also monitoring recovery efforts, as are several private firms (e.g., KPMG and Deloitte and Touche) contracted through the state.

New Orleans Economic Development Policies

The City of New Orleans's economic development efforts have been spearheaded by Mayor Nagin's office, building on recommendations from the Bring Back New Orleans Commission and national associations such as the Urban Land Institute. Additionally, the state, through the LRA, is developing the *Unified New Orleans Plan* for bringing federal, state, and local agencies together to guide investment and rebuilding in the New Orleans area. Once completed, this infrastructure plan will be submitted to the City Planning Commission, the city council, and the mayor's office for review, and then it will go to the LRA for approval (*Unified New Orleans Plan* 2006). Whelan (2006) argues that although political wrangling has caused some divergence, common ground exists in two areas. First, all parties agree that recovery should be undertaken with a focus on sustainable development, avoiding past environmental incursions by the petrochemical, oil, and gas industries. Further, this sustainable development should include "smart growth" in the form of mass transit development. Second, all agree that recovery must concentrate on developing a more balanced economy and become less dependent on traditional industries such as petrochemical, oil, and gas industries.

In an attempt to capitalize on these common interests, the mayor's office unveiled a blueprint for recovery for the city, estimated to cost $1.1 billion in its first phase (Krupa and Donze 2007). The plan proposes to use public money to spur private investment in targeted zones, with $300 million for loans, grants, and other incentives aimed at encouraging entrepreneurs and developers in key industries. Funding relies on bonding and state grants, along with the Federal Emergency Management Agency financing most of the plan. The mayor's plan has been received warmly by state and local officials, but it depends on the federal government waiving the 10 percent local jurisdiction match of funds for infrastructure projects financed by the Federal Emergency Management Agency ("A Waiver for New Orleans" 2007).[5]

Future Prospects

Although economic recovery has begun and there are positive signs, much remains to be done. Political squabbling has been an issue throughout the recovery process, stalling the implementation of the housing recovery effort. As of February 2007, only 258 checks totaling $14.4 million had been issued by the state. By contrast, the state of Mississippi had issued 11,827 checks totaling $665 million (Scott 2007, 81). Louisiana's Road Home Program has received scathing criticism from federal authorities for sluggish allocation of housing funds to homeowners (Scott and Moller 2007). These problems proved to be the undoing of Gov. Kathleen Blanco, who did not seek reelection in fall 2007. As of January 2008, nearly half of the Road Home applicants were still waiting to receive grants (Brookings Institution Metropolitan Policy Program 2008).

Greater cooperation among the various levels of government in Louisiana will be the key to recovery. The political skirmishes of the past couple years have slowed the pace of recovery in the state and affected regions, especially in comparison with regional efforts elsewhere (Scott 2007). Collaboration is crucial not only for recovery but for recruiting new industry and sustaining local businesses—and for keeping both competitive. But this competitive economic sector cannot come at the cost of Louisiana's future streams of revenue. While these initiatives offer a number of tax incentives for attracting and sustaining business in the area, their long-term impact on the state's tax base is uncertain.

Recently, the state has been enjoying an exceptional budget surplus that is to be dedicated toward improvements in education and infrastructure (Scott and Moller 2007). These investments are sure to improve the state's economic well-being, but more research is needed to assess the contribution of these new incentives to economic development, especially in comparison with other states in the region affected by the hurricanes. Given these unprecedented economic development policies, businesses may remain hesitant to set up shop in an area that is still struggling to recover amid the politics that have characterized the state and New Orleans MSA.

A promising sign, however, is the recovery of the Port of New Orleans to pre-Katrina activity levels. The Port of New Orleans is not only vital to the state's recovery but also a crucial port of entry for the nation's imports (Port of New Orleans 2006; Scott 2007). The Port of New Orleans's cargo activity supported $37 billion in economic benefits to the country and generated $2.8 billion in federal tax revenue in 2005 (Friedman 2005). By 2006, the port had regained 100 percent of cargo ship calls, well above industry estimates (Port of New Orleans 2006). In fact, the port exceeded its five-year average by 4 percent for 2006 (Port of New Orleans 2007). The importance of the Port of New Orleans to the state's recovery efforts was reiterated by the port's president and CEO, Gary Lagrange: "One thing that we all learned from Hurricane Katrina is that everything is connected. . . . This city's future, the state's future and this port's future are all intertwined" (Port of New Orleans 2006).

While Louisiana and the Gulf Coast region continue recovery efforts following the natural disasters of 2005, there is much to be learned from the experience thus far. Although the final impact of the economic recovery legislation is not yet known, it should serve as a boilerplate for future disaster recovery efforts. For Louisiana, economic recovery has been challenging, especially given the political wrangling among politicians and public managers at the state and local levels. Future recovery efforts must get past the political process in order to expedite much-needed support in the hardest-hit areas. The lessons drawn from this case study highlight the need for well-planned efforts that can be carried out collaboratively among public, private, and nonprofit entities. Recent scholarship has underscored the importance of collaborative public management for solving societies' most critical problems (Agranoff and McGuire 1999; 2001; Milward and Provan 2000; O'Toole 1997). To the extent that federal, state, and local officials can collaborate in putting together well-thought-out plans to advance economic recovery in the wake of national catastrophes, the better off susceptible communities will be.

Notes

1. Only 26 percent of homeowners in Louisiana had flood insurance (Scott 2007).

2. Thirty-seven parishes in the Katrina and/or Rita zones of Louisiana are designated by the GO Zone Act as warranting individual or public assistance (LED 2007).

3. GO Zone Bonds may be issued by the State of Louisiana or any of its political subdivisions, including statewide issuers and local public trust or industrial development boards. All bonds must be recommended by the LED and approved by the governor and the Louisiana State Bond Commission. See gozoneguide.com.

4. The state and respective federal agencies have also approved funding for infrastructure and hazard mitigation totaling $2.3 billion. While not covered in this chapter, this funding nonetheless will have an economic impact on related industries as well.

5. According to Nossiter (2007), $324 million of the $1.1 billion recovery plan is contingent upon Congress waiving the 10 percent match. Bonds already approved by city residents would make up $260 million, and a new bond sale based on selling city property holdings to developers would bring in another $300 million. The city is asking the state for further assistance in funding the plan (Krupa 2007).

References

Agranoff, Robert, and Michael McGuire. 1999. Managing in network settings. *Policy Studies Review* 16:18–41.

_____ . 2001. Big questions in public network management research. *Journal of Public Administration Research and Theory* 11:295–326.

Associated Press. 2008. *Louisiana posts strong personal income growth*. March 27. blog.nola.com/tpmoney/2008/03/la_posts_strong_personal_incom.html. Accessed April 10.

Brookings Institution Metropolitan Policy Program. 2006. *Special edition of the Katrina index: A one-year review of the key indicators of recovery in post-storm New Orleans.* www3.brookings.edu/metro/pubs/20060822_KatrinaES.pdf. Accessed March 21, 2007.

_____ . 2007. 2008. *The Katrina index: Tracking recovery of New Orleans and the metro area.* www.gnocdc.org/KI/KatrinaIndex.pdf. Accessed April 12, 2007; April 10 and 16, 2008.

Chang, S. 1984. Do disaster areas benefit from disasters? *Growth and Change* 15: 24–31.

Friedman, G. 2005. *New Orleans: A geopolitical prize*. www.stratfor.com/news/archive/050903-geopolitics_katrina.php. Accessed March 30, 2007.

Jurkiewicz, C. J., ed. 2007. Administrative failure in the wake of Katrina. *Public Administration Review* 67 (special issue): 1–212.

Kiel, L. D., and D. J. Watson. 2006. Introduction: Focus section on natural disasters and economic development. *Economic Development Quarterly* 20:208–10.

Krupa, M. 2007. N.O. asking state to chip in on plan; road projects among priorities for legislature. *Times-Picayune*, April 5, 1.

Krupa, M., and F. Donze. 2007. Leaders stand united behind recovery plan; blueprint addresses fears of abandonment. *Times-Picayune*, March 30, 1.

Lenze, David G. 2006. *Personal income for metropolitan areas 2005*. Washington, DC: U.S. Bureau of Economic Analysis.

Louisiana Economic Development. 2003. *Restoration Tax Abatement: The facts.* www.led.louisiana.gov/uploads/pdf/RTA%20Fact%207-04.pdf. Accessed March 23, 2007.

_____ . 2006a. *The Gulf Opportunity Zone (GO Zone) Act of 2005: Louisiana economic impact.* www.lded.state.la.us/uploads/pdf/GulfOpportunityZoneActof 2005.pdf. Accessed April 3, 2007.

_____ . 2006b. *Industrial property tax exemption: The facts.* www.lded.state. la.us/uploads/docs/ITEP%20The%20Facts%2010-2006.doc. Accessed March 23, 2007.

_____ . 2006c. *The Louisiana Gulf Opportunity Zone business guide.* gozone guide.com. Accessed March 23, 2007.

_____ . 2006d. *The official guide to doing business in Louisiana.* www.business guidela.com/incentives.html. Accessed March 23, 2007.

_____ . 2006e. *Quality Jobs Program: The facts.* www.lded.state.la.us/uploads/ docs/QJ%20Facts.doc. Accessed March 23, 2007.

_____ . 2007. *Enterprise Zone Program: The facts.* www.lded.state.la.us/ uploads/docs/2007%20EZ%20Facts.doc. Accessed March 23.

Louisiana Recovery Authority. 2006. *Presentation to the Joint Steering and Executive Committees on Disaster Planning, Crisis Management, Recovery and Revitalization.* www.lra.louisiana.gov/assets/SelectCmtePresentation102306.pdf. Accessed March 21, 2007.

Milward, H. Brinton, and Keith G. Provan. 2000. Governing the hollow state. *Journal of Public Administration Research and Theory* 10:359–80.

Nossiter, A. 2007. New Orleans proposes to invest in 17 areas. *The New York Times*, March 30, A16.

O'Toole, Laurence J., Jr. 1997. Treating networks seriously: Practical and research-based agendas in public administration. *Public Administration Review* 57: 45–52.

Port of New Orleans. 2006. *Lagrange looks to future, cites recovery milestones in annual address.* 63.243.21.112:8083/prsrel021506.pdf. Accessed March 21, 2007.

_____ . 2007. *2006 cargo figures illustrate fast-paced recovery.* 63.243.21.112: 8083/prsrel032807.pdf. Accessed March 30.

Richardson, James A. 2006. *What's needed for post-Katrina recovery.* www.fsround. org/publications/pdfs/RichardsonStudy-FINAL.pdf. Accessed March 23, 2007.

Scott, L. C. 2007. *Advancing in the aftermath IV: Tracking the recovery from Katrina and Rita.* www.lorenscottassociates.com/Reports/AdvancingInTheAftermath.pdf. Accessed April 12.

Scott, R. T., and J. Moller. 2007. Road Home snag broke Blanco; It was "final straw" in series of setbacks. *Times Picayune National*, March 22. factiva.com. Accessed April 22, 2008.

Skidmore, M., and Toya, H. 2002. Do natural disasters promote long-run growth? *Economic Inquiry* 40:664–87.

Unified New Orleans Plan. 2006. www.willdoo-storage.com/Plans/CityWide/UNOPexecsum.pdf. Accessed April 3, 2007.

"A waiver for New Orleans." 2007. *The Washington Post*, April 1, B6.

Waugh, W. L., Jr., and R. B. Smith. 2006. Economic development and reconstruction on the Gulf after Katrina. *Economic Development Quarterly* 20:211–18.

Webb, G. R., K. T. Tierney, and J. M. Dahlhamer. 2002. Predicting long-term business recovery from disaster: A comparison of the Loma Prieta earthquake and Hurricane Andrew. *Environmental Hazards* 4:45–58.

Whelan, R. K. 2006. An old economy for the "new" New Orleans? Post-Hurricane Katrina economic development efforts. In *There is no such thing as a natural disaster: Race, class, and Hurricane Katrina*, ed. C. Hartman and G. D. Squires, 215–31. New York: Routledge.

White, J. 2007. Grant checks disbursed to small business owners; about 200 collect checks under state program. *Times-PicayuneMoney*, April 19, 1.

CHAPTER 11

A New Stadium, A New City:
The Dallas Cowboys' Quest for a New Playing Field

Kimberly Aaron

The appeal of professional sports can be characterized by the "thrill of victory" and the "agony of defeat." Cities endure similar thrills and agonies as they compete with one another to attract major league football teams and the economic development opportunities generally associated with them. However, the outcomes in the economic development game are not as absolute as on-the-field wins and losses. Whether a city's "thrill" will be worth the investment is not always clear in the short run. Other development opportunities may be sacrificed to meet the demand for public resources that comes with the development of major league stadiums.

In November 2004, voters in Arlington, Texas, approved a $325 million proposal for the city to partner with the Dallas Cowboys football franchise in the development and construction of a football stadium that would be the new home for the team. This vote ended years of speculation regarding whether the Cowboys would remain at Texas Stadium in Irving, Texas, their home field since October 1971, or seek a greener playing field in North Texas.

Jerry Jones, the owner of the Cowboys franchise, shook up Texas football in 1989 when he acquired the Cowboys and immediately fired long-time coach Tom Landry. Jones's ownership of the Cowboys began with controversy, and controversy has been the hallmark of his ownership as the team has gone through players and coaches and experienced successes and failures on the field. Controversy continued as the franchise began actively looking for a new home in 2003. The lease at Texas Stadium, owned by the City of Irving, would be expiring, and Jones had set a goal to be playing in a new stadium within five years.

This case study examines the events that led to the team's selection of Arlington as the home for its new stadium.

Sports Facilities, Public Subsidies, and Economic Development Opportunities

The conclusions from research regarding the benefits to cities of professional sports franchises vary as much as the opinions of government officials and citizens on the subject. For every researcher who can identify both tangible and intangible benefits, another can delineate equally compelling disadvantages to local communities. Regardless, major league sports are big business, and the stadiums in which they play are part of that business. As early as 1974, Noll identified that government policy provides the sports industry with a special status and plays a "crucial role in shaping the business by permitting restrictions on market competition, enacting tax policies that [allow] sports franchises to be tax shelters, and providing facilities at rents significantly below costs" (1974, vii).

Privately built stadiums are becoming more uncommon as the public sector funds more sports facilities with sales taxes and property taxes or special taxes such as those assessed on hotel rooms, car rentals, and tobacco sales (Swindell and Rosentraub 1998). According to Keating (1999), more than $20 billion has been spent on stadiums, with approximately $14.7 billion of that amount attributable to tangible government subsidies. An economist with the Federal Reserve Bank of St. Louis estimated that "between $14 billion and $16 billion is expected to be spent on post-1999 stadiums and arenas, with somewhere between $9 billion and $11 billion of this amount coming from public coffers" (Zaretsky 2001, 1).

According to Swindell and Rosentraub (1998, 12), public officials support the development of stadiums because they believe that these facilities "(1) generate economic growth through high levels of new spending in a region, (2) create a large number of jobs, (3) revitalize declining central business districts, and (4) change land-use patterns." However, they conclude from their research that "sports teams and the facilities they use produce very limited economic benefits," with players and owners being the prime beneficiaries of the public investment (1998, 19). Baade's (1994, 2) conclusion from his brief review of the literature, supported by his own empirical research, is that there is "no factual basis for the conventional argument that professional sports stadiums and teams have a significant impact on a region's economic growth."

Countering the argument of sports naysayers is Santo's (2005) finding that a positive relationship exists between the presence of sports stadiums and regional income. Carlino and Coulson (2004) also conclude that professional sports franchises can be "good investments" when considering the quality-of-life attributes associated with the franchises, such as civic pride. Further, they posit that higher quality of life leads to higher rents in the cities that have National Football League (NFL) teams. Swindell and Rosentraub (1998) are skeptical of arguments that consider the value of intangible benefits such as "civic pride." Their research indicates that fans value such benefits more highly than the public at large, who pays for the stadium. While Baade and Dye (2001, 13) are willing to acknowledge that intangible benefits exist, they believe that "tangible economic grounds" must be used to justify public funding.

An advocate of stadium development, Chema (1996) believes that existing research may have limited application because it focuses on nonurban facilities that are set apart from a concentrated city infrastructure. He states that development strategies, including the formation of a sports team or establishment of a sports venue, "can and will provide significant economic value" to a city when it is "part of a critical mass of attractions designed to lure people into the urban core" (Chema 1996, 20). Interestingly, Chema cites Arlington as an exception to a trend for successful ballparks being located in "urban settings" (1996, 20). In his work with Austrian (2002, 561), Rosentraub—generally critical of sports facility development—concedes that "some level of development activity" was refocused in the downtown areas of the two cities that were the subject of the authors' research when the sports facilities were part of a larger hospitality development.

Rich (1998) observes that as stadium development grows, its demand on public resources increases. Johnson and Frey (1985, 219) state that since 1980 "more than half of the cities with sports franchises have been confronted by the owners . . . with demands for increased subsidies." However, if there is so much disagreement over the benefits of such development, why are cities willing to allow this drain on public funds to attract and retain sports franchises? Political thinking still relies on the premise that sports facilities build a city's reputation and drive economic development. Regardless of research to the contrary, expenditures have been "rationalized" on the premise that professional sports teams stimulate economies and create jobs (Baade 1996). In their analysis of the justification of sports investments in North America and Europe, Gratton, Shibli, and Coleman (2005) determined that cities have had an easy time of "selling" investments in sports to voters by citing an economic development strategy that depends on attracting tourists to the area. In an editorial referencing the U.S. sports experience, Thornby (2002, 814) remarks on the importance of "mega-events" in city marketing that "raise the profile of a city . . . and promote tourism."

Yet, questions arise when public money generates profits for team owners and athletes. Zaretsky (2001) believes that sports teams are not good investments for cities. Baade and Dye (2001) suggest that the competition among cities as they vie for teams pushes up public funding, resulting in the long-term prospect of reduced income to the city that "wins" the economic contest. Swindell and Rosentraub (1998) observe that the work of many policy analysts suggests that the projected economic returns associated with stadium development are optimistic at best, while Keating (1999, 1) states that "the lone beneficiaries of sports subsidies are team owners and players." This disparity of perceptions and opinions on the benefits of public investments in sports facilities had a significant effect on the route the Cowboys took to their new stadium location.

A New Stadium for the Cowboys

Texas is a state that takes football seriously. Starting with Pee Wee Football associations, children are indoctrinated into the sport, both as participants and observers. The love of the sport continues from elementary school through high school and into college. Although there are a multitude of favored teams in the state, in the 1970s and 1980s, Texas had one professional football team that was claimed by the nation: the Dallas Cowboys, dubbed American's Team.

In 1960, the NFL awarded an expansion franchise to Clint Murchison Jr. and Bedford Wynne. The new franchise was named the Dallas Cowboys. Games were played in the 76,000-seat Cotton Bowl stadium at Fair Park in southeastern Dallas. Fair Park is a 227-acre area owned by the City of Dallas that houses museums, performance halls, and recreational facilities. It also is home to the Cotton Bowl Classic football game and the State Fair of Texas. The Cotton Bowl stadium was built in 1930 and became known as Fair Park Stadium. The stadium was renovated in 1936, and additions were made in 1948, 1949, and 1993. Today the stadium has approximately 68,000 permanent seats. The Cowboys' first sell-out game at the Cotton Bowl was in 1965.

In 1967, the Cowboys announced plans to build Texas Stadium in Irving, Texas, a western suburb of Dallas. The new stadium, which would be exclusively for the team's use, was projected to be ready by 1970 and would be financed through a bond option plan. The actual ground breaking on the stadium occurred in 1969, and the first game was played in 1971. In 1984, the Cowboys announced that they were moving their headquarters operations and training facility to Valley Ranch, an area in North Irving. The following year, Murchison sold the team to an 11-member limited partnership headed by Bum Bright. In

1985, improvements were made to Texas Stadium, and the new head-quarters and training facility opened.

Considering the tradition of local ownership, some Texans were surprised when Jerry Jones acquired the Cowboys in 1989. Like many Texans, Jones had made his fortune in oil and gas (but in Oklahoma) and he loved football. He had played college football in Arkansas, where he lived at the time he acquired the Cowboys franchise. Jones had a reputation as a tough, successful businessman. His decisions and actions as owner of the Cowboys furthered that reputation as the team made changes on and off the field.

A Tale of Two Cities

The Site

Jones began to signal his interest in upgrading Texas Stadium in 1996 when he suggested that Irving pull out of the Dallas Area Rapid Transit system so that the one-cent sales tax on the system could be saved for later use in refurbishing Texas Stadium. The City of Irving, with its proximity to the Dallas–Fort Worth Airport, did not want to miss an opportunity to participate in rail development that would eventually provide connections to the large international airport. Stadium talk quieted until 2003, when Jones began actively looking for a new home for the Cowboys.

In August 2003, local media reports announced that the Cowboys would meet with the Dallas City Council early in September to discuss the possible construction of a new stadium. Jones indicated that he might be willing to leave Irving and build a state-of-the-art stadium in Dallas with the right incentives. County commissioners in Dallas were particularly interested in the discussion, as the county has the power to raise public cash through increases in hotel and rental car taxes countywide. Site speculation focused on a location in downtown Dallas near the Trinity River where two major interstates intersected.

Speculation continued through the end of the year regarding the likelihood that the Cowboys would remain in Irving or move back to their namesake city. Mayor Laura Miller of Dallas expressed concern regarding the recent opening of the Gaylord Texan Hotel in Grapevine, a northern suburb (Levinthal 2003). The Gaylord Texan Hotel offered state-of-the-art convention facilities that could accommodate up to 5,000 guests. Since its opening, Dallas's hotel occupancy rate had dropped below 55 percent. Miller was concerned that voters might resist the funding of a stadium rumored to cost $1 billion through an increase in hotel taxes when the occupancy rates of Dallas hotels were dropping.

Early in 2004, Jones invited the mayors of almost every city in Dallas County to Valley Ranch. At that time, Jones unveiled the concept for the new stadium, with costs estimated at $650 million. Jones's expectation was that increases in hotel and rental car taxes would fund development costs. Several attendees expressed concerns about traffic congestion in the downtown Dallas area. A few business leaders echoed Mayor Miller's earlier concerns regarding the effect an increase in hotel and rental car taxes would have on Dallas's convention business. Mary Kay, one of Dallas's largest corporations, sent a letter to the Dallas Convention and Visitors Bureau indicating that if hotel taxes were to increase, the company would stop holding some of its regular meetings in the city. The Convention and Visitors Bureau endorsed the stadium complex as a way to revitalize downtown Dallas but did not necessarily support financing it with the hotel tax. Mayor Miller stated her opposition to the tax hike, and Dallas County Judge Margaret Kelleher suggested taxing users of the new stadium to fund the development project. While some individuals and organizations expressed their reservations about the project, many others appeared to see it as an economic boon. The team's managers hoped that a final agreement on the stadium would be in place by the spring and that the issue would be placed on the ballot for the November elections.

The first public meeting on the stadium development was held early in February 2004. On the same day, the Cowboys issued a statement indicating that they were looking forward to starting the negotiation process with the leaders of the City of Dallas and Dallas County and optimistically stated that the project could be a "win-win" for Dallas County, its citizens, and the Cowboys. The local hotel association was skeptical, however, that the projected returns on the project would be adequate for everyone, particularly as the Cowboys had not presented detailed plans for the development. While the county commissioners, who had critical taxation powers, wished to see the plan before they could identify the sources of funding, they also wanted to gain approval from the state legislature to raise more funds. The team's managers intended to reveal the detailed plans in the next few weeks. Meanwhile, Irving officials made overtures to the Cowboys in an effort to retain the franchise in the city. An Irving city council member stated that his city would not get out of the stadium business quietly and noted that about $100 million was earmarked for a new convention center that could be used for a stadium. Further, Irving could increase its own hotel tax without involving the county commissioners in the process.

By mid-February, the Cowboys were making it known that a downtown Dallas location or Las Colinas, an upscale commercial and residential area of Irving, were preferred sites for the new stadium. The team's representatives were making the rounds at city and county offices, trying to build support for the stadium project. Team representatives also met with Dallas officials at Fair Park for a tour and general discussion. The mayor and some city council members were pushing a return to the Fair Park location and the Cotton Bowl stadium for the Cowboys instead of the downtown location. The city had estimated the costs to develop the industrial site near downtown Dallas at a little over $200 million. Fair Park would require less public investment. From managers' perspective, for Fair Park to be a viable location, it would need to persuade not only the county to ask for a vote on taxes and fees but also Mayor Miller and the city council to create a tax increment financing district to plow newly generated tax funds back into the complex. Further, team officials were concerned that Fair Park would allow them to build a stadium only, with no room for additional development.

Finally, the city needed to persuade those who lived in Fair Park that it would be good for them to have the Cowboys as their next-door neighbors. While some citizens believed the Cowboys would be good for the community, others believed residents could lose their homes to the development and that the traffic congestion in the area would become unmanageable. Irving city council members welcomed this shift in potential locations for the stadium within Dallas, contending that it made the case for keeping the Cowboys in Irving stronger. Irving's belief was that eliminating the downtown site made the renovation of Texas Stadium a better alternative.

Funding

By the end of February, county commissioners in Dallas were under increasing pressure to rely on a source in addition to the higher hotel and car rental taxes to pay for the stadium. The primary alternative was a ticket tax, but voters might view such a tax unfavorably. Voters in Houston had voted down a ticket tax for a new basketball arena in 1999.

A more challenging obstacle was that the county commissioners and city council members in Dallas could not agree on a location or a funding approach. While many commissioners and council members supported the Fair Park location, Commissioner John Wiley Price, a controversial and influential political figure, said that he would oppose the Cowboys at Fair Park because he believed a massive redevelopment plan would not fit into Fair Park. Without the additional development generating sales tax revenue and property tax revenue, little long-term economic stimulus would result. In an attempt to gain a better understanding of the development opportunity, the county commissioners hired lawyers, financial advisors, and underwriters to assist in their evaluation and guide plans. They also requested that the Cowboys reimburse them for the costs they would incur in performing an evaluation.

The Cowboys aggressively promoted the idea of return to Dallas. In March, the team sent a mailer to 100,000 Dallas County voters touting the Cowboys and emphasizing Jones's goal to bring the Super Bowl and the NCAA finals to Dallas. Initial cost estimates for the development included a $600 million stadium, with another $400 million for additional development including hotels, shops, team museums, and public fields. Meanwhile, the City of Dallas revealed a proposed economic development strategy calling for the protection of Fair Park's existing assets for reinvestment. As a part of this strategy, some areas within Fair Park would become tax increment financing districts. In an effort organized by Mayor Pro Tem Don Hill, local civic leaders met at City Hall in an attempt to put together a deal that would bring the Cowboys to Fair Park. Adding support to the initiative, the Board of the Cotton Bowl Classic called for the construction of the team's new stadium at Fair Park.

While Dallas city and county officials were debating among themselves, Irving officials continued to believe that because of the relationship the city had with the Cowboys, they were in the catbird's seat. Irving had two options: a Las Colinas location or the renovation of Texas Stadium. However, like the county commissioners and city council members in Dallas, Irving city officials could not agree on which site would be the best location and how far the city should go to retain the franchise. Irving's mayor estimated the price to renovate Texas Stadium at about $225 million. While the Las Colinas location (which was available for sale) would be a more costly alternative, it would provide space for additional development. City officials believed that such development could be financed through naming rights, user fees, or an increase in hotel taxes. In addition, Irving could offer as much as $60 million in infrastructure funds at the Las Colinas site through tax increment financing. However, Irving's mayor, like Mayor Miller, said that while he wanted to keep the Cowboys, the city was not willing to pay any price to do so. At any rate, Cowboys management appeared committed to finding a new address for the team's playing field.

By mid-March, negotiations between Dallas County officials and the Cowboys had ground to a halt over money. The Cowboys refused to reimburse the county for the costs of the lawyers, financial advisors, and consultants who were supporting the county in the negotiations. County officials wanted a guarantee before discussions continued that the county would be reimbursed. Regardless of this apparent stalemate, the Cowboys continued to investigate the Fair Park location, looking at various sites and discussing scheduling conflicts with the State Fair. By late March, a major hurdle was cleared when the Cowboys agreed to reimburse the county up to $500,000 for legal and consulting fees incurred during negotiations. With this issue behind them, Cowboys management thought it could announce a site for the stadium as early as April—Fair Park, the downtown Dallas location, or Las Colinas—and put the proposal on the November ballot. At that time, a Cowboys spokesperson stated that no site had been ruled out and no one site was ahead of the other. Dallas officials, with the exception of Commissioner Price, were pushing for Fair Park.

After a couple of quiet months, Mayor Miller, Jones, and other Cowboys officials met in June to discuss further the Fair Park location. At that time, the mayor told Cowboys management that Dallas would not pay for half of the stadium. Shortly after this meeting, it was announced that the Cowboys had terminated stadium development discussions with the City of Dallas, Cowboys officials having concluded that productive negotiations were not possible. Dallas officials said that the Cowboys never provided requested financial information and were forcing city and county officials to make their decision too quickly. Meanwhile, Irving did not have the financial resources to develop the stadium that the Cowboys had envisioned.

The Road to Arlington

Shortly after the Cowboys terminated discussions with Dallas, the team announced that it had agreed to negotiate exclusively with Arlington. Arlington, located in Tarrant County, is home to the Ballpark in Arlington, the playing field for the Texas Rangers baseball team. The Ballpark sits next to the Six Flags over Texas amusement park on a major thoroughfare. Arlington took advantage of Dallas's flagging momentum to promote its existing entertainment attractions and its experience in working with the Texas Rangers. The negotiations with Arlington were to continue until August—the deadline for placing proposed tax increases on the November ballot. This action caught Dallas and Irving by surprise. Dallas business executives, including members of the Dallas Citizens Council, attempted to negotiate with the Cowboys directly but had little success as they did not have the power to initiate stadium funding. Some Dallas city council members urged the mayor to kickstart negotiations unilaterally. Business leaders and council members felt that Dallas had not done what it needed to in order to strike a deal with the team. One council member characterized Dallas as not having a strategy for dealing with the Cowboys. Meanwhile, Irving officials reiterated their interest in keeping the team and indicated that they would like to enter into negotiations if discussions with Arlington faltered.

Negotiations with Arlington moved quickly. Facing an August 18 deadline, the Arlington city council met in a closed session early in the month to create the first draft of a master agreement with the

Cowboys. A mailer was sent to every house in Arlington with a registered voter promoting the Cowboys and the possibilities of attracting a Superbowl game, the NCAA finals, the Cotton Bowl Classics football game, and the high-drawing University of Texas–Oklahoma University (Texas-OU) football game, known as the Red River Shoot-Out. At this time, officials in Arlington were awaiting a cost-benefit study from Economics Research Association that would assess the economic impact that the new stadium would have on the city and had not yet decided whether to place the stadium issue on the November ballot. The council was considering increasing hotel and car rental taxes to a legal limit of 15 percent from 13 percent and 10 percent, respectively, and raising sales tax from 7.5 percent to the 8 percent legal limit. The Irving city council, in an attempt to remain a player in the negotiations, instructed city officials to approach county commissioners in Dallas about building the stadium in Irving.

By the second week in August, the study by the Economics Research Association had been reviewed, and Arlington officials and the Cowboys announced that they had agreed on all major aspects of the deal. The city council passed a resolution outlining details of the financing plan. The resolution would need to go to the state comptroller's office before it could be presented to voters, but this requirement was perceived to be a formality. The agreed-upon costs to Arlington were $325 million to be paid for with the tax increases, as well as user taxes that included a $3 tax on the parking fee at the stadium and a tax of up to 10 percent on each ticket sold. The Cowboys would pay any cost overruns and rent to the city of $2 million per year starting in 2009, when the 90,000-seat stadium would be completed. Arlington would also receive 5 percent from the naming rights on the stadium, up to $500,000 per year. The team's charities would spend $16.5 million over the life of the agreement on athletic fields for youth and other youth education programs in the city. The agreement would run for 30 years with options for two 10-year extensions. Arlington would use its powers of eminent domain as necessary to acquire the land, budgeted for $42 million.

Arlington city council members believed that the economic benefit of constructing the stadium justified sending the proposal to the voters. The cost-benefit study estimated that the proposal would generate $238 million annually in spending in the city and would result in an estimated gain of 807 long-term jobs averaging $38,000 per year. Tarrant County would see $416 million more in revenue annually and the creation of 1,940 ongoing jobs. One-time construction impacts were projected at $72 million for Arlington and $349 million for Tarrant

County. The estimated increase in tax dollars flowing into Arlington's general fund would be about $1.8 million to $2.9 million depending on how many extra events were scheduled in the stadium. The projected tax revenues were significant to Arlington, as the city was projecting a $16 million deficit for the year starting in October and needed to rejuvenate itself.

While most Arlington city council members liked the Economics Research Association's report, outside analysts felt the report overestimated the stadium's impact (Getz, Mosier, and Yip 2004). In addition, there was one obvious error in the study: it identified the Houston Oilers as playing in Reliant Stadium in Houston. The Oilers moved to Tennessee in 1997, and the Texans had played in Reliant Stadium since 2002. This error, though not having a direct effect on the financial projections, cast doubt on the integrity of the report. Further, although the analysis was prepared for the City of Arlington, the Cowboys had provided many of the assumptions on which the consultants had based their financial projections. These assumptions included estimations regarding the number of events (e.g., concerts, festivals, and other sporting events) that would occur each year, parking demand, and increases in ticket prices, as well as forecasts regarding income from concessions. However, the members of the Arlington city council did not let any concerns regarding potential bias in the team's assumptions influence their decision to move forward.

In response to Arlington's announcement, the Dallas city council urged the mayor to create a Cowboys stadium task force. Officials said that if the deal fell through with Arlington, they might be willing to pick up the pieces but not with the financial package that Arlington was offering. The Dallas mayor said that the meeting with Jones earlier in the summer had made it clear to her that the Cowboys were going to find a town that would pay for a significant amount of the stadium. She continued to hold the position that Dallas was not going to pay for half of the project. Meanwhile, Irving city council members were wondering if their city should have been more forceful in efforts to retain the Cowboys. City officials were hoping that the Arlington stadium referendum would fail. With seemingly blind optimism, they indicated that they wanted to continue to consider pursuing stadium development in Las Colinas. However, the Irving mayor suspected that communications between the city and the Cowboys had been limited because the Cowboys did not believe that Irving could raise sufficient funds. Irving's sales tax was at its maximum, and increasing the hotel tax would generate only about $80 million. Irving would have to partner with Dallas County to raise money. Managers' discussions with the county had fared little better than their conversations with the City of Dallas.

Shortly after the announcement was made that a tentative agreement had been struck between Arlington and the Cowboys, the Arlington city council formally approved the master agreement in an 8-1 vote. They also agreed unanimously to put the proposed tax increases to a referendum vote in November. Only one city council member expressed reservations about the master agreement because of the assumptions in the economic report and the lack of empirical data.

Reaching the Goal

With optimism high, speculation began to develop regarding the Cowboys project. In October, a deal was announced among the Cowboys, the Rangers, and Southwest Sports Realty for a sports and entertainment center. On the same day, Mark Rosentraub, dean of the College of Urban Affairs at Cleveland State University and an expert on the economic impacts of financing sports facilities, released the results of his own study of the deal (Giddons 2004). In his report, Rosentraub contended that the Cowboys-Arlington agreement did not make sense and appeared to be built on flawed public and economic policy. Rosentraub estimated that the deal would end up costing Arlington $290 million over the next 30 years. As a result of his research with Swindell, Rosentraub advocated that investments of public funds in sports facilities be limited to special tax districts adjacent to the facilities so that those individuals and entities benefiting directly from the facility would be paying the bulk of the fees and taxes (Swindell and Rosentraub 1998). Offering a slightly different perspective from Rosentraub, the Texas Comptroller's office released a study saying that a Superbowl in Arlington in 2011 would add $419 million to the state's economy; however, the study did not include information regarding the amount that would go to Arlington.

As expected, Arlington voters approved stadium funding with 55 percent of the vote. The victory was credited to not only a strong pro-stadium campaign (that as of the end of October had spent $4.6 million) but also the unified front presented by the city council. Arlington was now looking forward to welcoming professional football and hopeful that additional tourist draws such as the Superbowl, NCAA finals, and other college sporting events would follow.

Meanwhile, Dallas officials said that they were committed to keeping college sports events at the Cotton Bowl stadium in Fair Park. The State Fair of Texas president expressed no concerns, saying he had a "gentlemen's agreement" with the Cowboys that the team would not pursue the Texas-OU game unless Dallas failed to renovate the Cotton Bowl. Cowboy officials responded that they were unaware of such an agreement; luring the Texas-OU game was part of the pitch to persuade

Arlington voters to approve the tax increase needed to pay for the stadium. The Arlington mayor said that the city would try to get any events that it could.

Arlington's vision for the new Cowboys stadium development was taking off. At the time of this writing, the 100,000-seat Cowboys stadium is scheduled to open for the 2009 season. Early in 2007, former Cowboys star quarterback Roger Staubach was named chair of the North Texas Superbowl XLV Bid Committee. The group, in an effort endorsed by the Dallas city council, is working to persuade the NFL to choose the new Cowboys stadium in Arlington as the site for the 2011 Superbowl. Shortly after the Staubach announcement, the Cotton Bowl Athletic Association voted to move the Cotton Bowl Classic football game to the new stadium in 2010. However, not everyone is stadium switching: the Texas-OU football game will remain at Fair Park's Cotton Bowl stadium at least through 2015.

Conclusion

Thornby (2002) suggests that to attract sports franchises, cities need to be focused in their efforts, have coalitions that can work together, and have the ability to respond to tight deadlines rather than be caught up in controversies over financial arrangements. Arlington's united front and quick response to the team's overtures signaled to voters that city leadership was serious about the opportunity to bring the Cowboys to the city, and voters responded favorably by approving funding for the stadium. Dallas city and county officials were never able to agree on any of the key issues they faced in attracting the team to its namesake city. Irving probably never had a decent shot at retaining the Cowboys. As Rich (1998, 2) posits, there is "little a city can do" to prevent a team from leaving once its owners have made the decision to relocate, and the Cowboys appeared to be looking for greener grass on which to play.

Disagreements exist over whether the failure of Dallas to build effective coalitions meant a missed opportunity or a dodged bullet. Whether Dallas and Irving suffer because of their inability to attract or retain the team will not be apparent for several years. As Rosentraub (2006) acknowledges, the taxpayers ultimately determine the value of professional sports stadiums. For the Dallas Cowboys, the citizens of Arlington made the decision in their favor, but whether Arlington will actually be the "winner" in this costly development game is yet to be determined. Development has experienced a slower start-up than expected, and as of early February 2007, 75 eminent domain challenges related to the land acquisition were pending in Tarrant County courts.

With the benefits of sports facilities accruing on a regional level, the "losing" cities of Dallas and Irving may continue to reap the benefits of the Cowboys' presence in North Texas without having had to make the investment needed to attract or retain the team. Baade (1994) emphasizes that officials should consider the "opportunity costs" of forgoing other development options when subsidizing a sports facility. In the November 2006 elections, the City of Dallas voted on the largest capital bond program in its history. Part of that bond package includes the funding of a major arts development in downtown Dallas, which the city may not have pursued had it invested its money in a new stadium for the Cowboys. Thus, Dallas has moved past the loss of the Cowboys franchise and is working to create a new image for the downtown area. Meanwhile, Irving officials' enthusiasm is growing as they investigate alternative uses for Texas stadium once the Cowboys depart for Arlington. Current plans that are under consideration include a Dallas Area Rapid Transit rail station and upscale residential development.

This case study holds several lessons for other communities. Cities may well consider how sports complex development opportunities fit into their long-term land-use and development plans. With both land and funds generally being finite assets, specific opportunities to pursue sports development complexes should be evaluated in light of not only what the city might gain from the development but also what could be lost in the way of other opportunities. Opportunity remains in the eye of the beholder.

References

Austrian, Ziona, and Mark S. Rosentraub. 2002. Cities, sports, and economic change: A retrospective assessment. *Journal of Urban Affairs* 24:549–63.

Baade, Robert A. 1994. Stadiums, professional sports, and economic development: Assessing the reality. In *Heartland policy study* 62. Chicago: The Heartland Institute.

_____. 1996. Professional sports as catalysts for metropolitan economic development. *Journal of Urban Affairs* 18:1–17.

Baade, Robert A., and Richard F. Dye. 2001 The impact of stadiums and professional sports on metropolitan area development. *Growth and Change* (spring): 1–14.

Carlino, Gerald N., and Edward Coulson. 2004. *Compensating differentials and the social benefits of the NFL*. Working paper no. 02-12/R. Philadelphia: Federal Reserve Bank of Philadelphia.

Chema, Thomas V. 1996. When professional sports justify the subsidy, a reply to Robert A. Baade. *Journal of Urban Affairs* 18:19–22.

Getz, Jim, Jeff Mosier, and Pamela Yip. 2004. Stadium study gets yeas, nays. *Dallas Morning News*, August 14, 1.

Giddons, David. 2004. Cowboys deal a loser. *Dallas Business Journal*, October 22. dallas.bizjournals.com/dallas/stories/2004/10/25/story1.html. Accessed March 30, 2008.

Gratton, Chris, Simon Shibli, and Richard Coleman. 2005. Sports and economic regeneration in cities. *Urban Studies* 42:985–99.

Johnson, Arthur T., and James H. Frey, eds. 1985. *Government and sport: The public policy issues.* Totowa, NJ: Rowman & Allanheld.

Keating, Raymond J. 1999. *Sports pork: The costly relationship between major league sports and government.* Policy analysis report no. 339. Washington, DC: The Cato Institute.

Levinthal, Dave. 2003. Dallas mayor calls for economic unity. *Dallas Morning News*, December 4. www.wfaa.com/cgi-bin/bi/gold-print.cgi. Accessed August 13, 2004.

Noll, Roger E., ed. 1974. *Government and the sports business.* Washington, DC: Brookings Institution.

Rich, Wilbur C. 1998. Professional sports, economic development and public policy. *Policy Studies Review* 15:1–2.

Rosentraub, Mark S. 2006. The local context of a sports strategy for economic development. *Economic Development Quarterly* 20:278–91.

Santo, Charles. 2005. The economic impact of sports stadiums: Recasting the analysis in context. *Journal of Urban Affairs* 27:177–91.

Swindell, David, and Mark S. Rosentraub. 1998. Who benefits from the presence of professional sports teams? The implications for public funding of stadiums and arenas. *Public Administration Review* 58:11–20.

Thornby, Andy. 2002. Urban regeneration and sports stadia. *European Planning Studies* 10:813–18.

Zaretsky, Adam M. 2001. Should cities pay for sports facilities? *The Regional Economist*. www.stls.frb.org/publications/re/2001/b/pages/lead-article.html. Accessed February 7, 2007.

CHAPTER 12

Birmingham: The Dome Debacle

Donna Milam Handley

The Birmingham-Jefferson Convention Complex (BJCC),
located in the heart of downtown Birmingham, Alabama, has been the
focus of an eight-year effort to enhance the economic prospects of
the city center. Debate has involved community stakeholders, funding
sources, and local government politicians, who struggled to determine
the feasibility of constructing a domed stadium to augment the existing convention center. Eventually it was decided that expansion of
the complex—not just a domed stadium—would make the city more
competitive with cities such as Atlanta, St. Louis, and even Los Angeles
(Bright 2004). Compromise has been reached, and a tentative plan is
now in place to establish an entertainment district. This case illustrates
how conflicting values, unstable governmental partnerships, and metropolitan planning disputes can be overcome to achieve a common goal of
economic prosperity.

Background

Founded in 1871 and known as the Magic City because it grew
and prospered so quickly, Birmingham was one of the main southern
cities to benefit from the boom of the industrial steel industry in the
early decades of the 19th century. Reduced demand for iron and steel
products during the Great Depression devastated the city's economy,
however. Birmingham was quickly deemed "the hardest hit city in the
nation" by President Hoover's administration ("Steel-Making," n.d.).

Birmingham was slow to recover from the Depression although
the federal government poured more than $350 million into the area in
an attempt to stimulate the economy ("Steel-Making," n.d.). Among the

projects that were federally funded was the restoration of the local statue of Vulcan, the Roman god of the forge, a symbol of the city's legacy. The statue was moved to a pedestal on Red Mountain, where it still stands today as the nation's largest statue second only to the Statue of Liberty (Bartlett 2004). Gradually the city began to recover as the industrial demands of World War II galvanized the manufacturing sector, in turn bolstering the local economy.

During the 1960s, Birmingham endured a tremendous struggle that further underscored the city's political, social, and economic issues and left an indelible mark on the history of the city and the state. The 1957 recession left the city struggling with high unemployment during the 1960s. Birmingham became known as one of the pivotal cities involved in the civil rights movement. National media attention was focused on the city in the wake of several horrific events, including a police riot in response to nonviolent protests against segregation in which fire hoses were used against demonstrators and hundreds of African American children were arrested. Tensions escalated in response to civil rights issues, and tragedy struck again when four young girls were killed in the bombing of the Sixteenth Street Baptist Church.

The need to improve the economic and social climate prompted many Birmingham natives to identify strategies to integrate racial harmony and economic prosperity into the city's future. Many had dreams for a revitalized city that incorporated culture and the arts, sporting events, entertainment districts, and other attractions for both local residents and visitors to the area. The Birmingham-Jefferson Convention Complex was designed to realize this vision.

History of the BJCC: 1967–98

The BJCC was a critical component within a revitalization plan that many Birmingham natives sought in order to change the economic status and public image of the city. The Alabama state legislature approved an enabling act in 1967 that created the BJCC Authority. Two years following the completion of the North Exhibition Hall in 1971, the concert hall and theater were added. The BJCC arena was built in 1976 with a capacity of 19,000, greatly enhancing Birmingham's marketability to attract various events to its local facilities.

Two decades later, a $160 million expansion was approved to add the Medical Forum, the East Exhibition Hall, and a hotel. The project was completed in 1992. Spectators currently enjoy a number of events housed within the complex's 220,000 square feet of exhibition halls, 3,000-seat concert hall, 1,000-seat theatre, and 19,000-seat arena (Bartlett 2004). Offices are located in the Medical Forum, adjacent to which is a 770-room hotel. These facilities serve the seven-county Birmingham metro area encompassing a population of just over 1.1 million. With the plan currently being considered by the BJCC board, these capacities would be greatly expanded.

The focus of the city once known as a center for steel and iron manufacturing has shifted from industry to health care, medical research, and banking (Bartlett 2004). The size and amenities offered by the BJCC helped establish Birmingham as a second-tier city in terms of economic development and hosting national and regional meetings and conventions. During the 1990s, up to 40 percent of the meeting space provided by the BJCC was used by national organizations. This exposure had an impact on Birmingham's strategy for continued national marketing and highlighted the city's potential for further economic growth.

In 1998, the BJCC board commissioned an independent study, the Metropolitan Area Projects Study, to assess the economic impacts of constructing an additional facility within the vicinity of the complex. A public referendum was held, and the plan proposed by the study group was defeated. In the years following the referendum, the BJCC board adopted another plan to expand the complex to include a 70,000-seat arena, as was originally recommended by the study group. The plan stipulated that the board own and operate the facility in conjunction with the existing buildings that make up the complex.

Four major issues influenced the outcome of the proposed expansion plan (Jack Fields, BJCC executive director, personal interview with author, April 26, 2007). First, the funding recommended for the facility would come from sales tax, which would require a one-cent increase. Second, debate arose in regard to who would actually own the facility; some argued that the BJCC Authority should own it, and others felt a private entity would be most appropriate. Third, the expansion plan fed rumors that the city intended to land an NFL franchise in another economic development effort. Fourth, citizens and city officials were unclear as to how other projects would affect the outcome of the expansion plan. Perhaps because of these uncertainties, the project was defeated in a public referendum by a 57 percent to 43 percent vote.

The prospect of hosting more sporting events—and especially acquiring a professional football franchise—led to the board's decision to feature construction of a domed stadium as part of the plan. Opponents of the plan argued that a tax-funded domed stadium was too expensive and that the cost burden should not be placed on public taxpayers by increasing local taxes. Advocates of the plan argued that the economic boost of bringing additional meetings and events to the area would be beneficial. Political divisiveness ensued, and the measure was stalled.

Revitalized Efforts toward Expansion

In the years between 1998 and 2006, several events took place that gave hope to advocates of the expansion. The Alabama legislature approved tax measures in 2002, 2003, and 2004 to increase rates for activities associated with tourism, such as lodging and alcohol taxes. The governor's verbal commitment to pursue additional funding for the project gave the BJCC board and state legislators even more hope. The county had been providing $10 million per year to fund the BJCC (a contract that is up for renewal in 2008), and the city had been providing $3 million per year. Further, BJCC officials were authorized to retain fees in lieu of taxes for lodging, alcohol sales, and ticket sales and concessions, which meant they did not pay these taxes to the state and instead could use them as a self-generating income base to benefit the complex. A car rental tax earmarked to provide additional revenues for the BJCC expansion had been approved by the legislature but not yet activated as of spring 2007. BJCC officials planned to introduce a bill to "trigger" funding from the car tax for the expansion during the 2007 legislative session.

The 1998 plan, known as Plan A, that emphasized expansion of the arena and construction of a dome had remained intact but had lain dormant despite attempts to increase funding. The proposal for a 70,000-seat arena made headlines again in 2004, as surrounding neighborhoods were experiencing renovations and growth. Media reports again reminded the public of the potential tourism dollars that the city was missing. At its existing capacity, the BJCC could host 35 percent of the nation's conventions and trade shows; an expanded complex would capture more than 70 percent of the market (Bartlett 2004). Hotel rooms in the immediate vicinity of the complex could accommodate close to 1,000; however, the BJCC lost the prospect of hosting national conventions because it did not meet this "magic number" (Fields, interview, April 26, 2007). In its efforts to keep Plan A on the local agenda, the BJCC Authority purchased additional land surrounding the complex's facilities in anticipation of the expansion. Thus, the plan moved forward while BJCC officials continued to wait on governmental approval at the state, county, and city levels to ensure support and continued funding to implement the plan.

A major obstacle to Plan A involved the negative connotations associated with the domed stadium. Opponents perceived the project as having limited use and catering to a select group (namely, sports fans), and they were unaware of the larger scope of the plan. Focus groups conducted by Connections Inc. in the fall of 2006 concluded that greater efforts to educate the public about the project would reduce the overwhelming opposition to it. The findings showed that the term "multipurpose facility" yielded a more positive response from citizens, and they were more receptive to the plan once they had been informed of the larger uses of the expanded convention complex (Williams 2007c). Most participants in the study were surprised to learn that more than 2.5 million people had visited the complex in 2005 (Williams 2007c), indicating a lack of knowledge about the volume of attendance at programs and shows held at the BJCC each year. Public education was a factor that had to be addressed in order to sell the plan to both citizens and elected officials.

By the end of 2006, BJCC officials had shifted their focus to a new strategy for expansion that included a new hotel and entertainment district. Due to delays in securing financing, BJCC board members opted to move forward with developing these auxiliary aspects of the plan. The layout of Plan A for the arena expansion was anticipated to cost approximately $623 million. Costs associated with Plan A included $435 million for the 70,000-seat dome and 160,000 square feet of exhibition space; $96 million to pay off existing bonds; $33 million for architecture, engineering, and design fees; $10 million for parking; and $9 million for street improvements (Williams 2007b). A new parking deck ($23 million) and a $17 million land-acquisition plan for future expansion were deemed optional and would not be necessary to implement later phases of the plan (Williams 2007b).

The decade of stalling on the plan for the expansion ultimately led BJCC board members to pursue an alternative plan (Plan B) in order to gain support for the project. Although they felt that the larger dome would better meet their long-term objectives for the facility, the lack of votes for support prompted them to consider construction of a scaled-back version of the dome. A consulting firm was hired in January 2007 to study the proposal for a smaller arena, which would provide only 40,000 seats instead of the larger 70,000 proposed in the original plan. The smaller arena would retain the same amount of exhibition space and would also support the entertainment district that had become the priority of the BJCC board. In a personal interview with the author, BJCC Executive Director Jack Fields stated that with the rise in construction costs that continued each year, the BJCC could not afford to wait much longer. The strategy to support an entertainment district and pursue expansion of the BJCC with a 40,000-seat arena seemed to be the most agreeable way to enhance the economic prospects of the area.

Political Struggles

In his 2007 State of the City address, Birmingham Mayor Bernard Kincaid included the BJCC expansion in his "Agenda for Progress," a positive step in building political consensus on the project (Williams

2007b). Kincaid pledged to work to bring the city, the Jefferson County Commission, and Governor Riley together to support the project. Fulfilling this promise proved to be a challenge, though. Two commissioners previously had run for office on a "no dome" platform. One commissioner was unfazed by the draft for a smaller version, stating that "a dome by any other name is still a dome." In addition, in the midst of an election year, Kincaid faced his own opponents on the Birmingham City Council, who were against the project.

The political struggles at the county level seemed to be the most daunting for the BJCC board to overcome. A critical part of the funding formula was provided by the county: $10 million each year had been allocated to the BJCC since 1989. This funding was a portion of the $65 million in revenues the county collects yearly from a half-percent occupational tax. However, the $10 million per year contract is set to expire in December 2008. Of the five county commissioners, only two voted to continue funding the BJCC in future years if the dome project continued.

Funding for the project became even more controversial when the *Birmingham News* reported that the occupational tax was in jeopardy of being repealed by the state legislature ("Fixing What They Broke" 2007):

> In 1999, during a feud between county commissioners and legislators over local legislators' attempt to spend county occupational tax money on pork projects, the legislature tried to pressure the county by passing an ill-conceived bill repealing the tax. The next year, a circuit court judge ruled the bill . . . was invalid because not enough legislators voted on it. Two years ago, the Alabama Supreme Court ruled that the legislature can set its own rules regarding how many votes are needed to pass legislation. That court ruling opened Jefferson County's occupational tax to legal challenge, county officials say. A ruling against the tax not only could mean the loss of the tax . . . but the county could be forced to repay many millions of dollars it has collected over the years.

Because it was uncertain whether the county would continue to receive $65 million in occupational taxes, the $10 million the BJCC received from the county could not be guaranteed. As a result, Jefferson County Commission President Betty Fine Collins, who had been in support of Plan B, changed her vote until the outcome of the 2007 legislative session, when it would be known whether the legislature would repeal the tax.

The Birmingham City Council had agreed to pledge $8.8 million per year for 30 years on the expansion if a plan were in place by March 2007. Otherwise, the council would pull funding and allocate the funds to other economic development projects. Because the future of the occupational tax in the state legislature was uncertain, however, the county commission decided to take no action on the project until June, after the legislative session was over. The varying timelines and agendas of city and county officials therefore posed a problem for the BJCC board.

There was some support for Plan B at the state level, however. Gov. Bob Riley indicated that he would back the project if city and county officials could agree on a plan. Rep. John Rogers asked the county to increase its contribution to $15 million per year (an additional $5 million each year over existing allocation levels), hinting that the future of the legislation on the county occupational tax was contingent upon the county's position on the BJCC dome project (Fields, interview, April 26, 2007). In light of state interest in the project, along with a revised plan for a smaller arena, hopes were revived for the possibility of expanding the BJCC and developing an entertainment district. With the arrival of Plan B, it appeared that the city and county were "singing from the same page for the first time" (Underwood 2007).

An Alternative Plan

Performa Entertainment Real Estate Inc., a Memphis-based firm, was hired to present a Plan B option to the BJCC board of directors during a retreat in February 2007 in Salt Lake City, where the group toured the Salt Palace Convention Center and the city's entertainment district. The trip was an educational retreat in which the Birmingham group learned more about how the convention center activities were coordinated. The contractors presented an updated cost analysis of the original plan for a 70,000-seat arena as well as projected costs for the smaller stadium, including renovations to the existing facilities.

The BJCC board responded positively to Plan B, which not only involved lower costs and afforded similar meeting and convention opportunities as those outlined in Plan A but also had local support. The cost to build the smaller arena would total approximately $380 million—about $120 million less than the larger facility. Costs of acquiring land, providing parking and infrastructure improvements, and renovating the BJCC would add an extra $50 million to the project ("Cartwheels for an Arena" 2007). A project of this size would enable the BJCC to have enough funds to pay annual debt service on bonds that would be required to finance the expansion. Committed funds for Plan B included $10 million per year from the county occupational tax and $8.8 million per year from the Birmingham City Council and three previously approved taxes, providing $521.3 million for the arena and an actual contingency surplus of $16 million (Williams 2007a).

In addition to lower costs, the scaled-down plan for the BJCC would provide relatively similar benefits in regard to its capacity to host meetings and conventions in Birmingham. This kind of facility is able to accommodate several types of special events: motor sports; football, basketball, and soccer; religious meetings; trade shows; and musical events and concerts (Fields, interview, April 26, 2007). The 40,000-seat arena would provide enough space to host motocross events, which would bring in the highest number of spectators, and local high school and University of Alabama football and baseball games. The city would potentially be placed on the rotation to host the Southeastern Conference basketball championships. The addition of the entertainment district with a new hotel with more rooms would draw attendees who want to be close to attractions and have the convenience of walking to and from meetings. The arena would offer more space (and therefore boost attendance at) consumer and trade shows, including gun and boat shows, which are currently hosted at the BJCC on a smaller scale. Another benefit of the arena is that events can take place simultaneously. Currently, for example, it may take a theatrical group two days to set up, one day for the performance, and one day to break down the set. In effect, the facility is being used for four days while drawing in revenues for only one day. With a larger arena, a concert or boat show could be going on at the same time, thereby increasing the number of attendees and revenues produced for the facility.

Local political support for the arena was mixed. Both Mayor Kincaid and County Commissioner President Collins voiced their support for Plan B. However, opponents to the plan contended that the arena would be too small. County Commissioner Larry Langford spoke against the new plan because it seemed the smaller arena could not be expanded to meet future needs. Several other commissioners and council members expressed similar concerns. Further, the complex would not be large enough to host the Magic City Classic football game, much less make it possible to land a national sports franchise. It was evident that politics was killing any "magic" the project might hold for the Magic City. Nevertheless, officials pressed on with promoting the project and educating local officials and citizens about the plan's potential.

Renewed Efforts

The efforts of the BJCC board to move forward with both Plan A and Plan B continued to be stalled by political wrangling. Local business leaders and private developers then stepped forward with an interest in the project. A business developer from Tennessee pledged $25 million to help make Plan B possible on two conditions: that he own the Social Security office buildings in Birmingham, which were soon becoming vacant, and that he offer to provide the funding if the state in turn agreed to lease office space in the buildings and continue to funnel a portion of state revenues toward the project. He also wanted to build a larger hotel in the vicinity of the BJCC that could be advertised to attract meetings and conventions.

A second group of investors also voiced interest in the project, with a focus on the entertainment district that would surround the BJCC. A project coordinator from the investor group presented a proposal at a city council meeting in March 2007. She claimed that the private investors she represented were ready to spend $1.5 billion on both the BJCC expansion and the entertainment district. However, they would only do so provided they formed their own board of directors and owned and operated the facilities. BJCC board and city officials rejected this offer. In addition, the coordinator could not provide the names of investors or a tangible plan for the development, which greatly discredited this option for investment.

While private interests were becoming more engaged in the project, the BJCC board was continuing its quest to acquire a plan to develop the entertainment district that would gain local government approval and appeal to both citizens and visitors to Birmingham. The BJCC board hired Performa to create a plan for the entertainment district near the downtown convention complex. Performa was responsible for the revitalization of the Memphis area and had a proven track record in developing projects of this size.

The contract was signed between the BJCC board and Performa, and by the end of March both the city council and county commission were in favor of moving forward with Performa's proposal—a $55 million project that would include restaurants, retail shops, night clubs, and apartments, along with a hotel located next to the BJCC. The project would be privately funded except for the land lease from the BJCC to Performa.

The Outcome

In its quest for an expanded facility and an entertainment district in the vicinity of the BJCC, the board of directors has made positive strides in the last several years. Local opinions varied on "the chicken-or-the-egg" strategy as to whether the entertainment district would evolve from the BJCC expansion and renovations, or vice versa. The BJCC chose to pursue the entertainment district first, which in turn would promote development, and they are hoping the success of the district will be magnified, thereby minimizing political struggles and quelling public controversy. Performa was willing to forge ahead in developing the entertainment district with or without the BJCC expansion.

As of April 2008, plans were progressing on the entertainment district, and Performa had planned to invest approximately $40 million, with the possibility of increasing to the targeted amount of $80 million as the project grows. The developers are seeking to finalize project financing and break ground by mid-2008. Estimates provide for an entertainment district to include restaurants, nightclubs, shops, and a courtyard for outside concerts and other events. The project is valued at $40 million and will include the construction of at least two new hotels, each valued at $20 million ("Entertaining the BJCC" 2007).

Efforts were stalled further in the wake of the Birmingham municipal elections in October 2007, when County Commissioner Larry Langford defeated Kincaid to become the city's new mayor. Langford's support for the project was indicative of the potential for cooperation with the city; however, his involvement led to additional changes as the project progressed. During his first weeks in office, Langford succeeded in obtaining council approval for tax increases that could potentially benefit the project. In November 2007, the council approved a one-cent sales tax increase and doubled the rate for business licenses within the City of Birmingham. However, city support of the 40,000-seat arena waned when Langford asserted that the larger domed stadium (as opposed to the smaller arena) would be in the city's best interest and that the BJCC site may not be the ideal location for the project. The new mayor summoned an independent study group in March 2008 to determine the best location for a stadium, stating that the city would support the project only if the city controlled the facility and if it were managed by a newly created Dome Authority.

Meanwhile, county officials' own financial woes mounted, contributing further to the BJCC's revenue problems. Jefferson County's failure to pay sewer bond debts created division in the commission on whether to continue funding the BJCC. In addition, by the end of March 2008, both Moody's and Standard and Poor's had downgraded the county sewer bonds, which indirectly led to downgrades of BJCC bonds from a 1989 facility expansion. (The BJCC bonds were downgraded because the county provided only partial revenues for the bonds.) In terms of the BJCC's future, these potential declines in revenue would reduce the funding available for the BJCC to expand its facility and maintain necessary upgrades to its existing space.

As the project slowly moves forward, the outcome will be contingent upon several actions. First, the BJCC will be significantly affected by the fate of the occupational tax bill that is being ignored in the legislature. Should the county be forced to stop receiving the funds from the tax—or, worse, have to pay back the taxes collected since 1999—there would be no county support for the expansion of the BJCC. Second, both the size and the location of the project will determine what types of events the area will draw and ultimately whether they will benefit the BJCC or go to competing facilities. Third, both city and county support is needed to finalize the project. Thus, the board continues to work on a plan that will build political consensus for the benefit of local economic development in downtown Birmingham.

Conclusion

Political disagreements have plagued Birmingham politics for decades, exacerbated in part by lack of leadership, which has created additional problems to do with crime and transportation and affected the viability of the industrial and manufacturing sectors. There appear to be few incentives or opportunities to make drastic changes that could further the economic, political, and social success of Birmingham and its surrounding areas.

The uncertain outcome of this case demonstrates a history of unstable leadership within the Birmingham community. Political leaders have maintained an environment of distrust and have on many occasions changed their opinions in regard to how to approach economic and community development. Business leaders have been slow to step forward to advocate change and promote unity that would benefit the greater downtown area.

Political divisiveness has seeped into the story of the BJCC. Besides political instability, the largest obstacle for the BJCC board to overcome has to do with control over the facility. Because state funding has not been forthcoming and political consensus in Birmingham is not likely to be reached in the near future, the BJCC has proceeded with plans without the guarantee of government support.

Yet despite nine years of delays, the BJCC board remains optimistic about both the development of the entertainment district and expansion of the arena. Since the 1960s, Birmingham residents have sought to overcome the city's tragic civil rights history and build an arts and entertainment center that will promote racial harmony and enhance the quality of life of both residents and visitors in the city. At last, this goal seems attainable.

The current climate of support provided by the business community may help Birmingham leaders realize the economic potential of this project and the benefit of a downtown location. The BJCC board has been consistent in its commitment to developing the downtown area and promoting its facilities. Moreover, it has shown itself to be flexible by adjusting its priorities and focusing on surrounding development that may be the impetus for expansion of the facility. The BJCC may indeed be heading in the right direction in terms of contributing to Birmingham's future economic development success. This case illustrates that there is no one way to complete an economic development project. The political, economic, and social environment will always influence the choices that developers make to reach their economic development goals.

References

Bartlett, Tony. 2004. The "Magic City" stages a star performance for groups. *Meetings South* (June). www.meetingsfocus.com/displayarticle.asp?id=3777. Accessed April 24, 2007.

Bright, Taylor. 2004. The dome debate: Will a multi-purpose facility and entertainment district make magic for the city? *Birmingham Post Herald*. www.postherald.com/dome.shtml. Accessed May 25, 2007.

"Cartwheels for an arena." 2007. *Birmingham News*, February 27. www.al.com. Accessed April 24.

"Entertaining the BJCC." 2007. *Birmingham News*, November 17. www.al.com. Accessed April 6, 2008.

"Fixing what they broke." 2007. *Birmingham News*, April 26. www.al.com. Accessed April 26.

"Local bills striking out." 2007. *Birmingham News*, May 26. www.al.com. Accessed May 28.

"Steel-making potential spurs growth." n.d. Birmingham Historical Society. www.citydata.com/us_cities/the_south/birmingham_history.html. Accessed April 24, 2007.

Underwood, J. 2007. Collins: BJCC expansion plans gaining momentum. *Birmingham News*, February 23. blog.al.com/spotnews/2007/02/collins_bjcc_expansion_plans_g/. Accessed May 25.

Williams, Roy L. 2007a. BJCC agrees on arena plans. *Birmingham News*, February 25. www.al.com. Accessed April 24.

_____. 2007b. Consulting firm hired for scaled-back plan. *Birmingham News*, January 11. www.al.com. Accessed April 24.

_____. 2007c. Focus groups give hope to BJCC planners. *Birmingham News*, December 14. www.al.com. Accessed April 8, 2008.

CHAPTER 13

Community Redevelopment of the Former Williams Air Force Base after BRAC

Paula J. Loomis and John C. Morris

The downsizing of the U.S. military following the end of the Cold War promised a substantial savings to the American taxpayer in the form of reduced military expenditures. As a result of the reduction in the number of active-duty troops, the United States soon found itself with many more military facilities than it needed. Just as the decision to site a new military installation in a particular place was often a political decision of great import, so too was the decision about which facilities to close. Congress and the Department of Defense began searching for a process by which the decisions about base closures could be removed from political influence as much as possible.

The result was the formation of the Base Realignment and Closure (BRAC) process. Under BRAC, an independent commission would study force requirements, conditions of existing facilities, and impacts on the local community and create a list of bases to be closed or realigned. Congress would then vote on the entire list, without the ability to amend the list in any way. The "winners" and "losers" would thus be determined on the basis of military need rather than the relative strength of a state's congressional delegation. To date, there have been four rounds of BRAC, which have resulted in the closure of more than 300 military facilities scattered from coast to coast. The number of facilities closed through this process means that many communities have struggled with the same basic question: What can we do with a former military property to make the best use of the facility?

In many communities, the military base provides an important, stable economic engine, providing jobs for local civilian workers, negotiating contracts with local businesses, and producing indirect benefits from the military members and their families who often live, shop, and work in the local community. When a base is closed, those economic benefits stop relatively quickly. The local government is responsible for redeveloping the former base (i.e., determining how to create an economic engine to replace or surpass the former base as a local force). Some local governments succeed; others struggle. This case study describes how the local governments near the former Williams Air Force Base (outside Phoenix, Arizona) succeeded and what lessons can be learned from their experience.

Once a base has been approved by Congress for BRAC, the base conversion process begins. Converting a base involves the Department of Defense, other federal agencies, state and local governments, regulators, and the local community. The first step is formation of a local redevelopment authority by the local government. The local redevelopment authority is responsible for base reuse planning activities, marketing, and implementation. It provides leadership, builds consensus, and serves as the community's point of contact with the Department of Defense. The department supports the local redevelopment authority's planning efforts through the Office of Economic Adjustment, which provides planning document funding and advice. The military has six years from the BRAC announcement to close the base (typically four to six years). Ideally, planning is complete and new tenants are identified before the military leaves.

History of Williams Air Force Base

Williams Air Force Base was constructed in 1941 to train combat pilots for World War II and operated as a flight training school from 1942 until it closed in 1993 as part of the 1991 BRAC decision. When Williams closed, the local economy lost 3,800 jobs (held by civilians who had worked on the base) and $300 million in annual economic activity. The Phoenix area's climate and favorable local economic environment and the amenities Williams offered to serve local aviation needs created a conducive redevelopment setting.

Williams is 30 miles southeast of Phoenix in East Valley. The warm, dry desert climate has little precipitation and 210 clear days each year—ideal weather for flight training and leisure activities (Coffman Associates et al. 1999, 1:27). East Valley includes the cities of Tempe, Guadalupe, Chandler, Gilbert, Queen Creek, and Mesa and unincorporated portions of Maricopa and Pinal Counties (Global Security 2007). In 1991, those cities were experiencing strong growth and employment. Mesa, northwest of Williams, was a golf mecca (City of Mesa 2007). Tempe, northeast of Williams, is home to Arizona State University.

Twenty percent of Tempe's workforce was employed in high-tech and research industries, and workers received double the salary of blue-collar workers (City of Tempe 2007). Mesa, Gilbert, and Queen Creek were some of the fastest-growing cities in the Phoenix metropolitan area. Queen Creek grew over 258 percent between 1980 and 1995.

In the 1990s, the Phoenix area was aggressively pursuing high-tech industries such as the software and aerospace industries. The potential annual business impact from five targeted "industry clusters" was projected to be $8.9 billion for the high-tech industry, $5.2 billion for the software industry, $3.5 billion for biotech-related industries, $3 billion for aerospace and aviation, and $3 billion for advanced business services (Williams Gateway Airport [WGA] 2007a). Firms in East Valley that provided executive, managerial, professional, specialty, and technical jobs included Motorola, Intel, Boeing Helicopter, Allied Signal, and Orbital Sciences (Coffman Associates et al. 1999, 1:24–26). These high-tech manufacturing and service corporations, along with Arizona State University's research organizations, produced high-value, low-weight airfreight (ideal cargo for air cargo carriers), creating an opportunity for Williams to support these activities (WGA 2007a).

In the 1990s, there were nine airports near Phoenix. Sky Harbor, located 19 miles northwest of Williams, was the largest and only commercial airport and served all major airlines and some general aviation. Sky Harbor had two runways and was projected to reach capacity by 2015, even with the addition of a third runway (EDAW Inc. 1992, 50). This situation created an opportunity for Williams and other airports near Phoenix to pick up excess commercial aviation activities that Sky Harbor could not handle. The other airports in the area handled general aviation or smaller aircraft. None had the runway capacity to handle large commercial or cargo aircraft (Coffman Associates et al. 1999, 1:20–22). Williams's runways, with a few additions, could handle commercial aircraft.

Williams covers 4,059 acres and is linked to Phoenix, Mesa, and Tempe via Powerline and Ellsworth Roads and Highway 60 (U.S. Environmental Protection Agency 2007; BRW Inc. 1996a, 1). In 1990, Williams's airside amenities to support aircraft operations included three parallel runways used for light military (non-cargo) aircraft, airfield lighting, and navigational aids that approximated commercial standards (WGA 2007a). Aircraft storage, aircraft parking aprons, fuel storage, aircraft rescue service, and firefighting facilities were among the landside amenities. Landside amenities that supported air-to-surface transitional activities included a control tower, aircraft storage (22,500 square feet), a hangar eligible for inclusion in the National Register of Historic Places, maintenance buildings, office space, and a fire station. Williams also had ample aircraft apron space (232,700 square yards) (Coffman Associates et al. 1999, 3:17–23).

The Local Reuse Authority Process

The successful redevelopment of Williams Airforce Base was due to not only its setting but also the early involvement by the governor of Arizona and the advice of Williams's Economic Reuse Planning Advisory Committee.[1] The decision to close Williams was part of the 1991 BRAC round. In 1991, Gov. John Symington appointed a 20-member economic reuse planning advisory committee as the local redevelopment authority. It included representatives from the neighboring cities, Maricopa County, and the State of Arizona; business leaders; and an additional 12 nonvoting members. The committee's stated goals were job creation and economic development. Through a public process, the committee adopted the Williams Economic Reuse Plan (WERP), which broadly outlined how the base was to be used. The plan specified that the base was to be an aerospace center, an educational training facility, and a "reliever" airport for Sky Harbor. Proposed aviation uses included commercial service, aircraft manufacturing, aircraft maintenance, air cargo operations, and flight training (WGA 2007b).

The committee also established an intergovernmental group in October 1992. This group drafted legislation to create the WGA Authority (established in 1994) and initiated a master plan in 1993 and a regional planning study of the surrounding communities. The intergovernmental group included representatives from Apache Junction, Chandler, Gilbert, Maricopa County, Mesa, Pinal County, Queen Creek, and the Maricopa Association of Governments. The mayors from Mesa, Gilbert, and Queen Creek and the governor of the Gila River Indian Community (and later, the mayor of Phoenix) served on the committee. The quick action by Governor Symington to establish the advisory committee—and the committee's quick action in turn to generate the WERP and establish the intergovernmental group—as well as the quality and breadth of the planning documents helped lead to Williams's successful redevelopment.

Early Planning Documents

The 1992 Williams Economic Reuse Plan

The WERP was the first planning document produced by EDAW Inc. to address the redevelopment of Williams Air Force Base. Its goals were to promote new economic activity, respond to community needs, achieve compatible land use, protect environmental resources, and provide for the plan's implementation. Early in the process, public meetings were held that emphasized the need to create jobs quickly. The Phoenix market was experiencing strong population and employment growth fueled by the service, trade, government, and manufacturing sectors. The East Valley was well positioned to capture a significant share of this growth. The plan projected that the Valley would capture 37 percent of overall growth, 18 percent of office space construction, and 33 percent of industrial space construction between 1990 and 2005. Williams's unique assets—its location in the Valley, the airfield, and training facilities—and the ability to transfer land and buildings through the public conveyance process (for education) at little cost made the base a logical location for an aerospace center that would serve industries in the Phoenix area and relieve the strain on Sky Harbor. Thus, the plan recommended that Williams be developed as an aerospace educational, training, and research center.

Once the basic direction for redevelopment was identified, the next task was to determine regional, state, and national aviation demand and whether Williams would concentrate on commercial, regional, general, cargo, or maintenance aviation. Several methods can be used to project aviation demand. One is a "straight-line" projection based on current regional requirements. This method could be used for estimating the general aviation requirements of the Phoenix and Williams airports. If we apply this method, Phoenix's general aviation operations in 1992 were projected to grow 1 percent per year.

Because they pertain to long-distance travel (i.e., air travel to move people and cargo quickly), national trends are another way in which aviation demand can be projected. Local or regional trends are inappropiate because they pertain only to short-distance travel (i.e., surface transportation to move people and cargo). For Williams, this method would apply to commercial air flights, regional jet service, and aircraft maintenance businesses since those sectors in Phoenix are driven more by national trends than local trends. It also would apply to cargo activities since no Phoenix airport served a large cargo load.

The Federal Aviation Administration (FAA) manages the National Plan of Integrated Airport Systems and publishes national aviation trends based on the economic performance of the United States. In 1992, the FAA predicted a 0.5 percent growth in the number of general aviation aircraft operations and a 2.5 percent growth in business flying hours (Phillips 1992). In terms of commercial aviation, the number of Sky Harbor's passengers had increased 12.7 percent per year from 1980 to 1990. The WERP showed a 6.5 percent growth in operations worldwide per year. With that growth, Sky Harbor would exceed capacity in

2015 with two runways and nearly reach capacity with three runways. Analysis also showed that if both Sky Harbor and WGA had commercial aviation, larger aircraft would operate out of Sky Harbor and regional jets out of WGA due to flight path configurations. National cargo demand was projected to grow between 7.5 percent and 8.5 percent and maintenance by 1.8 percent per year through 2000 (EDAW Inc. 1992, 47–51).

With these trends and the existing facilities at Williams in mind, the EDAW recommended that aviation uses include flight training, aircraft maintenance, retrofitting, and some general aviation, expanding to commercial and cargo aviation after the runway could be expanded to accommodate commercial and cargo aircraft. Educational institutions that were projected to use the facilities included Arizona State University, the Maricopa County Community College System, aeronautical colleges, and a new state college system. The only commercial and retail services recommended were those that served the aviation or educational communities, such as hotels. Over a 20-year period, the EDAW estimated that the plan would generate 17,339 jobs, $435 million in wages, private development of 5,220,700 square feet, and $50 million in local taxes (EDAW Inc. 1992, 47–51).

The 1993 Williams Master Plan

The second planning document was the 1993 master plan. It was built on the WERP but included much more detail and 20-year projections. Development of the plan was funded by the Aeronautics Division of the Arizona Department of Transportation and the WGA Authority. Technical work was conducted by airport consultants, including Coffman Associates, Ross and Baruzzini Engineering, and Gilbertson Associates (1993). Aviation uses and the rationale behind them were the same as described in the WERP. The EDAW further recommended that Williams create a Military Reuse Zone to offer income tax credits, reduced property taxes on qualified property, and exemption of transaction privileges to prime contractors for construction of certain facilities and that Williams apply to create a Foreign Trade Zone.

The plan's details included upgrades to increase the airfield capacity and accommodate commercial and cargo aircraft in the long term. The layout of an airport's runways (i.e., length and pavement strength) and taxiways directly affects an airfield's capacity. Exit taxiways have a significant impact on airfield capacity; if properly spaced, they allow aircraft to exit the runway quickly. Williams's existing parallel runways allowed for simultaneous operations, but they needed to be lengthened to accommodate commercial and cargo aircraft. The plan called for one runway to be extended to 12,000 feet. In addition, the number of taxiways would be increased to accommodate commercial aircraft.

Williams's runway lighting and the airfield identification system also would be upgraded in the long run (Coffman Associates et al. 1999, 5:1–9). Landside facilities, except the existing terminal building, would not be upgraded until tenants were identified. The terminal would be minimally reworked to accommodate a general aviation passenger terminal, pilot's lounge, and flight planning office. To attract cargo, Williams would have to construct a specifically designed warehouse, and utilities and roads eventually would have to be upgraded (WGA 2007a). The plan also called for a new freeway to be located a half mile from the airport (Coffman Associates et al. 1993).

The Williams campus master plan was initiated in May 1994 for a 753-acre multi-institutional campus (BRW Inc. 1996b). The Arizona State University East Campus, Mesa Community College, Chandler-Gilbert Community College, and the U.S. Air Force Research Laboratory would all be located on the site of the former base. Training operations began in 1994 (Coffman Associates et al. 1999, 1:6). In July 1996, WGA established a military reuse zone. One thousand jobs had been created by 1996, with an official forecast of jobs totaling 17,000 over 20 years (Martin and Stainbrook 2001). In 1996, WGA won the Facility of the Year Award from the National Association of Installation Development, an organization that focuses on military base reuse. By 1997, the airport had generated $1.5 million in income—well ahead of production forecasts (Martin and Stainbrook 2001)—and was classified in the National Plan of Integrated Airport Systems as a reliever airport (Coffman Associates et al. 1999, 1:5)

WGA was very successful in attracting tenants. They included Native American Air Ambulance Inc., U.S. Air Parts, Extex (an FAA-approved turbine engine parts manufacturer), Boeing (an avionics upgrade unit), McDonnell Douglas (an F/A-18 structural repair unit), Pathcor (manufacturers of specialized electronic guidance recording equipment), U.S. Bearing and Fabrication Distributors, Simula (manufacturers of occupant safety systems), and Jetstrip. Research, educational, and training tenants included Raytheon (research and flight simulators), Boeing/FedEx (MD-10 flight test program), Advanced Training Systems International, Symvionics Inc. (flight simulators and training systems), Phoenix Composites Inc. (which assists builders of experimental aircraft), and Am-Safe (which conducts tests on new technology for aircraft safety systems) (Coffman Associates et al. 1999, 1:5). Advanced Training Systems Inc. (providers of tactical aviation training), Airline Transport Professionals (providers of flight training toward advanced flight ratings), Maricopa Community College (which offers pilot certifications and associate degrees in airway science technology and aviation maintenance technology), and Chandler-Gilbert Community College (which partners with the University of North Dakota for flight training and Emery-Riddle University for aviation maintenance) are also tenants (Coffman Associates et al. 1999, 1:4).

Airport development included reconstruction of one runway and new runway lighting and signage. Pathcor planned to develop a new facility along the southwest end of the apron. Other hangars were used for industrial and commercial tenants. WGA provides fueling and line services including aircraft towing, wash rack, and auxiliary power unit services 24 hours a day. It maintains a pilot's lounge, flight planning area, flight deck pilot shop, and flight deck care area. Aircraft painting is provided by Ratts Air Service. Phoenix Composites is responsible for maintenance services, and the City of Mesa provides aircraft rescue and fire fighting assistance. A service road was extended around the airfield to allow emergency, airport maintenance, and security vehicles access without crossing the runways. Concurrent with the Sossaman Road construction was the extension of new utility lines (Coffman Associates et al. 1999, 1:12–17).

Since 1992, the WGA Authority has received $39.2 million in grants-in-aid and contributed $3.2 million in matching funds. Maricopa County has contributed $500,000 toward the expansion of Ray Road and Sossaman Road and $60,000 for the Williams Area Transportation Study. The educational institutions have contributed $96,725 (Coffman Associates et al. 1999, 1:12–17).

Later Planning Documents

The 1996 Williams Regional Planning Study

With all the new construction in the Valley and at Williams, it was important not only to include the surrounding communities in the planning process but also to consider their interests in the plans themselves to ensure that Williams's development did not hinder community development. The 1996 Williams Regional Planning Study was drafted to address these matters. The plan encompassed a six-mile radius from WGA, including the communities of Apache Junction, Chandler, Gilbert, Mesa, and Queen Creek. It provided systematic guidelines for the airport's overall development and its relationship to the surrounding communities. Its goals were to maximize economic development, minimize future land-use conflicts, and establish a regional land-use framework that would enhance residents' quality of life. From research and public workshops, the three goals were developed, and a plan was subsequently presented to a broad range of interest groups.

Development on Williams was in line with the 1993 master plan. The final 1993 master plan was a combination of the preferred elements of all three goals (BRW Inc. 1996a). It is interesting to note that the land-use aspect of the 1996 plan did not affect local community land-use plans except for areas within the designated 65-decibel Day-Night Noise Level area (Chandler-Gilbert Community College 2003). The plan effectively reassured residents that airport noise would not be a problem and ensured there would be no conflicts between the proposed land-use plans for the airport and communities' land-use plans.

The 1999 WGA Master Plan

Because the 1996 master plan was completed before the airport opened, a second master plan was developed to refine WGA's role within the aviation system, security requirements, and future development estimates and to update the timetable. The plan was funded and developed by the same team that drafted the 1993 master plan. Public input was coordinated through the Planning Advisory Committee (Coffman Associates et al. 1999, i).

The first decision was whether WGA would continue with goals from the first master plan or alter its direction. The team considered three alternatives to the plan that was eventually adopted. Transfer of the aviation demand to other airports was one option. This alternative was considered undesirable because other Phoenix airports were unable to accommodate the aircraft load at Williams. Also, the continued growth expected by the major employers as well as the infusion of new industries into East Valley underscored the need for a highly functional airport at WGA. The second alternative was to develop an entirely new airport. This option was found to be less feasible than accommodating demand at other regional airports. Even if the additional expense to relocate the airport could be justified, it was unlikely that an ideal location could be found due to environmental concerns.[2] A third alternative—keeping the airport in its present condition—was not selected because if WGA stayed at its current capacity, Sky Harbor would exceed its capacity and experience significant delays (Coffman Associates et al. 1999, 4:2–19).

The team also considered the advantage and disadvantages identified by the Kiehl Hendrickson Group, an airport consulting company, in its 1997 study, "Arizona's Emerging Airport: Williams Gateway" (see Box 1). The study also noted that the dominance of low-fare carriers at Sky Harbor and the expansion of international services were factors WGA had to overcome or position around. Many cities across

Box 1: Williams Gateway Airport Strengths and Weaknesses

Strengths	• Location and proximity to population growth, solid potential for driving economic growth in East Valley • Operating cost advantages [compared with] Sky Harbor • The likelihood of increasing amounts of delay and noise-related constraints at Sky Harbor • Potential for establishment of a commuter rail line from downtown Phoenix and Tempe • Operating flexibility at WGA • Strong and growing base of academic and aviation-related commercial business
Weaknesses	• Underdeveloped passenger terminal facility • Unfinished FAA (Federal Aviation Regulation Part 139) certification • Undeveloped passenger support services • Relatively remote location and lack of readily accessible and convenient freeway access • On-site access challenges • Confusing name recognition

Source: Kiehl Hendrickson Group (1997).

the country have accounted for these factors by operating two airports (Kiehl Hendrickson 1997). Because they are in close proximity to each other, this scenario would apply to Sky Harbor and WGA.

Next, the team reevaluated national and regional aviation demand, as it did in 1993. In terms of commercial aviation, Sky Harbor's passenger traffic had increased since 1993 at an annual growth rate of 9.7 percent and was forecasted to increase at an average annual rate of 3.8 percent through 2020. Accommodating this large local origin-destination traffic would provide an opportunity for growth for WGA. In its report, the Kiehl Hendrickson Group estimated that charter services would increase from 2,700 to 5,400 and suggested that charter operators serving groups, package tours, and international and domestic markets without existing scheduled service would be the best customers for WGA. It noted that carriers specializing in niche markets (serving particular routes such as Los Angeles to Phoenix) offered fewer opportunities.[3]

Serving air cargo operations also was identified by the Kiehl Hendrickson Group and in the WGA 1999 master plan as an option for WGA to exploit. The air cargo industry was deregulated in 1977. Since then, integrated all-cargo airlines have emerged that combine traditional all-cargo airlines with freight forwarders (previously, passenger airlines carried the majority of airfreight in the "belly" of the scheduled aircraft). Cargo was still thought to be a good long-term market for WGA.

General aviation support was another area of opportunity for WGA. The number of aircraft registered in Maricopa County that were based at WGA had increased since the airport opened in 1994. The Maricopa County Association of Governments' Regional Aviation System Plan projected an increase of 2,859 in 1997 to 3,832 in 2015, a 1.6 percent annual growth rate (cited in Coffman Associates et al. 1999, 2:17–20). The number of aircraft based at WGA was anticipated to increase to 243 by 2020. This study did not project large increases in research, education, or training related to aviation.

The final 1999 master plan identified the need for new scheduled passenger regional and cargo service in addition to maintenance of the airport's current educational, research, and maintenance activities. It projected growth in nonscheduled charter activities (including commercial passenger) and increases in the number of air cargo freight forwarders. Further, it noted the need to establish a regional distribution station and a general aviation fleet composed of single-engine piston aircraft, turboprops, jets, and helicopters that eventually would number approximately 800 (Coffman Associates et al. 1999, 5:1–11).

Next, the team developed alternatives for airside and landside facilities. A 12,500-foot runway was recommended to allow for the largest and heaviest cargo aircraft. With this extension, only a small number of cargo aircraft would experience payload or fuel limitations during the warmest summer months.[4] The longest runway would be located adjacent to the new passenger terminal and cargo facilities on the east side. The plan included several taxiway improvements: a parallel taxiway along the east side to provide access to the future landside development, 3 new taxiways for the center runway, 10 new taxiways for the west runway, and 2 partial parallel taxiway segments to provide access to the full length of the runway. All taxiways would be updated to 75 feet to accommodate large aircraft. Other improvements would include the installation of precision-approach path indicators and a system to provide half-mile visibility of the airport for aircraft (Coffman Associates et al. 1999, 5:1–5).

Landside facility improvements would include renovating the existing terminal as an interim passenger terminal until a new east side terminal could be constructed. The new terminal would include aircraft ticketing and automobile rental facilities, airline offices, a hold room, retail space, and areas to accommodate security screenings, mechanized baggage claim, and outbound baggage devices. When renovated, the terminal could serve up to 100,000 passenger enplanements annually and could be expanded to 250,000 enplanements. The new east side terminal would have second-level loading, 6,409 parking spaces, and a terminal loop road connecting the airport to the San Tan Freeway. Cargo would initially be on the west side, with a new 23,000-square-yard apron and regional distribution station planned for the east side. General aviation development would be reserved for the north and middle apron areas and the west side. General aviation hangars would be located along the western edge of the north apron, with future fixed-based operator facilities (i.e., aircraft maintenance, flight training, and charter services) planned for development along the middle apron, which also would serve itinerant general aviation. The area southwest of the runway would be reserved for industrial and commercial development; aviation manufacturing, aircraft maintenance and modification, and aircraft testing; and education, research, and corporate office facilities. A fuel farm was planned for the south end of the airport (Coffman Associates et al. 1999, 5:5–13).

The timeline was not linked to specific dates but rather to achieving the forecasted activity level. These planning horizons matched the anticipated investment amounts designated in the financial plan: short ($7.79 million), intermediate ($34.4 million), and long ($29.8 million) term. The financial plan called for implementing the FAA Airport Improvement Program (Coffman Associates et al. 1999, 6:2–11).

Current Status of WGA

WGA has continued its path of success. In 2006, Williams had 280,760 operations, making it the 39th-busiest airport in the United States (WGA 2007c). (Sky Harbor had 614,000 operations, making it the fifth busiest nationally.) Since 1999, WGA has initiated commercial passenger service; attained Transportation Security Administration certification; received User Free Airport status; welcomed the world's largest aircraft, the Antonov 225; maintained a facilities occupancy rate of 96 percent; established a $200,000 cooperative marketing partnership with Sky Harbor; and been recognized by FAA for five consecutive years of perfect Federal Aviation Regulation Part 139 compliance (WGA 2004). There are more than 1,000 jobs on the base, and the economic impact on the community is $300 million annually (WGA 2007c). WGA won the Airport Authority 2004 Award for Excellence, one of four presented internationally, and its control tower won two FAA awards: the Willie F. Card Contract Tower of the Year and Air Traffic Controller of the Year (WGA 2006a).

Facilitywise, the existing terminal was remodeled as the interim airport terminal (WGA 2007a). WGA constructed an $11.3 million cargo ramp and associated taxiway; executed a lease for a private developer to construct a 40,000-square-foot cargo facility; established a U.S. Customs cargo inspection facility; completed construction of a new hangar and office and entryway features, including artwork, landscaping, and signage; broke ground on a new office and warehouse building; and executed leases with private developers for three more hangars (WGA 2004). The WGA Authority set development in motion for 52 acres of nonaviation land near the south end of the airport, which is projected to generate an additional 1,500 jobs. The WGA Authority signed an agreement with Reliance-Williams Gateway LLC to build over 500,000 square feet of new buildings, including 50,000 square feet of speculative office and warehouse space. More than 20 aviation companies operate at WGA, and the Williams area is projected to have more than 100,000 jobs by the year 2035.

WGA has had a great impact on the local economy. It has created jobs, produced income, and influenced regional spending. Direct benefits include the supply of aviation goods and services including flight instruction; provision of air ambulance services; aircraft maintenance, repair, and modification; and aviation-related manufacturing. Indirect benefits are created by visitors who arrive via the airport for business or personal reasons and spend money locally. Induced benefits from WGA are created by traditional multiplier effects such as increased wages, tax revenues, and demand for goods and services. WGA also creates benefits that are not easy to measure. Air transportation provides freedom for individuals to travel, makes the local economy more competitive, and provides businesses ready access to markets, materials, and international commerce. It also brings enhanced medical care, law enforcement, and timely cargo delivery (Coffman Associates et al. 1999, 6:11–20).[5] WGA's future plans include reaching 338,000 operations and two million emplanements by 2020 (WGA 2007c). (Sky Harbor is expected to reach 545,768 operations and 17.6 million emplanements.) Maricopa County forecasts more than 500,000 new residents east of WGA by 2020 (WGA 2007c).

Conclusion

Five themes emerge from this case study of the redevelopment of Williams Air Force Base that may be instructive for communities that are losing a major employer. First, early, active planning is important—especially securing early financial support from the state. In the Williams example, the State of Arizona and local community officials started planning immediately after the 1991 BRAC announcement. Governor Symington established the Williams Economic Reuse Planning Advisory

Committee, which published the WERP in 1992 and the first master plan in 1993—a very short time period in which to develop the planning documents. Starting the planning process early does not mean that the community has unconditionally accepted the closure. Rather, starting early provides the community the maximum amount of time possible to consider and research alternatives. Also, starting early means a community can submit grant applications earlier (thereby providing a better chance of funding) and may get its choice of consultants.

As Boles (1994, 54) observes, "Only through extensive effort to organize early can a community hope to stay current with the constantly changing BRAC process." Starting early has benefits even if the base does not close. Plans can be revised in anticipation of closure. For example, Rickenbacker near Columbus, Ohio, had three false starts that gave it multiple opportunities to review its plans before the base closed.

Second, correctly identifying a market "niche" is critical. The niche must be narrow enough to differentiate the property from nearby property but broad enough to attract many potential companies. The niche must also contain industries that are synergetic. The WERP and first master plan identified WGA's niche as education, research, and maintenance related to general, regional, and cargo aviation. This definition was not so specific that plans could not be flexible.

Third, communities need to take advantage of state and federal funds and be "first to the plate." The planners of Williams's redevelopment took great advantage of not only state and federal funds to establish a campus of the Chandler-Gilbert Community College at WGA but also FAA development funds. Many states have closed bases, and communities that have been involved later in the process have had to compete with communities near bases that closed earlier. Brooks Air Force Base in Texas closed after Kelly Air Force Base (which was located five miles from Brooks), making the Brooks closure more difficult than if Kelly had not closed.[6]

Fourth, redevelopment takes a great deal of planning. In all, the redevelopment of WGA involved nine planning documents. The Williams Economic Reuse Planning Advisory Committee and the WGA Authority did a very good job of thoroughly analyzing all their activities. If they erred at all, it was on the side of having too many plans. However, in the grand scheme, the cost of an extra plan is far less than miscalculating a development opportunity.

Fifth, the role of luck cannot be underestimated. The communities around Williams have been lucky. They are lucky that they are located in an area that is growing and that has a climate favorable to aviation activities. In the long run, they also were lucky that Williams closed. The closure provided a more cost-effective way to establish a reliever airport for Sky Harbor than constructing a new airport.

Williams is a good example of how a community should face redevelopment when a base or a major employer leaves. Phoenix and the State of Arizona acted swiftly, accepting the closure and pressing for redevelopment. They acted smartly, taking advantage of Williams's strengths relative to the region and national trends. Finally, they acted inclusively, involving the local communities and state agencies.

Notes

1. Copies of the WGA master plans and other plans can be obtained through the Williams Gateway Public Information Office at 480-988-7600 or by contacting the firms that developed them directly (WGA 2006b).

2. Because Williams was an existing airfield, environmental issues to do with noise levels and water drainage had already been addressed.

3. The Kiehl Hendrickson Group recommended that a different customer base (nonscheduled groups versus scheduled airline passengers) be targeted.

4. Airfield surfaces (i.e., runways, taxiways, and aprons) are composed of either asphalt or concrete. In very hot climates, the surface becomes soft and is easily damaged when large, heavy aircraft tires strike the surface during landing or when taxiing or parking. The surface can be displaced by tires pressing down on the surface, creating grooves or trenches. The only option under these conditions is to reduce the weight of the aircraft by reducing either the weight of its cargo or the amount of fuel carried on board.

5. Because these services exist at WGA, they can be made available to surrounding communities through memoranda of understanding. These arrangements are commonplace in many communities.

6. The two former bases are less than 20 miles apart and compete for tenants, state and city funds, public and media attention, and priority among city officials.

References

Boles, Anthony. 1994. Base realignment and closure: An interactive model for co-operative community planning and reuse. MA thesis, San Diego State University.

BRW Inc. 1996a. *Williams regional planning study*. Phoenix, AZ: BRW Inc.

_____. 1996b. *Williams campus master plan*. Phoenix, AZ: BRW Inc.

Chandler-Gilbert Community College. 2003. *Master plan, 2004–2013*. www.cgc.maricopa.edu/planning/master. Accessed May 25, 2007.

City of Mesa. 2007. www.ci.mesa.az.us. Accessed January 17.

City of Tempe. 2007. Community overview. www.tempe.gov/business/overview. Accessed May 25.

Coffman Associates with Ross Baruzzini Engineering Inc. and Gilbertson Associates. 1993. *Williams Air Force Base master plan.* Scottsdale, AZ: Coffman Associates et al.

_____. 1999. *Williams Gateway Airport, airport master plan.* Scottsdale, AZ: Coffman Associates et al.

EDAW Inc. 1992. *Williams Air Force Base economic reuse plan.* San Francisco, CA: EDAW Inc.

Global Security. 2007. *Williams AFB.* www.globalsecurity.org/military/facility/williams. Accessed January 26.

Kiehl Hendrickson Group. 1997. *Arizona's emerging airport: Williams Gateway.* Washington, DC: Kiehl Hendrickson Group.

Martin, Maryann, and Anita Stainbrook. 2001. *Success stories: A look at community progress.* www.nemw.org/cmclean5.htm. Accessed January 26.

Phillips, Edward H. 1992. Business aircraft sales linked to global economic recovery. *Aviation Week and Space Technology* 136:136.

U.S. Environmental Protection Agency. 2007. Williams AFB, Arizona. EPA ID AZ7570028582. yosemite.epa.gov/r9/sfund/overview.nsf/3395id3dc70d6ecd882 5650f005dc903/048. Accessed January 17.

Williams Gateway Airport. 2004. Williams Gateway named "Airport of the Year." News release, April 29. www.flywga.org/pressreleases.asp. Accessed January 17, 2007.

_____. 2006a. Williams Gateway is 42nd busiest airport in the U.S.; noise complaints down significantly. News release, January 23. www.flywga.org/press-releases.asp. Accessed January 17, 2007.

_____. 2006b. *Media guide.* Mesa, AZ: Williams Gateway Airport.

_____. 2007a. www.flywga.org. Accessed January 17.

_____. 2007b. History. www.flywga/history.org. Accessed January 17.

_____. 2007c. Frequently asked questions. www.flywga/faq.org. Accessed January 17.

CHAPTER 14

Nonprofit Organizations and Local Economic Development:
A Community-Building Effort in Dallas

Alicia C. Schortgen

Nonprofit organizations play a significant role in building local economies. With more than 1.3 million tax-exempt organizations in the United States accounting for 4.2 percent of the country's gross domestic product, nonprofit organizations are involved in nearly all aspects of community outreach and service provision. Local economic development leaders rely on nonprofit professionals for a number of resources including policy advocacy, gathering volunteers, and overall public relations support. But what happens when economic development interests collide with community needs? Often those most adversely affected by economic development decisions are low-income or elderly residents whose property is targeted for revitalization efforts. While federal funding initiatives such as Community Development Block Grants seek to mitigate some of these effects, local governments competing for economic development opportunities tend to relegate displaced residents to an afterthought in planning.

Some cities have made serving the needs of low-income residents a priority in their economic development plans. At the height of Cleveland, Ohio's, development in the 1970s, the city's planning commission recognized the adverse effect of its downtown development on Cleveland's poor and elderly population and insisted that the private developers guarantee jobs to local residents. The city addressed the transit-dependency of its urban residents in its plans and established Cleveland's Regional Transit Authority in 1975. The Cleveland City Planning Commission "wanted new development to leverage clear benefits to Cleveland's poor and working-class people and not simply exchange new bricks for old at substantial cost to the public treasury" (Krumholz 1999, 88).

A decade later in 1985, Jersey City, New Jersey, recognized that the city's development efforts resulted in a rapidly inflated rental market where cheap rental apartments were being converted into upscale multi-family housing complexes. Jersey City's then-director of Housing and Economic Development, Rick Cohen, established a linkage program whereby developers were required to set aside affordable housing units in their developments or contribute to a low-income housing trust fund. The results were impressive: "By the time Cohen was finished with his four-year stint as director, Jersey City had a $14 million trust fund for low-income housing and a newly instituted shelter system for the home-less" (Krumholz 1999, 89).

While the textbook model of economic development "assumes rational planning and a broad range of technical studies" (Krumholz 1999, 83), a more pragmatic approach to community building requires political savvy and grassroots efforts to accomplish urban planning goals. According to Krumholz (1999, 84), "The textbook model of local economic development seems deeply flawed in practice. . . . Leadership is provided by private developers or real estate entrepreneurs seeking their own objectives, rather than public officials and citizens seeking public objectives." The self-interested behavior of private companies in economic development is sometimes restrained by local policies, but citizen groups must be proactive in pursuing their desired development outcomes. The introduction of nonprofit organizations into the local development landscape over the past several decades has brought in-creased focus on public objectives, especially with regard to populations that have been adversely affected by economic development efforts.

Development in large urban areas is often propelled by the careful interaction of nonprofit organizations and government agencies. Important to urban growth is the successful implementation of housing policy, which necessitates cooperation among the public, private, and nonprofit sectors. Since its passage by Congress in 1974, the Housing and Community Development Act has provided a catalyst for non-discrimination in urban communities and encouraged participation and cooperation in the creation of housing policy. In its current form, the law provides, among many other programs, block grant opportuni-ties through partnership projects. Over the past 20 years, public admin-istrators have looked to nonprofit community development organiza-tions to compensate for decreasing governmental resources. Although cooperative housing initiatives exist across the United States, their results are mixed.

This case study explores the relationship between the public and nonprofit sectors in efforts to develop housing in Dallas, especially in urban low-income areas, which are becoming more gentrified. The case concerns a Dallas-based community development corporation that plans to convert a 15-story downtown high-rise building into affordable housing and intends to set aside a number of units for homeless individuals and families. Specifically, the case illustrates the grassroots approach to development, which maintains that decisions regarding economic growth and development should be made by communities themselves rather than dictated by higher levels of government. It also shows how the city has been dealing with the concerns of various parties regarding the effects of such a project on local economic development.

Nonprofit-Sector Values

The inherent values of the nonprofit sector make it a unique contributor to the economic development landscape. Philanthropic organizations throughout America's history have promoted community needs and sought to balance the interests of multiple interest groups. Over the past three decades, nonprofit organizations have grown significantly in number, size, and scope, and many have entered into direct competition with the public and private sectors. What differentiates the nonprofit sector is its focus away from profit-making incentives and majoritarian constraints. Moreover, as Eberly (2000, 3) comments, "Few things are more important to America's social order than the dynamic role voluntary associations have played in creating a stronger society."

Three specific values of the nonprofit sector help us understand the role of philanthropic organizations in local economic development: fostering the notion of civil society, providing social capital, and serving multiple stakeholders. First, the sector seeks to preserve the values of civil society outside the limitations of government structure. Seligman (1992, 16) observes that "[d]espite the differing theoretical perspectives and political agendas, what nevertheless makes the idea of civil society so attractive to so many social thinkers is its assumed synthesis of private and public 'good' of the individual and social desiderata. The idea of civil society thus embodies for many an ethical ideal of the social order, one that, if not overcomes, at least harmonizes, the conflicting demands of individual interest and social good."

Participation in civil society allows individuals to seek the interests of their community. Voluntary associations are a unique by-product of democratic societies and help to meet the needs of like-minded citizens. In his discussion of Alexis de Tocqueville's appreciation for American voluntary association, Eberly (2000, 26) writes, "Associations represented an independent source of political power and as such exercised a powerful check against either powerful private interests or tyranny by political majorities."

A second value unique to the nonprofit sector is the provision of social capital, which is often seen as a necessary derivative of civil society institutions (Eberly 2000). The concept of social capital is rooted in social science practices and most commonly refers to the investment of individuals in their networks, resulting in a cooperative benefit. Despite conventional wisdom on the subject, scholars have yet to reach consensus on its definition. According to Putnam (2000, 125), social capital may be described as the "honesty and trust [that] lubricate the inevitable frictions of social life."

Social capital exists at various levels of interaction and is most homogeneous at the neighborhood level. Social networks within communities possess information that may not be known at higher levels of governance, thus allowing these smaller entities to better enforce contracts and solve problems through collective action in some situations (Bowles and Gintis 2002). As such, by providing social capital, nonprofit organizations can help local government officials appreciate specific community values and conflicts.

A final benefit of the involvement of nonprofit organizations in economic and community development results from the sector's diverse stakeholder interests. The third sector enjoys more overlap among clients, funders, and interested parties than either the private or public sectors. The nonprofit stakeholder spectrum ranges from donors to grantors, from clients to volunteers. Nonprofit managers often struggle to balance their organizational objectives with the needs of all concerned, especially given the increasing competition between and among sectors. The benefit of the multiple stakeholder "burden" is that the nonprofit sector, especially local and grassroots organizations, may directly represent the interests of parties in such complicated policy matters as economic development.

Competition among Sectors

Do community development corporations compete directly with local government economic development efforts? Is the relationship complementary or controversial? Local governments certainly compete with one another to entice developers and businesses to choose their cities or counties when locating capital structures and capital ventures. But how do policymakers balance economic development and affordable housing needs? According to Basolo (2000, 323), "Public choice theory predicts that local decision makers will favor developmental policy such as economic development programs over redistributive policy such as affordable housing programs."

In modern cities, policymakers have realized that the choice between housing and development need not be zero-summed. Olberding (2002) suggests that the "third wave" of regional economic development strategies is less competitive and more cooperative. Such regional partnerships comprise local governments, private-sector firms, and nonprofit organizations. The focus of more recent economic development strategies has been away from specific policy concerns and toward multiorganizational alignment. The objective of such organizations is "to find new institutional and organizational arrangements with sufficient scope, responsiveness, and flexibility to provide the foundation for economic development" (Clarke and Siaz 1996, 543).

This new foundation for economic development exists within various North Texas cities as well as regionally. The North Texas Commission is a nonprofit consortium that seeks to enhance and promote the economic vitality and quality of life of the Dallas–Fort Worth Metroplex by providing leadership, acting as a catalyst for regional cooperation, identifying regional problems and issues, and helping address these problems and issues (see the North Texas Commission Web site at www.ntc-dfw.org). While the North Texas Commission is not directly responsible for overseeing development projects in the region, the organization provides information to interested member groups and brings together various parties to facilitate discussion and planning. The existence of an organization like the North Texas Commission in the Dallas area ensures partnership among the three sectors to achieve healthy economic development.

Community Development Corporations

Congressional interest in housing development began in 1937 with the U.S. Housing Act (P.L. 71, 81st Congress, 63 Stat. 413: 42 U.S.C. 1441). A response to the nation's social state during the Great Depression, the Housing Act ordained that the federal government "remedy the unsafe and unsanitary housing conditions and the acute shortage of decent, safe, and sanitary dwellings for families of lower income." Over the subsequent eight decades, community housing administration has evolved into a complex network of intersecting agencies and stakeholder groups. The most prevalent organizations in low-income housing development are community development corporations. The community development corporation movement was born in 1968 out of a series of IMPACT (Instructional Model to Prepare Adept Certified Teachers in Special Education) grants to newly minted community development corporations in Cleveland, Ohio, and Brooklyn, New York. Currently, there are more than 4,000 independently incorporated community development corporations in the United States.

Community development nonprofits represent one of the fastest-growing philanthropic sectors. While unique when compared with more typical service organizations, nonprofit community development organizations share the sector's values of volunteer governance and community focus. Robinson (1996) cites several achievements of community development corporations, including an increased respect for clientele and serving as political watchdog. According to Robinson (1996, 1658), "Neighbourhood residents generally report that the attitude of [community development corporation] management towards traditionally ill-treated, impoverished residents is one of commitment and respect." Community development corporations play a critical role in local economic development, especially in terms of providing affordable and available housing in urban neighborhoods.

Community development corporations have been criticized in the literature for being too easily influenced by the interests of property owners, funders, and local governments (e.g., Goetz and Sydney 1994; Stoecker 1997). This case study of the downtown Dallas high-rise project explores this criticism. Specifically considered are Dallas's political climate, the community's concern over the location of the building, and the nonprofit's dependence on local government approval for the success of the development.

Dallas Dynamics

The City of Dallas has a dynamic history. Founded in 1841 by John Neely Bryan as a trading post along the Trinity River, Dallas quickly burgeoned into a thriving settlement. The city's population tripled to more than 10,000 by 1880, and the construction of two railroad lines helped maintain steady industrial growth in the area. As people began to move north into the city, Dallas became the world's hub of the leather and buffalo-hide trade. Service and support organizations such as banks and insurance companies began to dominate the Dallas economy late in the 19th century. Today, in addition to a large service industry, telecommunications technology companies maintain a significant presence in the city.

As the ninth-largest city in the United States, Dallas faces challenges similar to other large urban areas. Eighteen percent of Dallas's residents live at or below the federal poverty line, and the city's median household annual income hovers around $38,000. Forty-three percent of Dallas residents own their home, and the U.S. Census Bureau estimates median residential property values in the area to be $89,800 per unit. While the cost of living in Dallas is relatively low, fair market rents remain out of reach for those living in poverty. The National Low Income Housing Coalition estimates the fair market rent for a one-bedroom apartment in Dallas County to be $678 per month. Thus, a household that brings in minimum wage income (at $5.15 per hour) and designates 40 percent of its income to housing costs would be required to work a minimum of 84 hours per week to afford a one-bedroom apartment in Dallas County. The Dallas County Housing Authority currently maintains 5,762 conventional public housing units and has distributed 17,414 Section Eight vouchers. There are approximately 9,500 people on the Dallas County public housing waiting list, and the average wait time for housing placement is 18 to 24 months.

Dallas is ranked among the nation's most ethnically diverse communities. The city's minority population is significant (26 percent African American and 36 percent Hispanic or Latino). Dallas County Housing Authority resident populations are much less diverse (87 percent African Americans, 6 percent white, and 6 percent Hispanic). Dallas's governing agencies are challenged to meet the various needs of the city's 1.2 million residents.

Like most other large cities, Dallas struggles to reconcile rising housing costs with the increasing homeless population. With more than 9,000 people lacking permanent accommodation in their community, Dallas residents are aware of the social issues associated with homelessness. In tackling these concerns, the city must consider the need to foster economic growth along with facilitating access to social services and combating the notoriety associated with shelters and subsidized housing projects.

To address the issues surrounding the growing homeless population and lack of affordable housing, one of the city's most recognized community housing development organizations, the Central Dallas Community Development Corporation, purchased an abandoned high-rise in the center of downtown. The nonprofit housing organization proposed to convert the 15-story building into small, individual housing units set aside primarily for the homeless and low-income tenants. The project was met with reactions ranging from ardent support to outright anger.

According to Hanson (2003, xv), "As one of the nation's newer metropolitan areas, largely built after the advent of the automobile and air conditioning, Dallas provide(s) an excellent opportunity for a natural experiment in how a post-industrial city copes with change." Despite recent interest in the evolution and growth of the city (e.g., Hanson 2003; Hill 1996; Hazel 1997), there has been little scholarly research on Dallas. According to the National Center for Charitable Statistics, Dallas County is home to more than 9,000 registered 501(c)(3) organizations, each with a unique mission, competing for the area's limited resources. With the significant saturation of nonprofit organizations in the area and its politically active business community, Dallas has had to balance the interests of these diverse groups and therefore provides a unique case study in which to examine innovative approaches to formulating community and economic development policy. Dallas was among the nation's first cities to draft and adopt a strategic plan to address homelessness. Dallas is also leading the country in providing permanent affordable housing options for low-income residents.

Economic Development and Homelessness in Dallas

The case of Dallas illustrates the conflict between meeting the increasing demand for low-income housing and encouraging economic development. Economic development priorities for the City of Dallas include a vast downtown development effort that targets residential and commercial growth. Downtown Dallas has been slow to reach its desired critical mass. At the same time, leaders in Dallas have sought to meet the needs of the area's low-income and homeless populations. Among the first cities in the nation to adopt a 10-year plan to end chronic homelessness, Dallas subsequently passed a multimillion dollar homeless assistance bond initiative.

Relationships among faith-based organizations, citizen coalitions, and business groups have been especially contentious in Dallas. Several key issues continue to divide the city, particularly with regard to homelessness. Business, government, and community groups have a "not-in-my-backyard" attitude toward the siting of the homeless assistance center in the downtown area. Similarly, the high-rise project studying Dallas stirred contention among local groups.

Homelessness continues to be at the forefront of political discussions in Dallas, and the city council has enacted numerous policies in an attempt to regulate the impact of homelessness on economic development potential in downtown areas. Although it is difficult to accurately measure homeless populations (e.g., Burt et al. 2001; Link et al. 1994; Toro and Warren 1999), estimates of the number of homeless in Dallas range from 3,000 to 8,000. The Dallas Area Continuum of Care, the primary funding apparatus for homeless service nonprofits in the area, estimates that nearly 3,000 homeless people receive services. A significant portion of both the homeless population and homeless service organizations are located in or near downtown Dallas—the area targeted for economic development. Therefore, Dallas's economic development efforts and low-income housing concerns often conflict.

Following the lead of other metropolitan areas such as New York and Phoenix, Dallas decided to formulate a long-term plan for addressing homelessness. In the summer of 2003, the United Way of Metropolitan Dallas convened representatives from a variety of organizations concerned with homelessness to discuss the city's tactics in addressing the issue. The Dallas City Council approved the Dallas Ten-Year Plan to Identify Goals, Strategies and Methodology to Impact and End Chronic Homelessness on May 12, 2004.

The primary outcomes necessary for successful implementation of the 10-year plan center on housing, including emergency, transitional, and permanent housing. Of these, permanent housing concerns are most costly and could force Dallas to make difficult compromises relative to other housing needs and economic development plans. Along with the 10-year plan, the city council approved significant tax abatement incentives for residential development plans that include low-income units in their capital projects.

In November 2005, Dallas voters approved a $23.8 million general obligation bond to fund single-room-occupancy apartments. The funds were issued in May 2006. Subsequently, in February 2007, after more than five years of debate on the issue, City of Dallas officials broke ground on the new homeless assistance center located in the 1800 block of Corsicana Street in downtown, just a few blocks from city hall. Scheduled to open in 2008, the new center will provide expanded services for nearly 400 people a day.

Some city council decisions have not been as favorable toward the homeless. In 2003, the Dallas City Council passed a law making panhandling illegal. Under pressure from the local business community, the council determined that aggressive panhandling was dangerous and invasive. In its investigation of the issue, *The Dallas Morning News* found that 2,652 panhandling citations were issued between April 2003 and November 2005. Of those, only eight resulted in paid fines. More than 500 of those people cited for panhandling served jail time in lieu of paying fines. In May 2007, the city council approved measures that tightened the earlier panhandling ordinance. The new measures included strict prohibitions on the verbal solicitation of money near restaurants or while someone is putting money into a parking meter (Levinthal 2007).

In August 2005, the city council approved a measure that made mobile food distributions illegal. Charitable organizations such as Hunger Busters distributed nearly 1,200 meals a week to the poor based on where the greatest numbers congregated. The council's measure required that organizations serve food only at approved locations or face a fine of $200 to $2,000 (Korosec 2005).

Public perceptions of the homeless in Dallas echo the sentiments of Thompsett et al. (2006, 60) in their study of attitudes, opinions, and knowledge regarding homelessness in the United States. The authors conclude, "The public appears to hold increasingly complex views of the homeless population and factors contributing to homelessness. Advocates may take heart that the general public is moving away from old stereotypes about homeless people and may be increasingly willing to support new policy initiatives directed at increasing availability of low-income housing or essential services for homeless individuals and families." While the adoption of the 10-year plan and subsequent actions indicate progress in addressing homelessness in Dallas, businesses and local leaders continue to struggle with balancing social service needs and downtown development.

City Walk at Akard

Central Dallas Ministries, a faith-based nonprofit organization focused on providing social services in Dallas's inner-city neighborhoods, formed the Central Dallas Community Development Corporation (CDCDC) in 2002 to expand its focus on affordable housing projects. As an independently recognized 501(c)(3) organization, the CDCDC seeks to mitigate Dallas's economic segregation by increasing the number of units of inner-city affordable housing. The CDCDC currently maintains four multifamily apartment complexes located in the city's most impoverished sections.

In an effort to promote its affordable housing mission in downtown Dallas, the CDCDC set its sights on an abandoned building near the center of the business district. Located at 511 North Akard, the 15-story 167,000-square-foot City Walk building will be transformed into the area's newest permanent housing project for homeless individuals and families. Upon completion in 2008, its 209 units will include 132 studio, 75 one-bedroom, and 2 two-bedroom apartments. Nine units will be priced at market rate, while the remaining 200 will be subsidized for low-income individuals and families.

Public hearings on the high-rise development attracted more than 100 area residents and business owners. The leading concerns of those attending hearings included whether the property would be professionally managed, whether tenants would be appropriately screened, and whether armed security would be provided (Horner 2006b). During the March 21, 2006, community hearing on the issue and under mounting concern over the project, the CDCDC agreed to reduce the number of units available to the homeless by half, from 100 to 50. Larry James, Central Dallas Ministries chief executive officer, maintained, "This is not a homeless shelter" (Horner 2006b).

On March 28, 2006, the Dallas City Council approved the City Walk at Akard project. At the council meeting, the head of a religious school located near the high-rise voiced opposition to the project. Supporting the cause throughout, Councilor Angela Hunt, in whose district the project will be developed said, "We must make sure our downtown welcomes people from all walks of life" (Horner 2006a). As part of the measure, the council agreed to provide up to $1 million from the city's November 2005 bond election funds to help finance the homeless assistance portion of the project. The Dallas City Council's affirmative voted also cleared the way for the CDCDC's receipt of a $750,000 federal community block grant (Webb 2006). Further, the city council agreed to support the developer's application for cost-reducing state tax credits. In exchange, "The nonprofit agency also [allowed] the city to approve a security plan, the choice of property manager, and the retailers expected to move into the bottom floor. Rent at City Walk will range from $348 to $1,000 a month" (Horner 2006b). As part of the compromise, the CDCDC agreed to conduct thorough criminal background checks on all residents and gave the City of Dallas the right to approve the building's security plan.

As of this writing, construction on City Walk at Akard was scheduled to begin in late 2007. Planners anticipate completion in the fall of 2008. The renovation is projected to cost more than $30 million using a combination of government and private grants and tax credits. To date, private companies and government entities have committed funding to the high-rise project. Despite some criticism from the community, the City Walk at Akard project is proving to be a viable contribution to the downtown Dallas landscape.

Conclusion

According to Hanson (2003, 373), "The independent sector is uniquely positioned to inject concerns for development of social and civic capital into deliberations about the city's welfare and to reinforce its moral arguments with resources that facilitate development of a rich network of intermediary social and civic institutions." The ability of the nonprofit sector to represent community concerns in planning and economic development is shown in this case study of a Dallas community development corporation's attempt to achieve its objectives while improving the lives of inhabitants. The study also shows that the unique values inherent to philanthropic organizations such as those in Dallas help facilitate the modern collaborative nature of the development process in which all three sectors work together.

Nonprofit organizations such as the CDCDC help preserve civil society through "harmoniz(ing) the conflicting demands of individual interest and social good" (Seligman 1992, 16). The CDCDC discovered throughout the high-rise planning process that civil society concerns occasionally conflict with multiple stakeholder concerns, especially over controversial issues like homelessness. Additionally, consistent with assumptions about the relationship between social capital and the nonprofit sector, the CDCDC has maintained its community focus and demonstrated the cooperative benefit of trust in disputatious situations.

Although the CDCDC's impact on the area's low-income population and overall economic development remains unclear, the planning process has been productive, wrought as it has been with necessary compromises among the nonprofit organization, citizen and business groups, and city administrators. The grassroots approach appears to be working in this case, despite the contentiousness among groups and the potential for community control to be undermined by reservations regarding the adverse effects of local economic development. The CDCDC's careful planning and focus on community building efforts to revitalize poor neighborhoods through collaboration and consensus is promising. The outcomes of this case study may help nonprofit managers and public administrators who are concerned with balancing the need for affordable housing and economic development understand the importance of negotiating citizen priorities and stakeholder interests in development efforts.

References

Basolo, Victoria. 2000. City spending on economic development versus affordable housing: Does inner-city competition or local politics drive decisions? *Journal of Urban Affairs* 22:317–22.

Bowles, Samuel, and Herbert Gintis. 2002. Social capital and community governance. *The Economic Journal* 112:419–36.

Burt, Martha R., Laudan Y. Aron, Edgar Lee, and Jesse Valente. 2001. *Helping America's homeless: Emergency shelter or affordable housing?* Washington, DC: Urban Institute Press.

Clarke, S. E., and M. R. Siaz. 1996. Economic development and infrastructure policy. In *Politics in the American states: A comparative analysis.* 6th ed., ed. V. Gray and H. Jacobs, 516–48. Washington, DC: Congressional Quarterly Press.

Eberly, Don E., ed. 2000. *The essential civil society reader: The classic essays.* Lanham, MD: Rowman & Littlefield.

Goetz, E. G., and M. Sydney. 1994. *Revenge of the property owners: Community development and the politics of property.* St. Paul: University of Minnesota Housing Program.

Hanson, Royce. 2003. *Civic culture and urban change: Governing Dallas.* Detroit: Wayne State University Press.

Hazel, Michael V. 1997. *Dallas: A history of "Big D."* Austin: Texas State Historical Association Press.

Hill, Patricia E. 1996. *Dallas: The making of a modern city.* Austin: University of Texas Press.

Horner, Kim. 2006a. Low income housing gets thumbs up. *Dallas Morning News*, March 28. www.dallasnews.com/cgi-bin/bi/gold_print.cgi. Accessed March 29.

————. 2006b. Proposed complex has skeptics. *Dallas Morning News*, March 21. www.dallasnews.com/cgi-bin/bi/gold_print.cgi. Accessed March 21.

Korosec, Thomas. 2005. Dallas law cracks down on feeding homeless; mobile units won't be parked outside City Hall or they'll face fine. *Houston Chronicle, Star Edition*, August 7, B-4.

Krumholz, Norman. 1999. Equitable approaches to local economic development. *Policy Studies Journal* 27:83–95.

Levinthal, Dave. 2007. Dallas gets tough on panhandlers. *Dallas Morning News*, May 23. www.dallasnews.com/cgi-bin/bi/gold_print.cgi. Accessed May 23.

Link, Bruce G., Ezra Susser, Ann Stueve, Jo Phelan, Robert E. Moore, and Elmer Struening. 1994. Lifetime and five-year prevalence of homelessness in the United States. *American Journal of Public Health* 84:1907–12.

Olberding, Julie Cencula. 2002. Diving into the "third waves" of regional governance and economic development strategies: A study of regional partnerships for economic development in U.S. metropolitan areas. *Economic Development Quarterly* 16:251–72.

Putnam, Robert D. 2000. *Bowling alone: The collapse and revival of American community.* New York: Simon & Schuster.

Robinson, Tony. 1996. Inner-city innovator: The non-profit community development corporation. *Urban Studies* 33:1647–70.

Seligman, Adam. 1992. *The idea of civil society.* New York: Free Press.

Stoecker, Randy. 1997. The CDC model of urban redevelopment: A critique and an alternative. *Journal of Urban Affairs* 19:1–22.

Thompsett, Carolyn J., Paul A. Toro, Melissa Guzicki, Manuel Manrique, and Jigna Zatakia. 2006. Homelessness in the United States: Assessing changes in prevalence and public opinion, 1993–2001. *American Journal of Community Psychology* 37:47–61.

Toro, Paul A., and Melissa G. Warren. 1999. Homelessness in the United States: Policy considerations. *Journal of Community Psychology* 29:119–36.

Webb, Cynthia D. 2006. Dallas City Council approves low-income housing project. *Dallas Business Journal*, March 28. www.bizjournals.com/dallas/stories/2006/03/27/daily18.html?t-printable. Accessed March 19, 2007.

CHAPTER 15

Rural Prison Sitings in North Carolina:
Competition and Community Leaders' Attitudes

Michele Hoyman, Jennifer Weaver, and Micah Weinberg

Prison sitings typically have been considered a "locally un-wanted land use" or a "not-in-my-backyard" issue, but counties and small towns across America are now competing—sometimes furiously—over the sitings of new public and private prisons (Pagel 1988; Walsh 1994). It may seem surprising that competition would erupt over prisons, but these institutions have become one of the few available economic development options for communities in rural America that have suffered the collapse of their manufacturing bases over the past decade. This case study explores how the process of competition for prison sitings in one state, North Carolina, can inform our knowledge of competition for such projects generally. The focus is on how community leaders conceptualize and gather information about prison sitings. The findings may add insight into why prisons have become economic development trophies.

Although prison sitings have grown in popularity as an economic development strategy, evidence of long-term favorable economic impacts that would rationalize this popularity is mixed at best (Besser and Hanson 2005; Blankenship and Yaranella 2004; Farrigan and Glasmeier 2007; Hooks et al. 2004; King, Mauer, and Huling 2003; Turner and Thayer 2003; Hoyman, Weaver and Weinberg 2007). Nevertheless, leaders still opt to attract prisons for the immediate-term jobs they bring, most often in states such as North Carolina, where prison jobs are public-sector jobs and therefore bring generous benefit packages. Leaders' enthusiasm for such projects has been dubbed the "public-sector-jobs-are-better" phenomenon (Kaatz and Morris 2000).

The quest for new prison sitings is primarily a rural phenomenon, with the vast majority of recent prison projects going to nonurban areas (Beale 1996). Rural areas are attractive for prison sitings because they have large land tracts, and more importantly, rural communities perceive prisons as one of the few viable options available for economic development. In Jones and Bachelor's parlance (1986), "the solution set" of acceptable traditional economic development options has shrunk so much that prisons are now a viable option within that solution set for rural areas. This case study analyzes the form that this competition takes in North Carolina as well as leaders' aspirations, fears, and preferences that fuel this competition.

Competition for Prisons

The focus here is on counties because prison-siting competition typically occurs among counties rather than cities, as is the case for sports stadiums (Rosentraub 1997; Danielson 1997). The type of siting arrangements (Ammons, Campbell, and Somoza 1992) and thus competition for prison sitings varies across states. In the Midwest, there are some extreme examples of open and fierce competition for prisons. In states such as Missouri and Illinois, host county contenders appear before the relevant state legislative committee to tout their community as the best site (Young 1994). Other states such as North Carolina have a more "quiet" process whereby the state places counties in a queue in which they wait their turn for a siting.

Stated in Reese and Fasenfest's (1997) terms, the decision to site prisons is a value choice, and how that value choice is defined can influence the degree of competition for a designated choice. One value choice pertains to the economic security of prison jobs. Communities that consider adding a prison desire jobs that are more stable and diverse than those within the more volatile manufacturing sector. It also may be the case that the values associated with "good" public administration or efficiency may be at odds with the values that would make good sense in terms of an equitable distribution of economic development opportunities across a state. For example, from the value of overall efficiency, it may be advisable to have a limited number of huge prison complexes, but from the value perspective of a governor who seeks political popularity, a wide dispersion of prisons across the state may appear both more equitable and more politically advantageous. This wide dispersion also lessens competition by making the opportunities more numerous. As other scholars have pointed out, bringing economic development opportunities to a state increases the vote margins for incumbent governors (Turner 2006).

As this case study shows, county leaders in North Carolina look to prison sitings as a chance to bring jobs to their communities, and they also have aspirations for the prison beyond these immediate jobs. The leaders hope that prisons will attract other retail business and fill the coffers of local businesses with income from the goods purchased by the prison. In addition, in North Carolina, many rural counties either lack countywide water and sewer systems, or the existing systems are outdated or inadequate. Previous studies have established that it is neither the poorest counties nor the highest percentage minority counties that seek and are granted prison sitings (Hoyman and Weinberg 2006). Counties with certain demographics such as low education, low population density, and a low percentage of home ownership were those that sought prisons. Several public and nonprofit organizations in North Carolina make infrastructure grants available to counties that have an economic development project that requires improved infrastructure. Prison sitings provide an opportunity to improve infrastructure. Finally, some claim that prison sitings in effect annex populations from urban areas to struggling rural areas (Gage 2000). Since many state and federal programs are allocated on a per capita basis, many areas with declining rural populations view prisons as a population windfall as well as an economic boon.

Prison incarceration has become a cottage industry, and prison space is being bought and sold, causing prisoners to be "exported" and "imported" across state lines. Three recent cases of interstate competition for "prison-bed commerce" are noteworthy. When overcrowding in Missouri prisons reached a peak in the 1990s, the legislature declined to build more prisons. To deal with mounting overcrowding concerns, Missouri prisoners were exported to private prisons overseen by the State of Texas. Later, prisoners were returned to Missouri after those exported prisoners won a court case in which it was ruled that prison conditions in Texas did not meet minimal constitutional standards (Blakely and Bumphus 2005). This example is typical of the pathologies of private prisons that are perhaps best characterized as both public and market failures (Morris 2007). In another case, the state of Virginia realized it had surplus prison beds and sold spots to other governments for $20,000 each. More recently, ads appeared in a midwestern state targeted at prison families in a state with overcrowded prisons. The ads highlighted good prison conditions in the state. Interstate prison competition is beginning, but it is too early to predict whether these purchases, sales, and swaps of prisoners will become a trend.

The Missouri-Texas case does highlight the public versus private prison dilemma. Communities do not usually have control over the choice to have a private or state-run prison. Communities may have input about whether to site a prison, but decisions about public versus private are made at the state level. For example, virtually all correctional facilities are state prisons in North Carolina. Two prisons were originally private but were later converted to state-administered prisons. Although some states may try to save money by contracting out prisons to private corporations, they often encounter problems because of their inability to provide effective oversight of privatized prisons.

There are distinct differences between state-administered and privately administered prisons. For state-administered prisons, the government sets pay and benefits for employees as well as standards for prisoner treatment. State-administered prisons generate no property tax revenue for the community. By contrast, privately administered prisons pay property taxes, and employee compensation and benefits vary. The government must conduct continuous oversight of private facilities to ensure they adhere to standards for prison treatment.

The State's Role in Prison Sitings

Siting a prison in the Midwest has become an openly competitive process in recent years. Intense competition for prison sitings usually means the prison is being viewed explicitly as an economic development vehicle. Such competitions often result in a community prevailing based on its state representative's seniority, the sympathy of other state representatives or state senators for that particular county, or its clout either within the state legislature or with the prison committee chair. It is clear that more communities are joining this competition every year. Of particular interest are localities that have shunned prisons and then later vigorously recruited them. Thies (1998) tells the story of Potosi, a town in Missouri that rejected a prison in the 1970s but later aggressively courted a new women's prison. The town began recruiting the prison after its two largest employers, a mine and a shoe factory, closed. The closing of these businesses had elevated the town's unemployment to 23 percent.

North Carolina handles prison sitings in a somewhat distinctive manner. The Department of Correction—not the state legislature—is the dominant actor. While individual legislators do occasionally perform a brokering role, they are not dominant players. Established practice in North Carolina dictates that the county pays for the plot of land and the provision of lines for sewage and water for the prison—an expensive outlay for the county. Finally, because the state views prison allocations as economic development projects, North Carolina chooses to construct numerous smaller prisons to spread jobs throughout the state rather than build fewer super prisons that may save the state money on capital expenditures for the facilities. This dispersion approach is not necessarily the most efficient one. However, criminology studies do show a relationship between large prisons and unrest. Local leaders have resisted the idea of closing prisons for the purpose of consolidation if it means losing jobs. For example, the former governor of Illinois encountered resistance from prison employee unions and communities themselves when he tried to close prisons in 2002 (Stanton 2002).

The North Carolina Case: "Quiet Competition"

Given county leaders' positive perceptions of prisons as economic development projects, why has North Carolina not experienced the open competition for prisons that some midwestern states have? The prison-siting process designed by the state may be one reason. In contrast to the open-competition model, North Carolina has been described as a "quiet"-siting state (Hoyman 2002), meaning that the Department of Correction discourages open competition among counties for prisons and attempts to accommodate the counties in the state that desire a prison as the need for prison construction arises.

In North Carolina, when state authorities determine a need for new prison construction, the Department of Correction sends out a request for proposal to all counties. When the Department of Correction receives responses to a proposal, officials inspect potential sites to ensure conformity to state specifications. The state also requires that the prison siting be politically acceptable to the community. A favorable majority vote from the county commission signals to state authorities that the community will accept the prison. Thus, in North Carolina prison siting is a voluntary process by the county. Other states such as Michigan have a mandatory process; that is, the state may exercise eminent domain to acquire land for the prison. Rabe's (1994) work on siting socially undesirable projects supports the notion that states that have a voluntary siting process and dispersed prison-siting patterns encounter the least resistance when taking on such projects. In this sense, then, North Carolina may be considered the "easiest" type of state in which to site prisons (Rabe 1994).

The Study

There are several reasons why North Carolina is a good case for research into rural prison sitings. Of the 100 counties in the state, 79 were designated as rural in the 1990 census. Twenty-four counties have considered prison sitings since 1970. Thus, this fairly large number of recent prison sitings provides a sufficient number of "observations" from a research perspective. Further, the one-state approach is advantageous because it holds institutional and state-specific variables constant (Nicholson-Crotty and Meier 2002). Also, North Carolina counties are powerful actors mirroring the national trend of devolution of certain social policy responsibilities to the substate level (Kelleher and Yackee 2004).

This study examines local leaders' attitudes toward prison sitings and why they view prison projects as potentially desirable or undesirable. Of the 79 rural counties, 15 have considered a siting since 1994, and 13 have actually sited a prison. Sitings that were considered earlier than 1994 were not included because of the difficulty in finding respondents who were familiar with those earlier decision processes.

Attitudes of Community Leaders

The questions that guided this research into why community leaders are favorable toward prison sitings were as follows: What are the perspectives of community leaders when defining prison issues? Do leaders define prisons in positive terms (benefits) or in negative terms (fears and costs)? How do leaders prioritize their opinions on prison issues? And, finally, how do community leaders' opinions compare with how they perceive the public's opinions on a prison siting?

The data for this study were gathered from 84 interviews conducted from February 2003 to August 2004 in 15 counties in North Carolina that had considered accepting a prison siting since 1994. Thirteen of these counties eventually sited a prison, although several of those sited are still under construction. Of the 84 leaders interviewed, 47 were elected, including chairs of county commissions, mayors, and state representatives. Twenty-three interviewees were appointed officials, including county managers and economic development directors. Other interviewees included business leaders, teachers, and newspaper editors and reporters.

The unit of analysis was the county leader even though the geographical and political unit that is empowered to make the siting decisions is the county. No referendum of the voters in a county is necessary to substantiate that the prison siting is popularly acceptable. All that is required is a majority vote of county commissioners. Therefore, it is the leadership, not the public at large, that initiates the pursuit of a project and signals the agreement to construct a prison.

Each interview was composed of both structured and open-ended questions targeted at county leaders. The kinds of county leaders responsible for facilitating the prison siting were slightly different in each county. A "snowball" sample was used to identify persons who were important actors in the decision-making process. County commissioners were contacted and then interviewed and asked to identify other key proponents and opponents of the prison project. These individuals were subsequently interviewed. A particular effort was made to reach not only those who favored the prison siting but also those who opposed it.

A prison siting can connote different issues for different people, consistent with the issue-definition literature (Kingdon 1995; Carmines and Stimson 1989). Respondents were asked to identify which issues (i.e., considerations) influenced their decision and to rank them. The question included 20 possible issues a leader might have considered when deciding to site a prison. These issues were drawn from the literature regarding how citizens and leaders view prison sitings. Issues were categorized as benefits, fears, and costs. "Benefits" include the number and types of jobs; job benefits, pay, security, and diversity; creation of spin-off industries and commerce; and hopes for additional state projects and property tax revenue. The "fear" category includes breakouts, influx of "undesirables," lower property values, increase in crime, stigma of being a prison town, and increase in traffic. "Costs" include cost of land; land preparation; sewage and water expenses; the burden on the educational system and associated property tax implications posed by in-migrant employees of the prison who are renters, not property owners; and local employers' loss of employees to the prison. The dataset for the leaders also contains information about the prison campaign process, including the ways in which counties consulted with other counties to assuage the public's fear of certain prison-siting issues. Finally, leaders were asked to identify and rank the issues their communities would consider in evaluating a prison siting.

The issues considered by leaders when siting prisons are shown in Table 1. Ninety percent of leaders identify job creation as an important criterion, along with job benefits packages, pay, security, and diversity. The sizable percentage of leaders who identified spin-off industries and commerce as important is indicative of leaders' aspirations that a prison siting will be a lucrative economic development project. Conversely, fewer leaders regarded a prison siting as an opportunity to garner more state projects in the future. This result is peculiar because leaders did indicate in interviews that they were fearful of rejecting a prison siting because the state might interpret the rejection as a signal to stop proposing other development projects.

Property tax revenue was named by 48 percent of leaders as a benefit of a prison siting. Because the transfer of the prison site to the state effectively removes the prison from the tax rolls, leaders may expect indirect revenue increases, believing that the prison will spur business growth or that prison employees who had been renting homes prior to working at the prison will ultimately purchase homes. Although

Table 1: Leadership Perceptions of Prison-Siting Issues and Leadership Views of Community Perceptions

Issue	Leadership Percent	(N)	Community Percent	(N)
Benefits				
Jobs	90	76	85	71
Job benefits	86	72	74	62
Job pay	81	68	80	67
Job security	96	81	76	64
Job diversity	64	54	56	47
Spin-off industries	60	50	51	43
Spin-off commerce	70	59	56	47
Additional state projects	54	45	46	39
Property tax revenue	48	40	43	36
Fears				
Breakouts	61	51	75	63
Influx of "undesirables"	57	48	64	54
Lower property values	55	46	65	55
Increase in crime	50	42	58	49
Stigma of prison town	60	50	68	57
Increased traffic	60	50	61	51
Costs				
Land cost	68	57	55	46
Land preparation	46	39	35	29
Sewage and water	70	59	60	50
Education of employees' children	38	32	36	30
Loss of employees to prison	49	41	49	41

N = 84.

community leaders do define the prison-siting issue in terms of fears or negative externalities, their fears appear to be dwarfed by their positive perceptions of the potential benefits of jobs.[1] Even though they were most fearful of the likelihood of breakouts, leaders reported that such incidents had not actually been a problem after the prison opened.

In terms of prison-siting costs, most leaders indicated that they were worried about the cost of the land (68 percent) and the cost of providing water and sewer infrastructure (70 percent). In general, leaders were not concerned about other costs like land preparation, financing the public education of in-migrants, or the fear of local employers losing employees to the prison because of its offer of superior pay and benefits.

Table 1 also reveals that a high degree of congruity exists between community leaders' attitudes and their perceptions of public attitudes. Fifty to 60 percent of leaders define a prison siting in terms of at least one fear. One interesting finding is the high congruence between leaders' own perceptions of the issues and leaders' report of the community's perceptions of issues.

Ranking of Prison-Siting Issues

Leaders were asked to rank as many as 20 different issues to measure the intensity of their perceptions regarding prison sitings. Issues that received a #1 ranking are shown in Table 2. Of the 64 leaders who participated, 57 ranked benefits, 2 ranked fears, and 5 ranked cost-related concerns as the top prison-siting issue. Forty-five respondents indicated jobs were the #1 issue related to prison sitings. Thus, the predominant way in which leaders perceived the issue could be described as "prison equals jobs."

Although community leaders' attitudes and their perceptions of public attitudes generally are congruent, there are two exceptions. First, the fear that prisons will lower property values was ranked #1 by only one leader, but leaders perceive this issue to be important to the public. Second, 12 leaders ranked fear of breakouts as the public's #1 concern, but none of the leaders reported the fear of breakouts as their own #1 fear.

Table 2: Leadership Ranking of Prison-Siting
Issues for Themselves and Their Community

Issue	#1 for Leadership	#1 for Community
Benefits		
Jobs	45	40
Job benefits	0	1
Job pay	2	2
Job security	1	1
Job diversity	2	2
Spin-off industries	1	0
Spin-off commerce	0	1
Additional state projects	1	0
Property tax revenue	5	1
Fears		
Breakouts	0	12
Influx of "undesirables"	0	0
Lower property values	1	3
Stigma of prison town	1	0
Increased traffic	0	0
Costs		
Land cost	4	3
Land preparation	0	0
Sewage and water	1	0
Loss of employees to prison	0	1

$N = 64$.

Role of Information

One of the main challenges a community faces when siting a prison is a large information deficit. The state has a great deal of information, having sited many prisons; a community, on the other hand, may have very little information if it is pursuing its first siting. Objective facts about the impacts of prisons are hard for community leaders to find. For example, early National Institute of Justice studies indicated that the negative externalities of sitings, such as breakouts or declines in property values, were largely mythical (K. Carlson 1988; 1990; P. Carlson 1988; 1990; 1991; 1992; Parcells and Farrington 1988; Lidman, Poole, and Roper 1988). However, the findings of these studies have not been widely disseminated. Consequently, they are largely unknown to community leaders throughout the nation. Practitioners may be unaware that there is clear consensus in the literature on the economic impacts of prisons: they do not provide long-term economic panaceas for struggling towns (Besser and Hanson 2005; Blankenship and Yaranella 2004; Farrigan and Glasmeier 2007; King, Mauer, and Huling 2003; Hooks et al. 2004; Turner and Thayer 2003; Hoyman, Weaver, and Weinberg 2007). To a certain degree, it is hard to reconcile the minimal long-term economic effects with the popularity of prisons (Hoyman, Weaver, and Weinberg 2007). Often, the decision to site a prison takes place amid a swirl of information and misinformation that includes rumors, promises, and fears about negative externalities.

Information asymmetry must be considered when analyzing county leaders' perceptions regarding issues related to prison sitings. The Department of Correction may convey a specific subset of the information a county needs to make a sound development decision. The information most often pertains to incarceration-related issues, such as fear of breakouts, without addressing the long-term impacts of prisons on communities. The following memo from one county manager to another manager who was considering a prison siting in 2003 illustrates the limited nature of such information (Ron George, county manager of Burke County):

1. There is no increase in crime.
2. Breakouts are rare. When there is an escape, the escapee wants to get out of the county as soon as possible.
3. Prison spending will equal $2,000,000 a year within the county.
4. Real estate values generally do not go down.

It is important to note that the Department of Correction does not provide any documentary evidence to support these tacit reassurances. No studies are cited to back up the department's claim regarding prison spending or its assertion that real estate values will not decrease, though evidence suggests that there will in fact be no decrease (K. Carlson 1988; 1990; P. Carlson 1988; 1990; 1991; 1992; Thies 2000). The retail spending effects cited in this memo were not supported by any data in any study.

County Consultations

One way for county leaders to gather useful information in order to compete effectively is to consult with other counties that have sited prisons. This study found that North Carolina county consultations were quite geographically dispersed. Rather than primarily consulting adjacent counties that had sited a prison in the past, leaders more often consulted counties that had recently sited a prison, regardless of geographic proximity. Out of 13 counties that consulted other counties regarding their experiences with the siting process, only 6 worked with adjacent counties. Of the 51 counties that were consulted, only 8 were adjacent to siting counties.

In addition, leaders were asked which issues they discussed with other counties. These issues fell into the same broad categories of benefits, costs, and fears. Although most leaders felt a prison siting would be beneficial in terms of bringing jobs to the community, most of their questions centered on the fear of breakouts and potential rise in crime rates. Leaders seemed willing to assume that jobs would come to the siting county but needed to rebut the fears in order to assuage the misgivings of their home constituents. They focused on refuting negatives rather than confirming positives. Though this tactic may have helped the county land the prison siting by garnering community acceptance, it may inadvertently have led counties to compete for unconfirmed benefits.

In terms of the consulting process, two themes emerge. First, while the Department of Correction's information is not intentionally inaccurate, it does not address community concerns about long-term economic effects. Second, communities engage in what could be called a simplistic search. Communities do not really seek out the truth on prison siting–related issues like jobs, but they go through the motions of assuaging fears. This type of approach is a bounded rational approach. For communities, this type of consultative process can be fast, free, and politically relevant. Consultations may not include a comprehensive "search for the truth" as regards long-term economic impacts, but they do focus on "deal breakers" (e.g., if there were evidence to fuel citizens' fears that crime would go up or surrounding real estate values would go down after a prison siting). That being said, had the counties consulted an "outsider" such as an independent agent or academic to help them in their decisions, they might not have received as timely information as that provided by peer counties.

Conclusion

North Carolina has a voluntary prison-siting process, and its siting patterns are dispersed. The process is less overtly competitive than it is in states in the Midwest, where communities openly compete for sitings. North Carolina is different from states in which the siting process is mandatory. North Carolina's Department of Correction prevents open competition by placing interested counties in a queue. So far, this queue has been short because new prisons have come online frequently and the state has been able to accommodate all comers without a long wait. The Department of Correction acts as a broker and engages in "quiet" sitings. If a prison has already been promised to a county, the department will signify to an interested county that it can have the next prison siting. Although occasionally a very senior state senator or leader has lured a project to a particular county, this occurrence is rarer than in overtly competitive states.

North Carolina has largely succeeded in creating this environment of minimal competition for two reasons: (1) its policy is to site many small prisons and no super-prison complexes and (2) rural area leaders view prisons as a good thing (i.e., a source of jobs). Eighty-five percent of interviewees equated prisons with jobs, and 78 percent felt that prisons mean jobs with good benefits packages. Although many leaders had fears to do with prison sitings (i.e., fear of breakouts, influx of "undesirables," lower property values, increase in crime, the stigmatization of being a prison town, and increases in traffic), those who expressed fears were far fewer than those who expressed enthusiasm regarding jobs.

The general literature on competition among many localities for a few designated prison sitings suggests that one disadvantage of competition is that host counties "race to the bottom"; that is, the high initial outlay needed to acquire the economic development project is continually raised, making the ultimate economic payoff increasingly uncertain. This situation does not hold in North Carolina because the Department of Correction brokers each siting (although the land costs associated with prison sitings and sewage and water costs are borne by the county). North Carolina provides an example of what economists refer to as a managed competition model. The North Carolina Division of Prisons has a queuing system whereby counties are asked to wait in line for the next prison. This system reduces the negative effects of direct competition. One negative effect occurs when the cost of a prison for a county goes up—and economic benefit goes down—with each additional competitor as each competitor promises more in an attempt to win the siting (Milward and Newman 1989; Thomas 1997). If there is a strong authority (usually a government entity) that is allocating these scarce commodities, as there is in North Carolina, some of the pathologies of the race to the bottom may be avoided.

Currently, there is very little competition among states for prisons. In fact, ironically, some states that have an oversupply of prison beds or prison spots are "selling" them to other states. Nevertheless, competition is a determining factor when it comes to prison sitings. Competition for state prisons usually occurs among counties, particularly rural counties, where a disproportionate number of new prisons are being sited. The strategy employed by counties in North Carolina of attracting prisons as economic development opportunities may be instructive for county governments in other states wishing to enhance their economic prospects.

Note

1. Negative externalities are costs associated with economic activities that are thrust on everyone in society. For example, a factory's release of toxic pollutants affects the community surrounding the factory as well as the factory's owner.

References

Ammons, David, Richard Campbell, and Sandra Somoza. 1992. *Selecting prison sites: State processes, site-selection criteria and local initiatives.* Athens: Carl Vinson Institute of Government, University of Georgia.

Beale, Calvin. 1996. Rural prisons: An update. *Rural Development Perspectives* 11: 25–27.

Besser, Terry L., and Margaret M. Hanson. 2005. The development of last resort: The impact of new state prisons on small town economics. *Journal of the Community Development Society* 35:1–16.

Blakely, Curtis R., and Vic W. Bumphus. 2005. An analysis of civil suits filed against private and public prisons: A comparison of Title 42 Section 1983 litigation. *Criminal Justice Policy Review* 16:74–87.

Blankenship, Susan E., and Ernest J. Yaranella. 2004. Prison recruitment as a policy tool of local economic development: A critical evaluation. *Contemporary Justice Review* 7:183–98.

Carlson, Katherine. 1988. Understanding community opposition to prison siting: More than fear and finances. *Correction Today* 50:84–90.

_____. 1990. *The impacts of a new prison on a small town: Twice blessed or double whammy? Final report of Clallam Bay Project.* Report no. 85-1J-CG- 0022. Washington, DC: National Institute of Justice.

Carlson, Peggy. 1988. Clallam Bay, Clallam County, and the Clallum Bay Correction Center. In *Impacts of Washington State's correctional communities,* ed. Russel M. Lidman and Barbara Poole, iii–viii, 251–71. Olympia: Washington State Institute for Public Policy.

_____. 1990. Prison escapes and community consequences: Results of a case study. *Federal Probation* 54:36–42.

_____. 1991. What happens and what counts: Residents' assessments of prison impacts on their communities. *Humboldt Journal of Social Relations* 17: 211–38.

_____. 1992. Doing good and looking bad: A case study of prison community relations. *Crime and Delinquency* 38:56–69.

Carmines, Edward G., and James A. Stimson. 1989. *Issue evolution: Race and the transformation of American politics.* Princeton: Princeton University Press.

Danielson, Michael N. 1997. *Home team: Professional sports and the American metropolis.* Princeton, NJ: Princeton University Press.

Farrigan, Tracey L., and Amy K. Glasmeier. 2007. The economic impact of the prison development boom on persistently poor rural places. *International Regional Studies Review* 30:274–99.

Gage, Beverly. 2000. Prisoner nation. *The Nation* 271, no. 3: 5–7.

Hooks, Gregory, Clayton Mosher, Thomas Rotolo, and Linda Lobao. 2004. The prison industry: Carceral expansion and employment in U.S. counties, 1969–1994. *Social Science Quarterly* 85:37–57.

Hoyman, Michele. 2002. Prisons in North Carolina: Are they a rational strategy for rural economic development? *International Journal of Economic Development* 4, no. 1. www.spaef.com/IJED_PUB/index.html. Accessed April 14, 2008.

Hoyman, Michele, and Micah Weinberg. 2006. The process of policy innovation: Prison sitings in rural North Carolina. *Policy Studies Journal* 34:95–112.

Hoyman, Michele, Jennifer Weaver, and Micah Weinberg. 2007. Locking in a good deal? The economic impacts of state prisons on rural economic development. Unpublished manuscript. University of North Carolina.

Jones, Bryan D., and Lynn W. Bachelor. 1986. *The sustaining hand: Community leadership and corporate power.* Lawrence: University Press of Kansas.

Kaatz, James B., and John C. Morris. 2000. The overpaid bureaucrat: Comparing public and private wages in Mississippi. *Public Personnel Management* 29: 129–46.

Kelleher, Christine, and Susan Yackee. 2004. An empirical assessment of devolution's policy impact. *Policy Studies Journal* 32:253–70.

King, Ryan S., Marc Mauer, and Tracy Huling. 2003. *Big prisons, small towns: Prison economics in rural America*. Washington, DC: The Sentencing Project.

Kingdon, John W. 1995. *Agendas, alternatives, and public policies*. 2nd ed. New York: HarperCollins.

Lidman, Russell, Mary Poole, and Peggy Roper, eds. 1988. *Impacts of Washington State's correctional communities*. Olympia: Washington State Institute for Public Policy.

Milward, H. B., and H. H. Newman. 1989. State incentive packages and the industrial location decision. *Economic Development Quarterly* 3:203–22.

Morris, John C. 2007. Government and market pathologies of privatization: The case of prison privatization. *Politics & Policy* 35:318–41.

Nicholson-Crotty, Sean, and Kenneth Meier. 2002. Size doesn't matter: In defense of single state studies. *State Politics and Policy Quarterly* 2:411–22.

Pagel, Al. 1988. Prejudices set aside . . . communities woo prisons. *Corrections Compendium* 12:1, 6–8.

Parcells, Pete R, and Keith Farrington. 1988. Washington State penitentiary at Walla Walla, Washington. In *Impacts of Washington State's correctional institutions*, ed. Russell Lidman, Mary E. Poole, and Peggy Roper. Olympia: Department of Community Development.

Rabe, Barry. 1994. *Beyond NIMBY: Hazardous waste siting in Canada and the United States*. Washington, DC: The Brookings Institution.

Reese, Laura, and David Fasenfest. 1997. What works best? Values and the evaluation of local economic development policy. *Economic Development Quarterly* 11:195–221.

Rosentraub, Mark S. 1997. *Major league losers: The real cost of sports and who's paying for it*. New York: Basic Books.

Stanton, Elizabeth. 2002. Illinois government proposes cuts. *New York Times*, February 21, 20.

Thies, Jeanie. 1998. The Big House in a small town: The economic and social impacts of a correctional facility on its host community. PhD diss., University of Missouri–St. Louis.

_____ . 2000. Prisons and host communities: Debunking the myths of prison sitings. *Corrections Today* 62:136–39.

Thomas, Kenneth. 1997. *Capital beyond borders: States and firms in the auto industry, 1960–94*. New York: St. Martin's Press.

Turner, R. 2006. The political economy of trophy industrial recruitment projects. Paper presented at the State Politics and Policy Conference, Lubbock, TX.

Turner, Robert C., and Dave Thayer. 2003. Are prisons a sound economic development strategy for New York? The views of rural policy makers. Paper presented at the annual meeting of the Northeastern Political Science Association, Philadelphia.

Walsh, Edward. 1994. Strapped small towns try to lock up prisons. *Washington Post*, December 24, A3.

Young, Virginia. 1994. Five rural towns competing for new state prisons. *St. Louis Post Dispatch*, February 26, 6B.

About the Authors

Kimberly A. Aaron has over 25 years of financial and operational management experience in the private, public, and nonprofit sectors. She has consulted extensively with a variety of private- and public-sector organizations and has served as a volunteer and on the boards of several nonprofit organizations. She is the associate dean of students at the University of Texas at Dallas and a lecturer in the School of Economics, Politics, and Public Policy, where she teaches in the public affairs program. She has an MBA (with a concentration in finance) from the University of Arkansas and a PhD in public affairs from the University of Texas at Dallas.

R. Paul Battaglio Jr. is an assistant professor in the public affairs program in the School of Economic, Political, and Policy Sciences at the University of Texas at Dallas. His research and teaching interests include comparative policy and administration, public human resource management, and comparative political attitudes. His work has appeared in the *Journal of Comparative Policy Analysis*, *Public Administration Review*, and the *Review of Public Personnel Administration*. Before entering academic life, he served for six years in the governor's office in Louisiana. He earned an MPA from Louisiana State University and a PhD in public administration from the University of Georgia.

Floun'say R. Caver is the manager of budgets at the Greater Cleveland Regional Transit Authority, where he supervises a staff of six analysts and leads the organization's performance and productivity activities. He also is a part-time instructor at the Levin College of Urban Affairs at Cleveland State University. Dr. Caver has been recognized in the

Crain's Cleveland Business "40 under 40" list and is a member of the Hiram College Board of Visitors. He earned his MPA from Cleveland State University and his PhD in public affairs from the University of Texas at Dallas.

Laura Czohara is a senior analyst with the Defense Capabilities and Management Team of the U.S. Government Accountability Office. She has taught undergraduate classes on the public policy process at Georgia State University. Ms. Czohara received her MA in social science administration from Case Western Reserve University.

Grace Gallucci is the deputy executive director of research, analysis, and policy development for the Chicago Regional Transportation Authority. She holds an MS in urban studies from Cleveland State University and a BS and MPA in business administration from the University of Dayton. Ms. Gallucci has been an adjunct professor at Cleveland State University and Kent State University. She is active in various professional organizations including the American Society for Public Administration and the American Public Transportation Association and has served on research panels for the Transportation Research Board of the National Academies of Science.

Donna Milam Handley is an assistant professor at the University of Alabama at Birmingham, where she teaches in the MPA program. She previously served as assistant director of economic development for the City of Auburn, Alabama. Her work has been published in *Public Administration Review, Municipal Finance Journal, Journal of Public Affairs Education*, and *Journal of Public Budgeting, Accounting, and Financial Management*. Dr. Handley's teaching and research interests include intergovernmental policy systems, community development, nonprofit management, public budgeting, and the federal grant system. She holds a PhD in public administration and public policy from Auburn University.

Wendy L. Hassett has over 12 years of experience in local government management. Currently, she is a clinical associate professor of public affairs in the School of Economic, Political, and Policy Sciences at the University of Texas at Dallas. Her scholarly work has appeared in *Public Administration Review, Public Performance and Management Review, Review of Public Personnel Administration, Journal of Public Budgeting, Accounting and Financial Management*, and other journals. She is coauthor of *Civic Battles: When Cities Change Their Form of Government* (PrAcademics Press 2007) and coeditor of *Local Government Management: Current Issues and Best Practices* (M.E. Sharpe 2003). Dr. Hassett earned her PhD in Public Administration and Public Policy at Auburn University.

Michele M. Hoyman is an associate professor of political science at the University of North Carolina at Chapel Hill. She has a PhD in political science from the University of Michigan. Her research interests are in rural economic development, equal employment policy, labor policy, and public personnel management. Dr. Hoyman is the author of *Power Steering: Global Automakers and the Transformation of Rural Communities* (University Press of Kansas 1997). She is a professional arbitrator.

John R. Lombard is an associate professor of urban studies and public administration and director of the E. V. Williams Center for Real Estate and Economic Development at Old Dominion University. He has presented and published papers on a variety of real estate and economic development topics and has been recognized by the International Economic Development Council for professional achievements and service to the profession. He serves on the editorial advisory board of the journal *Applied Economic Development* and *Site Selection Magazine*. Dr. Lombard received his MA and PhD in geography from the State University of New York at Buffalo.

Paula J. Loomis teaches architecture at Hampton University; manages the Virginia Beach office for EDAW, a worldwide planning and economic development firm; and is a colonel in the U.S. Air Force Reserve, a fellow of the American Institute of Architects, and a member of the American Planning Association. She was the lead engineer/deputy in the U.S. Air Force's Base Transition Office for BRAC 2005. Ms. Loomis holds a BA in environmental design, master's degrees in architecture and construction management, and an MBA in urban studies at Old Dominion University, where she is also pursuing her PhD.

Heike Mayer is an assistant professor in the urban affairs and planning program at Virginia Tech's Alexandria Center. Her research interests focus on the factors shaping the economic competitiveness of cities and regions, particularly the internal strengths of cities and regions to develop their economies. Her work has been published in the *Economic Development Quarterly*, *Economic Development Journal*, *Journal of the American Planning Association*, and *Journal of Urban Affairs*. She received her PhD in urban studies from Portland State University.

Julia Melkers teaches and conducts research in the areas of public management, organizational theory, economic development, and science and technology. In her work, she has addressed issues of effective performance measurement of state economic development programs and technology-based programs. Her work has been published in *Public Administration Review*, *Urban Studies Review*, *Policy Studies Journal*,

Public Budgeting and Finance, and *Journal of Public Administration Research and Theory*, among others. Dr. Melkers also serves on the editorial boards of *Research Evaluation, Evaluation and Program Planning, State and Local Government Review*, and *Economic Development Quarterly*. She has a PhD in public administration from Syracuse University.

John C. Morris is an associate professor and graduate program director in the Department of Urban Studies and Public Administration at Old Dominion University. He spent several years as a policy evaluator in Washington, D.C., and has been affiliated with the Center for Governmental Services at Auburn University and the John C. Stennis Institute of Government at Mississippi State University. His research interests include public-private partnerships, environmental policy, and organizational theory. Dr. Morris has published articles in journals such as *Public Administration Review, Journal of Politics, Policy Studies Journal, Politics and Policy, Public Works Management & Policy*, and *Environmental Politics*, among others. He holds a PhD in public policy and administration from Auburn University.

Laura A. Reese is a professor of political science and director of the global urban studies program at Michigan State. Her main research and teaching areas are urban politics and public policy, economic development, and local governance and management in Canada and the United States. She has conducted large-scale evaluations for the Economic Development Administration, U.S. Department of Commerce. Her research on substate economic development programs has examined tax increment finance authorities and industrial tax abatements. Dr. Reese has written several books and articles in these areas and has engaged in public personnel administration focusing on implementation of sexual harassment policy. She received her PhD in political science from Wayne State University.

Gary Sands, an associate professor of planning at Wayne State University, has more than 30 years of experience as an academic researcher and consultant to government agencies in the fields of housing and economic development. He has undertaken funded research on a variety of local economic development programs, including renaissance zones, neighborhood enterprise zones, industrial property tax abatements, and tax increment finance authorities. In particular, he has examined the relationship between local government regulations and incentive programs and the characteristics of private development activity. Dr. Sands has published articles on housing and local economic development issues in Canada and the United States. He received his PhD in housing and public policy from Cornell University.

Alicia C. Schortgen is an assistant professor of public affairs at the University of Texas at Dallas. Alicia earned her BS in political science from Texas A & M University and an MPA and a PhD in public affairs from the University of Texas at Dallas. Her research interests include philanthropic behavior, intersectoral relationships, the history of non-profit organizations in America, nonprofit accountability and outcome measurement, and leadership and executive behavior in government. In addition to her academic interest in the sector, Dr. Schortgen has extensive professional and volunteer experience in nonprofit management and fundraising.

Bob Sharp is a PhD candidate at Old Dominion University in the Department of Urban Studies and Public Administration. He holds an MPA from the University of Wyoming and has over 25 years' experience in government and volunteer organizations. His research interests include management processes and organizational change. Mr. Sharp is a member of the American Society for Public Administration and currently works as a management consultant for Hitachi Medical Systems.

Joe A. Sumners is director of the Economic and Community Development Institute at Auburn University. He also serves as executive director of the I-85 Corridor Alliance, a regional partnership of communities, educational institutions, and businesses located along Interstate 85 from the Georgia state line to Montgomery, Alabama. He serves as a technical advisor to Gov. Bob Riley's Alabama Rural Action Commission and is president of the board of directors of the Alabama Communities of Excellence program. He is an active consultant, writer, and public speaker. Dr. Sumners received his BA and MA in public administration from Auburn University and his PhD in political science from the University of Georgia.

Douglas J. Watson is a professor and director of the public affairs program at the University of Texas at Dallas. He is coeditor of *Local Government Management: Current Issues and Best Practices* (M.E. Sharpe 2003), *Spending a Lifetime: The Careers of City Managers* (Carl Vinson Institute of Government 2006), and *Civic Battles: When Cities Change Their Form of Government* (PrAcademics Press 2007), and four other books. His work has appeared in *Public Administration Review, Review of Public Personnel Administration*, and other journals. Dr. Watson was a local government practitioner for 30 years (1971–2003) and served as city manager of Auburn, Alabama, for the last 21 years of his tenure.

Jennifer Weaver is a fifth-year doctoral student in political science at the University of North Carolina. She served as a research associate on the prisons in North Carolina project. Her other research interests include poverty and social welfare. Her dissertation is on the predictors of variation in criminal justice policies across the states.

Micah Weinberg is a doctoral candidate in political science at the University of North Carolina. The subject of his dissertation is the partisan speech of state governors. His work focusing on state and local politics and public policy has been published in *Policy Studies Journal*.